EUREKA!

EUREKA!

A Dictionary of Latin and Greek Elements in English Words

MARY BYRNE

DAVID & CHARLES
Newton Abbot   London

For A.A.B. and E.B.

British Cataloguing in Publication Data

Byrne, Mary
  Eureka!: a dictionary of Latin and Greek
  elements in English words.
  1. Vocabulary 2. English language –
  Foreign elements – Greek 3. English
  language – Foreign elements – Latin
  I. Title
  428.1   PE1582.A3

  ISBN 0-7153-8831-2

Typeset by Typesetters (Birmingham) Ltd
Smethwick, West Midlands
and printed in Great Britain
by Billings & Sons Limited, Worcester
for David & Charles Publishers plc
Brunel House Newton Abbot Devon

Introduction

At one time, an understanding of the 'classical' languages and a knowledge of the history, literature and way of life of ancient Greece and Rome were held to be the essential foundation of any education that aspired to anything more than the 'three Rs' (at least for men – a good education for women being seen, until recently, as something quite different). This conviction has waned over the years, however, and it is now generally held – no doubt accurately – that the time of the majority of school pupils is better spent on other matters.

The disappearance of Latin and Greek from school curricula has not been without losses, though, and the major one is linguistic. Ask those who did learn Latin, or both Latin and Greek, at school whether this has been useful to them in any way, and they are likely to mention that it has helped them in their use of English.

Even a cursory glance through the pages of this book will give an idea of how much of our vocabulary derives from the classical languages. The influence of Latin on English began when England was part of the Roman Empire, but a more significant linguistic stimulus was the conversion of the country to Christianity by missionaries such as St Augustine. This put seventh-century and eighth-century England back in touch with continental culture – and Latin, its lingua franca. Norman French, which arrived in force after the Conquest, was another major route by which Latin words reached English, and Greek came into its own in the sixteenth-century revival of classical learning. At this time there was wholesale conscious borrowing from both Greek and Latin, and a tradition was established of turning to the classical languages for new scientific and technical vocabulary. This is a tradition that continues to the present day ('television', 'video', 'stereophonic' and 'microcomputer' are examples that spring immediately to mind).

So people who have studied Latin and Greek at school are likely to say that the experience helps them to understand English words, especially abstract and scientific and other technical terms, and to use English more accurately. They may also say – though this is a point they are more likely to take for granted – that a knowledge of where the words they use come from, of the elements of which words are made up, enhances their appreciation of English and the pleasure they take in using it.

The main aim of this book is to make accessible to those who have never studied Latin and Greek, or whose exposure to them has been very limited, some of the linguistic knowledge and pleasure that actually having learned the languages used to impart to large numbers of people. It is hoped that it will also be of interest to those learning English at an advanced level, and to English-speakers learning any of the European languages substantially derived from Latin (such as French, Italian and Spanish). An added source of interest are the English words that make some reference to the mythology, literature, history or way of life of ancient Greece and Rome, and the reader will perhaps be surprised by how many such references lie hidden in our everyday vocabulary.

SOME NOTES ON THE ENTRIES

Each entry consists of a number of examples of English words derived from a particular Latin or Greek word (or from a group of Latin or Greek words closely related to each other). The first point to be made is that the brief explanations of meaning following the English examples are not strict definitions such as are found in a normal dictionary, but are intended to show the route (sometimes obvious, sometimes tortuous) by which the modern meaning of an English word can be traced back to the basic meaning of its Latin or Greek ancestors.

Some explanation of the forms in which Latin and Greek words are given is required. Taking nouns and adjectives first, many readers will be familiar with the fact that the form of a

6

Latin or Greek noun or adjective varies slightly depending on the role it plays in a particular sentence (whether it is the subject, direct object, indirect object, or whatever). In some words, only the ending varies, but in other words a new stem is introduced for some of the forms. There is no need to go into the intricacies of this system here; the important point is simply that English words deriving from Latin and Greek nouns and adjectives are often formed on the subsidiary stem rather than the basic one. The Latin word *iter* (journey), for example, has the subsidiary stem *itiner-*, and it is on this longer stem that the English words 'itinerary' and 'itinerant' are formed. The entries in this book include, where relevant, both the basic noun or adjective and the second stem.

Similarly, English words deriving from Latin verbs are often formed on the stem used to form the past participle of the verb, rather than the basic stem. The Latin verb *flectere* (to bend, stem *flect-*), for example, has the past participle *flexus* (bent), formed on the stem *flex-*. Derivative English words may have been formed on either of the two stems (*flect-* or *flex-*): 'deflect', 'flexible', 'reflect', 'reflex', for example. So again, where relevant, both the infinitive (*flectere* – to bend), which gives the basic stem, and the past-participle stem (*flex-*) are given.

Many English words derived from Latin and Greek are direct copies, as it were, of Latin or Greek composite words made up of a prefix formed from a preposition (such as *ab* away from, *ante* before, *de* from, *ex* out of, *pre* before, *post* after, *syn* together with) and another word. The point to note here is that these prefixes formed from prepositions tend to be capable of carrying a great variety of subtleties of sense (apart from the basic senses of the preposition), subtleties that are not always easily pinned down. They may, for example, carry a suggestion of a change of state, or of the completion of an action or process; or simply give the word more force. Where the suggestion is one of a change of state, the convenience has usually been adopted in this book of 'translating' the prefix by 'make...' Where a prefix is being used with some sort of strengthening effect, or to suggest completeness or completion, it has generally been 'translated' by the word 'thoroughly'. (Thus, abbreviate 'make short'; demonstrate, 'show thoroughly'.)

7

Finally, those who have some acquaintance with Latin or Greek may be surprised (and purists may be shocked) to see that no attempt has been made to indicate whether vowels are 'long' or 'short'. This would be a serious omission in a work intended as a tool for those actually learning one of the languages, but for the purposes of this book it has been deemed more helpful to present the Latin and Greek words in the simplest form possible.

FURTHER READING

The *Oxford English Dictionary* is an obvious source of further enlightenment for readers who want to know more about the origins of English. Also recommended are two standard dictionaries of etymology (both of which have been invaluable tools in the preparation of this book): *The Oxford Dictionary of English Etymology*, ed C. T. Onions (OUP, 1966) and *Origins: A Short Etymological Dictionary of Modern English*, Eric Partridge (Routledge & Kegan Paul, 4th ed 1966).

A

A, AN Gk *a-, an-* – a prefix that negates that which follows (and so can be translated by 'not', 'un-', -less', 'without' etc). Eg **abyss** bottomless (gulf etc), **agnostic** (person) without knowledge – ie who does not believe that we have knowledge of any spiritual reality behind the material world, **ahistorical** not historical, **akinesia** (state of being) without (voluntary) movement, **amoral** without morals, **amorphous** shapeless, **anaemia** (US **anemia**) bloodlessness – ie lack of blood, **anaesthetised** (US **anesthetised**) without (physical) feeling, **anarchy** (state of being) without rule – ie lawlessness, **anodyne** (inducing) painlessness – or avoiding trouble or controversy, **anonymous** nameless – ie unsigned, with no named author, **apathy** feelinglessness – ie failure to be stirred by something, **apolitical** not political, **arrhythmia** irregularity (of the heart-beat), **asphyxia** pulselessness – ie state in which one is unable to breathe, **asylum** (place with) no right-of-seizure – ie place where one cannot be seized, place of refuge, **asymmetrical** not symmetrical, **atheist** no-god (believer) – ie person who believes that there is no god, **atom** (particle) not (able to be) cut – ie particle so small that it cannot be divided and is thus the ultimate particle of matter (or so it used to be thought), **atrophied** not nourished – ie wasted away, **atypical** untypical

A Eg **avert** – see AB

A Eg **abbreviate, annex, ascend** – see AD

AB, ABS, A Lat *a, ab, abs* away, from, away from. Eg **abduct** lead away – ie carry off, kidnap, **aberration** a wandering away from (the right path, or the usual path), **abhor** shudder away from, **abject** thrown away – ie thrown down, base, miserable, **abjure** swear away – ie renounce, **ablution** a washing away (of dirt), **abnegate** deny away – ie renounce, **abnormal** away from (ie not in line with) the norm, **abrupt** broken away – ie broken off, sharp, sudden, **abscond** hide (oneself) away, **absent** being away, **absorb** swallow away – ie suck up, **abstemious** (keeping) away from strong drink – ie restrained regarding food, drink etc, **abstinence** a holding

9

away from – ie a holding back, a refraining (from, eg, food, sex), **abstract** drawn away – ie removed (from the concrete), existing only as a mental concept, (etc), **abstruse** thrust away – ie hidden, difficult to understand, **avert** turn away – or ward off (a disaster etc)

ACADEM Gk *Akademos* – name of a Greek hero, after whom was named the grove in Athens where Plato (see PLATONIC) taught. This ancient place of learning has given English the words **academy, academic** etc

ACER(B), ACID, ACRI(D), ACU Lat *acer, acr-* sharp, bitter; *acerbus* bitter, sour; *acidus* sharp, sour; *acuere, acut-* to sharpen to a point; *acus* needle; or related Latin words. Eg **acerbic** bitter, sour, **acid** sour, **acrid** bitter, **acrimony** bitterness, **acumen** sharpened point – ie sharpness (of mind), **acupuncture** a needle pricking – ie sticking needles into the skin for medical purposes, **acute** sharpened to a point – ie (of an illness) coming to a sharp point or crisis, (of someone's mind) sharp, **exacerbate** (make) (more) bitter – ie make worse

ACRO Gk *akros* outermost, topmost, highest. Eg **acrobat** walker (at the) highest – ie walker on tiptoe, rope-dancer, gymnast, **acronym** name (formed by the) outermost (letters of other words) – ie word made up of the initial letters of a series of other words, **acrophobia** fear of the highest (places) – ie fear of heights, **acropolis** highest city – ie upper city, citadel, **acrostic** (poem or puzzle in which other words are formed by the) outermost (letters of the) lines – ie in which the first or last letters of each line spell other words

ACT, AG Lat *agere, act-* to drive, do, set in motion; *agilis* easily set in motion; *agitare, agitat-* to put in constant motion. Eg **act** do, **action** a doing, **active** (given to) doing, **actual** relating to (or existing in) doings (ie fact), **agenda** (things) to be done, **agent** doer, **agile** easily set in motion, **agitated** in constant motion, **proactive** driving forward – ie initiating, **react** do back – ie do something in response, **transact** drive across – ie drive through, carry out (eg a piece of business)

ACU Eg **acupuncture, acute** – see ACER(B)

10

AD, A (or AB, AC, AF, AG, AL, AN, AP, AR, AS, AT before 'b', 'c', 'f' etc) Lat *ad* to, towards, against, at. As a prefix, *ad* (and the other forms given above) can also suggest a change 'to' a condition ('make...'). Eg **abbreviate** make short – ie shorten, **accept** take to (oneself), **accumulate** heap to – ie heap up, **adhere** stick to, **adjacent** lying towards (ie beside or near), **adjunct** (thing) joined to, **ad lib** (abbreviation of *ad libitum*) 'at pleasure' – ie as one wants, as much as one wants, or (as a verb) to speak without preparation, **admire** wonder at, **ad nauseam** 'to (the point of) sickness', **advent** a coming to – ie an arrival, **advertise** turn (people's attention) towards, **affect** do to – ie act upon, **affluence** a flowing towards – ie a flowing plentifully, wealth, **aggression** a stepping against – ie an attack, **allocate** place to – ie assign to a place, **annex** (thing) tied to (ie joined on to) (something else), **annihilate** make (into) nothing – ie destroy completely, **appreciate** (give) a price to – ie to give a value to, be aware of the value of, or to go up in value, **ascend** climb to – ie climb up, **assimilate** make like (the rest) – ie absorb, **attenuate** make thin – or weaken

ADELPH Gk *adelphos* brother (plural *adelphi* brothers and sisters). Eg **Christadelphians** Brothers/sisters (in) Christ – name of a religious sect, **Philadelphia** (land of) brotherly (and sisterly) love, **triadelphous** (having) (stamens in the form of) three brothers/sisters – ie having three bundles of stamens

AEM Eg **anaemia, leucaemia** – see (H)AEM(O)

AER(O) Gk *aer* air. Eg **aerate** (put) air (into), **aerial** relating to the air, **aerodynamics** dynamics of air (ie gases), **aeronautics** air-sailing – ie travel in the air

(A)ESTH Gk *aisthesthai* to feel, perceive. Eg **aesthete** (US **esthete**) perceiver (of beauty), **aesthetic** (US **esthetic**) relating to perception (of beauty), **anaesthesia** (US **anesthesia**) feelingless (state) (of the body)

(A)EV Lat *aevum* age. Eg **coeval** (of or belonging to an) age together – ie of or belonging to the same age, **longevity** long age – ie long life, **medi(a)eval** relating to (or belonging to etc)

11

the middle ages, **prim(a)eval** relating to (or belonging to etc) the first ages

AG Eg **agenda, agent, agile, agitated** – see ACT

AGOG Gk *agein* to lead. Eg **demagogue** leader of the people, **hypnagogic** sleep-leading – ie sleep-bringing, or relating to the process of falling asleep, **pedagogue** boy-leader – ie (in ancient Greece) the slave who took a boy to and from school; hence, a tutor or teacher, **synagogue** a leading together – ie a bringing together, a building for coming together (by Jews, for worship)

AGON Gk *agon* assembly, contest, struggle; *agonistes* combatant, rival, actor. Eg **agonise** struggle – or suffer torment (eg in the mind), **agony** a struggle – or torment, **antagonise** struggle against – or arouse hostility in, **protagonist** first (ie chief) actor – ie the chief person in a drama, conflict etc; or (loosely) a champion or advocate of a cause

AGORA, EGYR Gk *agora* (place of) assembly, market-place; *panegyris* general assembly. Eg **agoraphobia** fear of assemblies (ie public places), **panegyric** (speech of praise suitable for proclamation at a) general assembly

AGR(I), AGR(O) Lat *ager, agr-* field. Eg **agrarian** relating to the fields, **agriculture** the tilling of the fields, **agronomics** field management – ie the science of land management, **agronomy** field management – ie the management of the resources of the countryside

ALB Lat *albus* white. Eg **alb** white (vestment), **albescent** whitish or whitening, **albino** (abnormally) white (person, animal) – ie one lacking in colouring pigment (in the skin etc), **album** white (tablet) – ie (in Roman times) a tablet on which edicts and announcements were written, (later) a book with blank pages, **albumen** white (of an egg)

ALG, ALGES Gk *algos* pain; *analgesia* painlessness. Eg **analgesia** painlessness, **myalgia** muscle pain, **neuralgia** nerve pain,

nostalgia return-home pain – ie home-sickness or longing for the past

ALI Lat *alius* other; *alias* at another time, otherwise; *alibi* in another place. Eg **alias** otherwise (or the name used when one is called otherwise than by one's real name – ie an assumed name), **alibi** (plea of having been) in another place, **alien** relating (or belonging) to another (person or place), **inter alia** 'among other (things)'

AL(IM), ALUMNUS Lat *alere* to nourish. Eg **alimentation** nourishment, **alimony** nourishment – ie a regular payment to a separated spouse, **alumnus** (person) nourished (by a particular school etc)

ALL(O) Gk *allos* other, another. Eg **allopathy** disease-treatment (on the principle of) otherness – ie treatment in which drugs etc are used that have the opposite effect on the body to that of the disease (see PATH(O)), **allotropy** (property of having) another turning (or another direction, another form) – ie property of existing in more than one form

ALPHA Gk *alpha* – first letter of the Greek alphabet. Eg **alphabet** – from the first two letters of the Greek alphabet (*alpha, beta* – equivalent to the English 'a, b')

ALT(E)R Lat *alter, altr-* the other (*alter ... alter* the one ... the other); or related Latin words. Eg **alter** (make) other – ie change, **altercation** (exchange in which) (first) one (then) the other (speaks) – ie a bandying of words, quarrel, **alter ego** other I – ie one's other self, **alternate** (first) one (then) the other – ie taking turns, **alternative** the other (in situations of choice), **altruism** (concern for) others

ALT(I) Lat *altus* high. Eg **altimeter** height measure – ie instrument for measuring height, **altitude** height, **exalt** (raise) forth high – ie raise up high

ALUMNUS see AL(IM)

13

AMB(I) Lat *ambo* both; *amb(i)* prefix – on both sides, both ways, around, about. Eg **ambidextrous** right(-handed) both sides – ie having both hands skilful, **ambient** going round – ie surrounding, **ambiguous** driving both ways – ie uncertain, having a double meaning, **ambit** a going round – ie an encompassing, the area encompassed, the scope of something, **ambition** a going round – ie (in ancient Rome) a going round to canvass votes; hence, a desire for office etc, **ambivalent** strong on both sides, (seeing) worth on both sides – ie both attracted and repelled by something, having 'mixed feelings' about something

AMBROSIA Gk *ambrosia* 'immortality' – the elixir of life that was the food of the gods (see also NECTAR). Hence in English the word **ambrosia** is applied to something tasting sweet and delicious

AMB(U)L Lat *ambulare* to go about, walk; or related Latin words. Eg **ambulance** (hospital) going about, **funambulist** rope walker, **noctambulist** night walker – ie sleep-walker, **perambulate** walk through (a place) – ie walk around (a place), walk around, go from place to place, **pram** (abbreviation of **perambulator**) (vehicle for) walking through (places) – ie for walking (a baby) around, **preamble** (text etc) walking before – ie coming before (the main text etc), **somnambulist** sleep-walker

AMIC, AM(OR), IMIC Lat *amare, amat-* to love; *amor* love; *amicus* friend. Eg **amateur** lover (of a sport etc, rather than one who does it for money), **amatory** relating to love, **amiable** lovable, **amicable** friendly, **amorous** loving or relating to love, **enamoured** in love, **inimical** unfriendly

AMPH(I) Gk *ampho* both, *amphi* on both sides, on all sides, around, about. Eg **amphibious** living on both sides (ie in water and on land), **amphitheatre** theatre on all sides – ie a theatre with rows of seating sloping upwards all round a central space

AMPL(I) Lat *amplus* large. Eg **ample** large, **amplify** make large, **amplitude** largeness – ie breadth, size

14

AN Eg **an(a)emia, anarchy** – see A

AN(A) Gk *ana* on, up, back, over again. Eg **anabaptist** (one who performs or believes in) dipping (ie baptism) over again – ie re-baptism in adulthood (or baptism only in adulthood), **anabolic** that throws up (ie builds up) (muscle tissue etc), **anachronistic** relating to back time – ie to a previous period, **anadromous** (of fish) running up(-river) (to spawn), **anagram** (new word formed by writing the) letters (of a word) back(wards) – or mixing them up, **analogy** (originally, in mathematics, a case of) (the same) ratio over again – hence, an equality of ratios or proportions, a correspondence, a corresponding case, **analysis** a loosing up – ie an unloosing, a separating out into different elements, **anatomy** a cutting up (of the body) – ie the science of the structure of the body, or a dividing up of something into its different elements, **anode** way up – see ION

ANCILLARY Lat *ancilla* maid-servant. Eg **ancillary** relating to (ie playing the role of) a maid-servant – ie playing a back-up role

ANDR(O) Gk *aner, andr-* man, male, husband. Eg **android** man-shaped (robot etc), **androgynous** man-woman – ie having the characteristics of both sexes, **monandrous** single-maled – ie having only one husband (or male mate) (at a time), or (of a plant) having only one stamen or fertilising organ

ANEM(O) Gk *anemos* wind. Eg **anemone** wind(-flower), **anemophilous** wind-beloved, wind-loving – ie wind-pollinated

ANGEL Gk *angelos* messenger; *euangelos* bearing good news (see EU). Eg **angel** messenger, **evangelist** bearer of good news

ANG(U)L Lat *angulus* corner. Eg **angle** corner, **quadrangle** four-cornered (figure, court etc), **rectangle** straight-cornered (figure) – ie right-angled figure, **triangle** three-cornered (figure)

ANIM Lat *animus* mind, spirit; *anima* spirit, soul. Eg **animal**

15

(thing with) spirit – ie living thing, **animated** spirited, **animism** (belief that objects and natural phenomena have a) soul, **animosity** (hostile) spirit – ie hostility, **equanimity** equal-mindedness – ie evenness of mind or temper, **inanimate** without spirit – ie without life, **magnanimous** great-minded – ie noble-minded, generous, **pusillanimous** weak-spririted, **unanimous** of one mind

ANISO Eg **anisophyllous** – see ISO

ANN, ENN Lat *annus* year. Eg **AD** (abbreviation of **anno domini**) (in the) year of (our) Lord, **annals** yearly (chronicles), **anniversary** yearly (re)turn (of a date), **annual** yearly, **annuity** yearly (payment), **biennial** (happening every) two years – or lasting two years, **centennial** (happening every) hundred years – or having lasted a hundred years; or (as a noun) hundredth anniversary, **millennium** a thousand years, **perennial** (lasting) through the year(s), **superannuated** above-yeared – ie over-yeared, too old

AN(N)U Lat *anus* ring. Eg **anus** ring(-shaped orifice), **annular** ring(-shaped)

ANT(E) Lat *ante* before. Eg **a.m.** (abbreviation of **ante meridiem**) before midday, **antecedent** going before, **ante-diluvian** before the Flood, **antenatal** before the birth, **anterior** more before – ie earlier, **anteroom** a before-room

ANTH(O) Gk *anthos* flower. Eg **anthology** a gathering of flowers – ie a collection of choice pieces (of writing), **chrysanthemum** golden flower, **polyanthus** many-flowered (plant)

ANTHROP(O) Gk *anthropos* human being, man (in sense: human being). Eg **anthropocentric** human-centred, **anthropology** science of humankind, **anthropomorphism** (the attribution of) human form (or characteristics) (to something that is not human), **misanthropist** human-hater – ie hater of humankind, people-hater, **philanthropist** human-lover – ie lover of humankind, person who does good works

ANT(I) Gk *anti* against, opposite. Eg **Antarctic** opposite the

Arctic, **antibiotic** against life – ie acting against living things, against micro-organisms, **anticlimax** the opposite of a climax (when one was expecting a climax), **antidote** (substance etc) given against (poison etc), **anti-hero** the opposite of a hero – ie chief character who is the opposite of heroic, **antipathy** feeling against (something or someone), **antipodean** (having) feet opposite – ie (of a person) living on the other side of the globe, **antithesis** a placing against – ie a placing of ideas in opposition to each other, an opposite idea, the opposite of something

APH Eg **aphorism** – AP(O)

APHROD Gk *Aphrodite* Aphrodite – name of the Greek goddess of love (especially sexual love), identified with the Roman Venus – see VEN(ER). Eg **aphrodisiac** (drug etc that excites) (sexual) love, **hermaphrodite** – see HERM

AP(O), APH Gk *apo* from, away, off; with various other subtleties of sense when used as a prefix. Eg **aphorism** a separating from – ie a marking of the boundaries (of something), a definition, a concise statement of a principle, a pithy saying, **apocalypse** an away-covering – ie an un-covering, revelation, **apocrypha** (things) hidden away – ie writings of unknown authorship or doubtful authenticity (applied specifically to certain scriptural texts), **apogee** (furthest point) from the earth – or the highest point or climax of something, **apostasy** a standing away from – ie abandon-ment (of one's religion etc), **apostle** (person) sent away (to preach etc), **apothecary** (keeper of a place for) putting away – ie store-keeper, druggist

AQUA, AQUE Lat *aqua* water. Eg **aquamarine** (name of a precious stone the colour of) sea-water – or the colour itself (blue-green), **aquarium** water(-tank) (for fish etc), **Aquarius** the Water(-Carrier) – sign of the zodiac, **aquatic** (living, taking place etc in or on) water, **aqueduct** a leading of (ie a channel for) water, **aqueous** watery, **subaqua** relating to underwater (sport)

ARBOR(I) Lat *arbor* tree. Eg **aboreal** relating to trees,

arboretum tree (plantation), **arboriculture** cultivation of trees

ARC(H) Lat *arcus* curve, bow (ie for arrows). Eg **arc** curve, **arch** curve, **archer** bow(-wielder)

ARCH Gk *-arches* or *-archos* ruler, ruling. Eg **anarchy** (state of being) without rule – ie lawlessness, **hierarchy** (ranked body of) sacred rulers (ie rulers in sacred matters – priests or angels) – or any body of individuals organised in ranks with differing degrees of power, **matriarch** mother ruler (of a family or clan), **monarch** sole ruler, **oligarchy** rule by the few, **patriarch** ruler of a family or clan (not, strictly speaking, 'father ruler', though the Greek word for a family or clan, *patria*, does come from the word for father, *pater*)

ARCH(A)(EO) Gk *archaios* ancient, primitive. Eg **arch(a)eology** study of ancient (things), **archaic** relating (or belonging) to ancient (times)

ARCH(I) Gk *archi-* first, chief. Eg **arch-** chief – ie master- (as in 'arch-villain'), **archangel** chief angel, **archbishop** chief bishop, **archduke** chief duke, **architect** chief builder – ie master-builder, designer of buildings

ARCT Gk *arktos* bear, the Great Bear, the pole star. Eg **arctic** relating to the Great Bear (ie to the north), **arctophile** lover of (teddy) bears

ARD, ARS Lat *ardere, ars-* to burn. Eg **ardent** burning, **ardour** burning (heat), **arson** burning

AREN Lat *arena* sand. Eg **arena** sandy (place) – eg the central space of an amphitheatre, **arenaceous** sandy

ARGENT(I) Lat *argentum* silver. Eg **argentiferous** silver-bearing, **Argentina** Silvery (Land)

ARISTO Gk *aristos* best. Eg **aristocracy** (class with power through a system of) rule by the best

18

ARITHM Gk *arithmos* number. Eg **arithmetic** numerical (art), **logarithm** ratio number

ARS Eg **arson** – see ARD

ART, ERT Lat *ars, art-* a skill. Eg **art** skill, **artifact** (object) made by skill (rather than nature), **artifice** a skilful making – ie contrivance, trickery etc, **artificial** made by skill (rather than nature), **artisan** skilled (person), **inert** unskilful – ie not given to movement or action (with a more specific technical meaning)

ARTHR(O) Gk *arthron* joint. Eg **arthralgia** joint pain, **arthritis** (inflammation of the) joints

ART(IC) Lat *artus* joint. Eg **article** joint – ie distinct part, distinct thing, (etc), **articulated** jointed – ie (of a lorry etc) divided into distinct parts, (of an idea etc) uttered distinctly

ASPER Lat *asper* rough. Eg **asperity** roughness, **exasperate** make rough – ie irritate

AST(E)R(O) Gk *aster* star. Eg **aster** star(-shaped flower), **asterisk** little star, **asteroid** star-shaped (body) – ie star-like tiny planet, **astrology** study of the stars (and their influence on human affairs), **astronaut** star-sailor – ie space-traveller, **astronomy** the arranging of the stars – ie the classification of the stars, the science of heavenly bodies, **astrophysics** physics of the stars, **disastrous** not starred – ie ill-starred, very unfortunate or unsuccessful

ASTHEN Eg **myasthenia, neurasthenia** – see STHEN

ATHL(ET) Gk *athlos* contest. Eg **athlete** contestant – ie (in the classical world) person who competed in the public games, **decathlon** ten(-event) contest, **pentathlon** five(-event) contest

ATLANT, ATLAS Gk *Atlas, Atlant-* Atlas – name of the god (one of the Titans – see TITAN) supposed to support the universe on his shoulders; hence the name of the mountain range in north-

19

west Africa, which was seen as holding up the heavens. The **Atlantic Ocean** takes its name from the mountain. The word **atlas** apparently came to be used for a book of maps as a result of the fact that a picture of Atlas supporting the world commonly appeared at the front of such books

ATTIC Gk *Attike* Attica – name of the Greek state of which Athens was the capital. The Eng noun **attic** was originally applied to a particular decorative structure above the main part of a face of a building, because the main face crowned by such a structure was usually of the 'Attic order' (an architectural style). Hence the term 'attic storey' for a top storey enclosed by the decorative structure, and then for a room in the roof of a house

AUD(IO) Lat *audire, audit-* to hear. Eg **audible** hearable, **audience** (people) hearing, **audiovisual** relating to hearing and seeing, **audit** a hearing – ie an examination of accounts (which was originally done orally), **audition** (the sense of, or an act of) hearing – or the trial hearing of an actor etc, **auditorium** (place for) hearing (a concert etc)

AUGUR Lat *augur* diviner, soothsayer – ie person who foretold the future by reading omens or signs, eg by observing the flight of birds or examining the innards of animals that had been sacrificed (see also AV). Eng **inaugurate** (to ceremoniously or formally initiate) derives from the ancient practice of taking the omens before embarking on important ventures and on important ceremonial occasions. Eng **augur** (to bode – well or ill) also derives from Lat *augur*

AUGUST The month of **August** derives its name from the Roman month *Augustus*, named in honour of the first Roman emperor, Augustus Caesar (see CAESAR)

AUR(I) Lat *auris* ear. Eg **aural** relating to the ear, **auriscope** ear viewer – ie instrument for examining the ear

AUR(I) Lat *aurum* gold. Eg **aureola** golden (crown) – ie halo, **auriferous** gold-bearing

20

AUSPIC Eg **auspicious** – see AV

AUSTR(AL) Lat *Auster* the south wind, (hence) the south. Eg **aurora australis** 'the southern aurora' – ie the southern lights, **Australia** the Southern (Land)

AUT(O) Gk *autos* self, by oneself. Eg **autistic** (turned in on) oneself, **autobiography** self life-writing, **autocrat** ruler by oneself (ie with complete power), **autograph** self writing – ie a person's own handwriting (especially his/her signature), **automatic** thinking for itself – ie acting of itself, or happening as a matter of course, **automobile** self-moving (vehicle), **autonomy** self-regulation – ie independence, **autopsy** a seeing-for-oneself – ie an examination (of a corpse), **auto-suggestion** suggestion by oneself (rather than by something outside oneself)

AV, AUSPIC Lat *avis (auis)* bird; *auspex, auspic-* person who 'sees birds' – ie one who observes the flight, cries etc of birds, looking for omens. Eg **auspicious** (of good omen, as suggested by) an observation of birds, **aviary** (place for) birds, **aviation** birding – ie flying

B

BACCH Gk *Bakchos* Bacchus (also called Dionysos) – name of the god of wine and the centre of a cult among both the Greeks and the Romans. His followers were known for their wine-induced frenzies and orgiastic rites. The Roman celebrations in his honour were called *Bacchanalia*; hence Eng **bacchanalia** is used to refer to drunken revels. Eng **bacchic** is used to mean drunken or riotous

BALL, BLEM, BOL Gk *ballein* (forming nouns in *-blema* and *-bol-*) to throw; or related Greek words. Eg **ballistic** thrown (through the air) – or relating to the throwing of things through the air, **emblem** (thing) thrown in (ie inserted) – as a sign or representation of something else, **embolism** (presence of) (blood clots etc) thrown in (ie inserted, put in the way, blocking), **hyperbole** a throwing over – ie a throwing beyond, overstatement, rhetorical exaggeration, **parabola** a throwing alongside (of a plane and a cone), **problem** (thing) thrown forward (to be dealt with) – ie a task, a difficulty, **symbol** (thing) thrown together (with something else – in such a way that the first represents the second) – ie a sign, mark etc

BARB Lat *barba* beard. Eg **barb** beard(-like thing) – ie pointed appendage etc, or a pointed remark, **barbel** (fish with) beard(-like appendages), **barber** (shaver of) beards

BAR(O), BAR(Y) Gk *baros* weight; *barys* heavy. Eg **baritone** heavy- (ie deep-)toned (voice), **barometer** weight measure – ie instrument for measuring pressure, **baryon** heavy (sub-atomic particle), **isobar** (line connecting places of) equal weight (ie pressure)

BASIL Gk *basileus* king; *basilikos* royal. Eg **basil** royal (plant), **basilica** (building with the groundplan of a) royal (palace), **basilisk** little king – perhaps because of a crown-like mark on the creature's head

BATH(Y) Gk *bathos* depth; *bathys* deep. Eg **bathos** (a fall from the heights to the) depths – ie from the sublime to the ridiculous, **bathymetry** deep measurement – ie science of sounding seas and lakes

BAT(T) Lat *bat(t)uere* to strike. Eg **abate** strike down – ie lessen, **abattoir** (place for) striking down (ie killing) (animals), **battle** a striking – ie a fight, **combat** a striking together – ie a striking of each other, fighting

BELL(I) Lat *bellum* war. Eg **bellicose** war(like), **belligerent** war-waging, **rebellion** a (making of) war back – ie a renewal of war by a conquered people, an uprising

BENE Lat *bene* well. Eg **benediction** a well-saying – ie a blessing, **benefactor** a well-doer – ie one who does good, **benefice** a well-doing – ie a favour, a grant (eg of a 'living', to a clergyman), a church 'living', **benefit** a well-doing – ie an advantage, **benevolent** well-wishing – ie good-willed towards others, **NB** (abbreviation of **nota bene**) mark well

BET(A) Gk *beta* – second letter of the Greek alphabet. Eg **alphabet** – from the first two letters of the Greek alphabet (*alpha, beta* – equivalent to the English 'a, b'), **beta rays** – streams of particles given off by radioactive substances

BI, BIN, BIS Lat prefix *bi* – two, twice; *bini* two together, two by two; *bis* twice. Eg **biceps** two-headed (muscle), **bicycle** two-circled (ie two-wheeled) (vehicle), **biennial** (happening every) two years – or lasting two years, **bigamous** twice married – ie married to two people at once, **bilateral** with/of/ on two sides, **bilingual** two-tongued – ie in (or speaking) two languages, **binary** two by two – or twofold, or based on two, **binoculars** (lenses for the) two eyes together, **bipartite** divided into two – ie having two parts, or affecting two parties, **biped** two-footed (creature), **biplane** plane (with) two (sets of wings), **biscuit** twice-cooked (bread), **bisect** to cut into two, **bisexual** twice sexual – ie sexual in two ways, sexually attracted to both sexes, **combine** (put) together two by two – ie couple together, join together

BIBL(IO) Gk *biblion* book. Eg **Bible** (The) Books, **bibliography** writing (relating to) books – ie a list of books, writing about books, **bibliophile** book-lover

BIN Eg **binary, binoculars** – see BI

BIO Gk *bios* life. Eg **amphibious** living on both sides (ie in water and on land), **antibiotic** against life – ie acting against living things, against micro-organisms, **biochemistry** chemistry of life (ie of living things), **biography** a life-writing – ie the story of someone's life, **biology** science of life (ie of living things), **biorhythm** life rhythm, **macrobiotic** (promoting) long life – applied to foods grown without chemical fertilisers, **microbe** small life – ie small living thing, **symbiosis** life together – ie a situation in which one creature lives attached to another creature (in such a way that the attachment is to the advantage of both of them)

BIS Eg **biscuit** – see BI

BLAST(O) Gk *blastos* bud, germ, sprout. Eg **blastogenesis**

23

(re)production (by) buds; (or) (re)production by germ – ie the passing on of hereditary characteristics by germ-plasm, **blastosphere** (or **blastula**) germ sphere – ie sphere of cells formed when a fertilised ovum divides, **myoblast** muscle germ – ie cell producing muscle tissue

BLEM Eg **emblem, problem** – see BALL

BOL Eg **embolism, symbol** – see BALL

BON Lat *bonus* good. Eg **bona fide** '(in) good faith' – ie genuine. Eng **bonus** (an extra payment etc) probably also derives from Lat *bonus*

BRACHY Gk *brachys* short. Eg **brachydactylous** (abnormally) short-fingered or short-toed

BRADY Gk *bradys* slow. Eg **bradycardia** (abnormally) slow heart(-beat)

BRANCHI(O) Gk *branchia*, gills. Eg **branchiate** gilled, **branchiopod** gill-footed – ie having gills on the feet, **dibranchiate** two-gilled, **dorsibranchiate** (having) gills on the back

BREV(I) Lat *brevis* short. Eg **abbreviate** make short – ie shorten, **brevipennate** short-winged, **brevity** shortness

C

CAB, CAPER, CAPR(I) Lat *caper, capr-* he-goat, *capra* she-goat. Eg **cab** – originally a shortened form of **cabriolet** (a type of light carriage so named because it leapt about – like a goat), **caper** – originally a shortened form of **capriole** (a leap like a goat's); hence to caper is to leap or frisk about, and a caper is a frisking about or playing around (etc), **Capricorn** the Goat-Horned – sign of the zodiac

CAC(O) Gk *kakos* bad. Eg **cacophony** bad (ie ugly) sound

CAD, CAS, CID Lat *cadere, cas-* to fall. Eg **accident** a falling to –

24

ie something that befalls one, a happening, (etc), **cadence** a falling (of sound) – in various senses, **case** a fall – ie a happening, instance, (etc), **coincident** falling upon together – ie happening together, **decadence** a falling down or falling away (from high standards etc), **deciduous** (subject to) falling down or falling off – ie (of a tree) losing all its leaves every year, **incident** a falling upon – ie a happening, **occasion** a falling down – ie something that falls in front of one, a favourable moment, (etc), **occident** (place of) the falling-down (sun) – ie place of the setting sun, the west, **recidivism** a falling back (into crime)

CAESAR, CZAR, KAISER Lat *Caesar* – name of a Roman family, the most famous member of which is the dictator Julius Caesar (see also JULY). The latter's adopted son Octavian became supreme ruler, in which role he was known as Augustus Caesar (Lat *augustus* venerable, majestic) (see also AUGUST), and subsequent emperors all took the name Caesar. Hence Lat *Caesar* became a general term for an emperor, giving us **kaiser** (German emperor) and **czar** (or **tsar**) (Russian emperor). The term **Caesarean (section)** apparently also derives from the name Caesar: one explanation lies in the legend that Julius Caesar was born in this way (though some confusion arises from the separate claim that the name Caesar came about in the first place because an ancestor of the family was himself cut – Lat *caesus* – from his mother's womb)

CAINOZOIC see **cene**

CALC Lat *calx, calc-* stone, lime, chalk; *calculus* little stone (eg one used for doing sums). Eg **calcareous** chalky, **calcium** (metal found in) chalk, **calculate** (use) little stones – ie do a sum, reckon, **calculus** little stone (forming in the body) – or a particular system of doing sums or reckoning

CALE Eg **calefacient** – see CALOR(1)

CALENDAR Derives from Lat *calendarium* account book, itself from *Calendae* (or *Kalendae*) – name of the first day of the Roman month, which was the day on which accounts were due

25

CALL(I), KAL Gk *kallos* beauty. Eg **calligraphy** beautiful writing, **callisthenics** (exercises promoting) beauty and strength, **kaleidoscope** beautiful-shape viewer – name of an optical toy making coloured patterns

CALOR(I), CALE Lat *calor* heat; *calere* to be warm, to be hot. Eg **calefacient** warm-making – ie warming, **calorie** (unit of) heat – used to express the energy value of foods, **calorimeter** heat measure – ie instrument for measuring heat

CALYP(T), CALY(X) Gk *kalyptein* to cover. Eg **apocalypse** an away-covering – ie an uncovering, revelation (and 'the Apocalypse' is the Revelation of St John, which described the end of the world), **calyx** covering (of a flower), **eucalyptus** well-covered (plant) – so named because each bud is 'covered' by a cap

CAMARA, CAMERA Lat *camera* (or *camara*) vault, (vaulted) chamber. Eg **bicameral** (eg of a parliament) (having) two chambers, **camera** – originally a shortened form of **camera obscura** ('dark chamber'), an optical instrument using the principle later used in photography, **camaraderie** chamber (-fellowship) – ie goodfellowship (such as one might have with a room-mate), **in camera** 'in chamber' – ie in a judge's private room (rather than in open court), in private

CAMP Lat *campus* plain, level field, field of battle. Eg **camp** field(-lodging) (originally, for soldiers), **campaign** (time in the) field – ie the time during which an army was out in the field (rather than back at headquarters), hence a series of military or other operations aimed at a particular result, **campus** field – ie the grounds and buildings of a college

CAN Lat *canis* dog. Eg **Canary (Islands)** Dog (Islands) – named from the large dogs on one of the islands, **canine** relating to dogs (or dog-like)

CANCER Lat *cancer* crab. Eg **Cancer** the Crab – sign of the zodiac, **cancer** crab – see CARCINO

CAND, INCEND, INCENS Lat *candere* to be shining white, shine, glow with heat; *candidus* shining white; *incendere, incens-* to set fire to. Eg **candid** shining white – ie frank, **candidate** (person dressed in) white – ie someone hoping for office (in ancient Rome such a person would wear a white toga), **incandescent** enwhitening – ie starting to glow with heat, glowing with heat, **incendiary** that sets on fire, **incensed** set on fire

CANT, CENT Lat *canere* to sing; *cantare* to sing; *cantus* song. Eg **accent** song (ie stress etc) (added) to (speech) – or the pronunciation etc characteristic of a region, (etc), **descant** a song apart – ie a tuneful accompaniment sung above the main tune, **incantation** a singing upon – ie a singing (or chanting) of a charm or spell over, a magic formula, **recant** back-sing – ie withdraw something one has said

CAP, CEPT, CIP Lat *capere, capt-* to take, seize; or related Latin words. Eg **accept** take to (oneself), **anticipate** take before – ie take up beforehand, deal with beforehand, or expect, (etc), **capacity** (ability to) take – ie ability to take in or hold, ability to take in mentally, or some other ability or power, **captive** seized (person), **captor** seizer, **conception** a taking together – ie a taking in (of male seed in the womb), a becoming pregnant, (etc), **exception** (someone or something) taken out – ie not included, **incipient** taking in – ie taking up, beginning, **intercept** seize between – ie seize something (or someone) on its (his/her) way from one place to another, **participate** take part, **perception** (power of) seizing thoroughly – ie power of 'grasping' things, becoming aware of things, **precept** (something) taken before(hand) – ie a warning, order, rule of action, **reception** a taking back – ie a taking to oneself, taking in, **recipe** 'take back!' – ie take in!, take! (the English word was originally a Latin instruction written at the beginning of medical prescriptions; hence it was applied to a medical formula, and then to a set of instructions for making a dish in cookery)

CAPER see CAB

CAPILL Lat *capillus* hair. Eg **capillary** relating to hair – or (eg of a blood-vessel) hairlike

27

CAPIT Lat *caput, capit-* head; *capitulum* little head. Eg **capital** relating to the head, (standing at the) head – ie (of a city) standing at the head, chief, major; (of a letter) such as stands at the head (of a sentence etc); (of punishment) involving the loss of the head (ie of one's life); or (as a noun) the 'head' or original funds invested in a business, accumulated funds, (etc), **capitation** (reckoning per) head, **capitulate** (draw up) little head(ing)s – ie draw up an agreement, make terms, surrender, **decapitate** de-head – ie behead, **per capita** by heads – ie for every head, for every person, **recapitulate** (draw up) little head(ing)s again – ie list again, go over the chief points of again. Also, Lat *Capitolium* (the **Capitol**) was the temple of Jupiter (see JOV) built at the 'head' (top) of the Tarpeian Hill (subsequently also known as the Capitoline Hill) in Rome; the seat of the American Congress is named after this building

CAPR(I) Eg **Capricorn** – see CAB

CARB(ON)(I) Lat *carbo, carbon-* coal, charcoal. Eg **carbon** – element of which charcoal is one form, **carboniferous** coal-bearing – ie coal- (or carbon-) producing

CARCINO Gk *karkinos* crab; *karkinoma* a cancer (apparently because the veins around a cancerous tumour were thought to resemble the limbs of a crab). Eg **carcinogenic** cancer-producing, **carcinology** study of crabs – ie study of crustaceans, **carcinoma** a cancer

CARDI(O) Gk *kardia* heart. Eg **bradycardia** (abnormally) slow heart(-beat), **cardiac** relating to the heart, **cardiogram** heart-writing – ie a tracing (made with a **cardiograph**) of heart-beats, **cardiology** science of the heart, **cardiovascular** relating to the heart and (blood-)vessels, **tachycardia** (abnormally) quick heart(-beat)

CARN(I) Lat *caro, carn-* flesh. Eg **carnage** (heap of) flesh – ie heap of dead bodies, slaughter, **carnal** relating to the flesh, **carnival** – apparently literally a 'lifting of flesh(-eating)' (a carnival was originally a festival just before the Lenten fast – during which no meat would be eaten), **carnivore** flesh-eater,

28

incarnate (made) into flesh – ie embodied in flesh, **reincarnation** a (making) into flesh again – ie rebirth in another body

CARP(O) Gk *karpos* fruit. Eg **carpophagous** fruit-eating, **monocarpic** one-fruited – ie fruiting once only, **pericarp** around-fruit – ie the wall of a fruit

CAS Eg **case, occasion** – see CAD

CAST, CEST Lat *castus* pure. Eg **castigate** (make) pure (by punishment or reprimand), **incest** impurity – specifically sexual intercourse with a close relative

CAT(A), CATH Gk *kata* down. Eg **cataclysm** a down-washing – ie a deluge, upheaval, **catadromous** (of fish) running down (-river) (to spawn), **catalogue** collect down – ie pick out, list, **catalyst** (substance bringing about a) loosening down – ie a dissolving, breaking down, chemical reaction, **catapult** (machine etc for) hurling down, **catarrh** a down-flow (from the nose etc), **catastrophe** downturn (in fortunes), **catheter** (tube) sent down (into the body), **cathode** way down – see ION

CAUD, CODA Lat *cauda* (or *coda*) tail. Eg **coda** tail(piece), **longicaudate** long-tailed

CAUL(I) Lat *caulis* stalk, cabbage-stalk. Eg **cauliform** stalk-shaped – ie stalk-like, **sclerocaulous** hard-stalked. Probably also deriving from Lat *caulis* is Eng **cauliflower** – 'flowered cabbage'

CAUST, CAUT Gk *kaustikos* burning; *kauterion* branding-iron; *kaiein* to burn. Eg **caustic** (capable of) burning – or corroding, **cauterise** (apply a) branding-iron – ie sear, **encaustic** (having colours) burnt in, **holocaust** whole burnt(-offering) – ie complete or wholesale destruction

CAUT, CAV Lat *cavere, caut-* to beware, be on one's guard. Eg **cautious** on one's guard, **caveat** 'let him/her beware' (as in *caveat emptor* 'let the buyer beware') – ie a warning, **precaution** a being on one's guard before – ie a measure taken beforehand to ward off possible ill

CAVAL Lat *caballus* horse. Eg **cavalcade** horse(back) (procession), **cavalry** horse(-soldiers)

CED, CEED, CES(s) Lat *cedere, cess-* to go, withdraw, yield. Eg **accede** go towards – ie agree (to something), or come to (a throne etc), **access** a going towards – ie an approach or entry, **antecedent** (thing) going before, **cede** yield, **cession** a yielding, **concede** (thoroughly) yield – ie give up, grant, **excess** a going out of (the limits) – ie a going beyond the limits, **incessant** without yielding – ie without stopping, **intercede** go between – ie plead with one person on behalf of another, **precedent** (case, instance etc) going before, **predecessor** (person) gone away before – ie previous holder of an office (etc), **proceed** go forward, **process** a going forward, **recede** go back – ie draw back, fade away, **recession** a going back – ie a withdrawal, fading away, or a slump in trade, **secede** go apart – ie withdraw (formally – from an alliance etc), **succeed** go under – ie go next, follow on; or advance, prosper, **successor** (person who) goes under – ie goes next, follows on

CELER Lat *celer* swift. Eg **accelerate** make swift(er), **celerity** swiftness, **decelerate** de-swift – ie make less swift

CEND, CENS Eg **incendiary, incensed** – see CAND

CENE, CAINO Gk *kainos* new, recent. Eg **Cainozoic** new-life – name of the Tertiary (third) great geological period (see zo(o)). The Cainozoic age is divided into five periods: **Eocene** dawn-new, **Oligocene** few-new (from the small number of fossil molluscs that have been found dating from this period), **Miocene** less-new (ie fewer-new – from the number of fossil molluscs, which is smaller than in later periods), **Pliocene** more-new (ie more fossil molluscs) and **Pleistocene** most-new (ie most fossil molluscs)

CENS Lat *censere* to give an opinion or judgement; *censor* censor – title of a Roman official responsible for the compilation of a list of the names and property of Roman citizens, for the punishment of offenders against morals, and for public works (roads, bridges etc) and the revenues of the state. Hence Eng

30

censor (person who inspects publications etc for material deemed morally or otherwise offensive), **censorship** etc, and also Eng **census** (population count)

CENT Eg **accent** – see CANT

CENT(I) Lat *centum* a hundred. (Note: in names of units, 'centi' is used in English to mean a hundredth part.) Eg **bicentennial** relating to two hundred years – or (as a noun) two-hundredth anniversary, **cent** hundred(th part, of a dollar), **centenary** relating to a hundred (years etc) – or (as a noun) hundredth anniversary, **centigrade** (relating to a system with a) hundred steps (ie degrees – between the freezing and boiling points of water), **centilitre** hundred(th part of a) litre, **centimetre** (US **centimeter**) hundred(th part of a) metre, **centipede** hundred-footed (creature), **centurion** (commander of) a hundred (soldiers), **century** a hundred (originally soldiers, then years etc), **per cent** (per hundred)

CEPHAL(O), ENCEPHAL(O) Gk *kephale* head. Eg **cephalic** relating to the head – or ('cephalic presentation') a head-downwards position of a baby in the womb just before birth, **encephalogram** in-head writing – ie X-ray photograph of the brain, **hydrocephalus** water (in the) head – ie 'water on the brain'

CEPT Eg **intercept, reception** – see CAP

CEREAL, CERES Lat *Ceres* Ceres – name of the Roman goddess of agriculture. The planet **Ceres** was named after her; and Lat *cerealis* (relating to Ceres) gives English the word **cereal** (edible grain)

CEREB(R)(O) Lat *cerebrum* brain. Eg **cerebral** relating to the brain, **cerebrovascular** relating to the brain and its (blood-) vessels

CERN, CRET Lat *cernere, cret-* to separate, sift. Eg **discern** separate apart – ie tell apart, distinguish, make out, **discrete** separated apart – ie distinct, **excreta** (that which has been) sifted out – ie discharged (from the bowels), **secret** separated

31

apart – ie set apart, hidden, **secretary** (person) separated apart – ie confidential assistant

CERVIC, CERVIX Lat *cervix, cervic-* neck. Eg **cervical** relating to the neck (of an organ – especially of the womb), **cervix** neck (of an organ – especially of the womb)

CES(S) Eg **excess, incessant** – see CED

CEST Eg **incest** – see CAST

CET(AC) Lat *cetus* whale; Gk *ketos* sea-monster, whale. Eg **cetacean** relating to whales, **spermaceti** whale's sperm – from a mistaken belief that this waxy substance found in the head of a whale was its semen

CETERA **et cetera** – see ET

CH(E)IR(O) Gk *cheir* hand. Eg **chiropodist** (one who treats) the hands and feet – now just the feet, **chiropractic** hand activity – ie manipulation (of the spine etc)

CHIMERA Gk *Chimaira* – name of a mythical fire-breathing monster with a goat's body (and a lion's head and a serpent for a tail), from Gk *chimaira* she-goat. Eng **chimera** came to be applied more generally to any wild or fanciful notion

CHIRO Eg **chiropodist** – see CH(E)IR(O)

CHLOR(O) Gk *chloros* pale green, yellowish green. Eg **chlorine** yellowish green (element), **chlorophyll** green (colouring matter of) leaves

CHOL(ER) Gk *chole* bile, anger. Eg **choler** bile or anger, **cholera** bilious (disease), **choleric** bilious (in both its senses), **cholesterol** bile solid – ie solid substance found in (amongst other places) bile-stones (gall-stones), **melancholy** (condition of having too much) black bile – ie a feeling of sadness, depression. In Greek, as in English, the association of bodily bile with anger arose from the theory that bile (a secretion of the liver, and seen as one of the 'humours' or fluids of the body) when malfunctioning or overexcited produces anger or irritability. In medieval physiology, the four 'cardinal humours' (chief fluids), the balance of which was supposed to influence temperament, were held to be blood, phlegm, bile and black bile (or 'melancholy'), the last of which does not actually exist. (See HUM, SANGUI(N))

CHOR(EO) Gk *choros* dancing-place, dance, dancing and song together, band of dancers and singers; *Terpsichore* Terpsichore ('dance-enjoying') – name of the Greek Muse of dancing and choral song (see MUSE). Eg **chorea** (St Vitus's) dance, **choreography** dance writing – ie the notation or composition of dance, **chorus** band of singers, **terpsichorean** relating to (the Muse of) dancing

CHROM(AT)(O) Gk *chroma, chromat-* colour. Eg **chromatic** relating to (or in) colours, **chromatopsia** colour sight – ie seeing in colour, **chromium** (element forming compounds of beautiful) colours, **chromosome** colour body – because the substance out of which chromosomes are formed (**chromatin**) is easily dyed

CHRON(O) Gk *chronos* time. Eg **anachronistic** (belonging to) back time – ie to a previous period, **chronic** (lasting a long) time (Note: to use 'chronic' to mean very bad, severe, is to use it loosely; 'chronic' illness, for example, is properly illness that goes on for a long time, not necessarily severe illness), **chronicles** time (books), **chronological** relating to the science of time – or arranged in order of time, **synchronise** (bring to a state of) times together – ie (of clocks etc) bring to the same time, put at the same time

CHRYS(O) Gk *chrysos* gold. Eg **chrysalis** golden (pupa) – now a pupa generally, **chrysanthemum** golden flower

CICERONE Lat *Cicero, Ciceron-* Cicero – name of a famous Roman orator, politician and philosopher (106-43 BC). It was the great man's verbal skills that led to his name being used for someone who shows visitors around ancient sites or other places of interest (in more modern phraseology – a tourist guide)

CID Eg **incident, occident** – see CAD

CID, CIS Lat *caedere, caes-* to cut, kill (see also CID below). Eg **circumcise** cut around – ie cut the foreskin of, **concise** (thoroughly) cut – ie cut up, divided into short sentences, said in few words, **decide** cut off – ie cut short, settle (a dispute etc), resolve, **excision** a cutting out, **incision** a cutting into, **incisive** (tending to) cut into – ie sharp, acute, **incisor** cutting-into (tooth) – ie a front or cutting tooth, **precise** cut in front – ie cut off, cut short, to the point, exact

CID Lat *-cidium* a killing, *-cida* killer, from *caedere* to kill (see CID above). Eg **fratricide** killing (or killer) of a brother, **fungicide** fungus-killer, **genocide** killing of a race, **herbicide** plant-killer, **homicide** killing (or killer) of a human being, **matricide** killing (or killer) of (one's own) mother, **spermicide** sperm-killer, **suicide** killing of oneself

CILI Lat *cilium* eyelid, eyelash; *supercilium* 'above the eyelid' – ie eyebrow. Eg **cilia** eyelash(-like appendages – to cells etc), **supercilious** eyebrowish – ie haughty, arrogant

CINE Eg **cinema** – see KIN(E)

CINER Lat *cinis, ciner-* ashes. Eg **cineraria** ashy (plants) – because of the ashy down on the leaves, **incinerate** (make) into ashes

CIP Eg **incipient, participate** – see CAP

CIRCA, CIRCUM Lat *circum* round, around; *circa* around, about. Eg **circa** around, about, **circuit** a going round, **circumcision** a cutting around – ie a cutting of the foreskin, **circumference** a bearing round – ie a boundary line round, **circumflex** bent-round (accent, over a letter), **circumlocution** a speaking round (instead of going straight to the point), **circumnavigate** sail round, **circumscribe** write (ie draw) (a line) round – ie define the limits of, limit, **circumspect** looking around – ie wary, cautious, **circumstance** (fact) standing round – ie surrounding fact

CIS Lat *cis* on this side. Eg **cisalpine** on this (ie the Roman) side of the Alps, **cisatlantic** on this side of the Atlantic, **cislunar** on this side of the moon – ie between the moon and the earth

CIS Eg **excision, precise** – see CID

CIT Lat *ciere, cit-* to set in motion, summon; *citare* to set in rapid motion, summon (urgently). Eg **cite** summon – ie quote or bring forward in evidence, **excite** summon forth – ie rouse, **incite** summon on – ie stir up, **recite** summon back – ie read aloud, repeat from memory, **resuscitate** summon (from) under(neath) again – ie summon up again, bring back to life

CIV Lat *civis* citizen; *civitas* city-state. Eg **civic** relating to citizens, **civil** relating to citizens – or befitting a citizen (ie polite), **civilian** (ordinary) citizen (as opposed to the military), **civility** (good) citizenship – ie politeness

CLAM Lat *clamare, clamat-* shout, cry (out). Eg **acclamation** a crying out at – ie a crying out in approval, applause, **clamour** a crying out, **declamatory** (thoroughly) crying out – ie rhetorical, rousing, **exclamation** a crying out, **proclamation** a crying forth – ie a calling out, an announcement, **reclamation** a crying back – ie a calling back, a winning back

CLAR(I) Lar *clarus* clear. Eg **clarify** make clear, **clarinet** little clear(-toned) (instrument), **clarity** clearness, **declare** (make) (thoroughly) clear

CLASM, CLAST Gk *klaein* to break. Eg **iconoclast** breaker of images – ie person who challenges cherished beliefs

CLAUSTR(O) Lat *claustrum* enclosure, from *claudere* to shut (see CLUD). Eg **claustral** relating to an enclosure (ie cloister), **claustrophobia** fear of enclosures (ie confined places)

CLAV(I) Lat *clavis* key. Eg **clavichord** key-and-string (instrument), **conclave** with-key (ie private) (room or gathering), **enclave** keyed-in (territory) – ie shut-in territory, territory surrounded by foreign territory, an enclosure

CLIN(O) Lat *clinare* to lean, bend; Gk *klinein* to lean, slope. Eg **clinometer** slope measure – ie instrument for measuring slopes, **decline** bend aside – ie turn away, **inclination** a leaning into, **matroclinous** leaning (towards the) mother – ie inherited from the mother, or more like the mother than the father, **recline** lean back

CLUD, CLUS Lat *claudere, claus-* to shut (see also CLAUSTR(O)). Eg **conclusion** a (thorough) shutting – ie a shutting up, bringing to an end, an inferring, **exclusion** a shutting out, **inclusion** a shutting in – ie a taking in, **preclude** shut in front (of something) – ie shut off, debar, block, rule out, **recluse** (person) shut back – ie shut away, **secluded** shut apart – ie shut off, shut away

CO Eg **coeducation, cohabit** – see COM

COCC Gk *kokkos* berry, seed. Eg **Staphylococcus** bunch-of-grapes berries – ie rounded bacteria clustered like bunches of grapes, **Streptococcus** twisted berries – ie rounded bacteria arranged in twisted chains

COC(T) Lat *coquere, coct-* to cook. Eg **concoct** cook together, (thoroughly) cook – ie digest, turn over in the mind, devise (a plan etc), **decoct** cook down – ie reduce by boiling, **precocious** cooked before – ie ripened too early, prematurely developed

CODA see CAUD

COGN Lat *cognoscere, cognit-* to know. Eg **cognition** (act or faculty of) knowing, **cognoscente** (person) knowing (art, literature etc) – ie connoisseur, **incognito** unknown – ie unidentified, disguised, **recognise** know again

COHORT Lat *cohors, cohort-* cohort – a division of the Roman army (see LEGION). Hence in English a **cohort** is a band of people (or sometimes a companion or follower)

COL Eg **piscicolous, terricolous** – see CULT

36

COL(L) Gk *kolla* glue. Eg **collagen** glue-producer – because this protein produces gelatine when boiled, **protocol** first (leaf) glued (to a volume) – see PROT(O)

COL(L) Lat *collum* neck. Eg **accolade** (movement) to the neck – ie an embrace around the neck, the embrace (now replaced by a touching of the shoulders with a sword) marking the conferring of a knighthood; hence an award or honour, public praise, **col** neck (between mountains), **collar** neck(band)

COLOSS, COLISEUM Gk *kolossos* (Lat *colossus*) gigantic statue; hence, Lat *colosseus* gigantic. Eg **colossal** gigantic, **colossus** gigantic statue (or person, organisation, etc). The origin of the use of the term **coliseum** (or **colosseum**) – 'gigantic (place)' – for a large place of entertainment was the emperor Vespasian's enormous amphitheatre in Rome

COM, CON, CO (or COL, COR – before 'l', 'r') Lat prefix *co- (con-* etc) with, together (or gives the word more force – 'thoroughly'). Eg **coeducation** education (of the sexes) together, **cohabit** live together, **coitus** a going together – ie sexual intercourse, **collaborate** work together, **compassion** a suffering with (another) – ie fellow-feeling for someone who is suffering, **compatriot** countryman/woman together – ie fellow countryman/woman, **concentric** (having a) centre together – ie having a common centre, **concord** (a having) hearts together – ie a being of one heart, harmony, agreement, **confident** (thoroughly) trusting – ie sure, self-assured, **correct** (thoroughly) straightened – ie in order, right, **consanguinity** (a having of) blood together – ie a having of the same blood, a blood relationship

COMET Gk *kometes* long-haired, from *komes* hair. A **comet** – 'long-haired (star)' – is so called in reference to its long tail

CON Eg **concord, confidence** – see COM

CON **pros and cons** – see CONTR(A)

COND Lat *condere, condit-* to put together, store, hide. Eg **abscond** hide away – ie take oneself away, run away, **recondite** hidden back – ie hidden away, obscure, profound

CONTR(A) Lat *contra* against. Eg **contraceptive** (measure) against (con)ception, **contradict** speak against – ie deny (a statement), **contrary** against – ie opposite, opposed, **contrast** stand against – ie put (two things) side by side (so that the differences between them are emphasised), **contravene** come against – ie go against, **controversy** a turning against – ie a dispute, **pros and cons (contras)** (reasons) for and against

COPI(A) Lat *copia* plenty; *cornu copiae* horn of plenty. In classical mythology this was the horn of the goat supposed to have suckled Jupiter (see JOVE); it was placed among the stars as a symbol of plenty. Eg **copious** plentiful, **cornucopia** horn of plenty – or a plentiful supply

COPRO Gk *kopros* dung. Eg **coprolalia** dung-talk – ie obsessive use of obscene language, **coprolite** dung stone – ie fossilised dung or stone resembling this, **coprophagous** dung-eating

CORD Lat *cor, cord-* heart. Eg **accord** (a bringing) (heart) to heart – ie a having hearts in harmony, agreement, **concord** (a having) hearts together – ie a being of one heart, harmony, agreement, **cordial** hearty – ie heartfelt, warm, or (as a noun) a drink reviving the heart, **discordant** (with) hearts apart – ie out of harmony, disagreeing, **record** (bring) back to heart – ie bring back to mind, make a note (etc) of something so that it can be brought back to mind

CORN Lat *cornu* horn. Eg **Capricorn** the Goat-Horned – sign of the zodiac, **corn** (on the foot) horny (skin), **cornea** horny (covering – of the eyeball), **corner** horn – ie point or angle, formed by the meeting of two converging lines, **cornet** little horn(-shaped musical instrument, wafer etc), **cornucopia** horn of plenty – see COPI(A), **unicorn** one-horned (creature)

COROLL, CORON Lat *corona* wreath, garland, crown; *corolla* little garland, little crown; *corollarium* garland of flowers (especially the garland of gilt or silvered flowers given to actors), hence gift, gratuity. Eg **corolla** little crown (of petals, in a flower), **corollary** gift – ie something that follows on freely, an obvious inference, consequence, **corona** crown – eg a coloured ring round the sun or moon, **coronary** (of arteries) crowning (the heart) – ie encircling it, **coronation** a crowning, **coroner** (originally, an officer responsible for the rights of the property of the) crown

CORP Lat *corpus, corpor-* body; *corpusculum* little body. Eg **corporal** (of punishment) bodily, **corporation** body (of people), **corps** body (of soldiers etc), **corpse** (dead) body, **corpulent** (well-)bodied – ie fat, **corpus** body (of literature etc), **corpuscle** little body (in the blood), **habeas corpus** – see HAB, **incorporate** (form or take) into a body

COSM(O) Gk *kosmos* order, good order, adornment, world, universe. Eg **cosmetic** relating to adornment – ie to outward appearances, **cosmonaut** sailor of the universe, **cosmopolitan** citizen of the world, **cosmos** the universe, **microcosm** small world ('microcosm' is now used to refer to any small-scale version of some larger, complex thing, but originally the 'small world' was specifically man, regarded as a miniature version of the **macrocosm** – the 'big world' or universe)

COST Lat *costa* rib, side. Eg **accost** (go) to the side of (someone) – ie approach someone, go up and speak to him/her, **infracostal** below the ribs, **intercostal** between the ribs

CRACY, CRAT Gk *-kratia* power, rule; *-krates* ruler. Eg **aristocracy** (class with power through a system of) rule by the best, **autocrat** ruler by oneself (ie with complete power), **bureaucracy** rule by the office (ie by officialdom), **democracy** rule by the people, **meritocracy** rule by (those with) merit (ie ability), **plutocracy** rule by the wealthy, **technocrat** ruler by technology – ie person with power because of technological expertise

CRAS Lat *cras* tomorrow. Eg **procrastinate** (put) forward (to) tomorrow – ie put off until tomorrow, put off

CRAT Eg **autocrat, technocrat** – see CRACY

CRED Lat *credere, credit-* to trust, believe. Eg **credence** belief, **credential** (entitlement to) belief or trust (etc), **credible** believable, **credit** belief – or a reputation or acknowledgement of trustworthiness or merit (etc), **creditable** trustable – ie worthy of trust or recognition, **credo** 'I believe' – ie what one believes, a set of beliefs, **creed** (what one) believes – or a set of beliefs, **credulous** believing (too readily), **incredible** unbelievable, **incredulous** unbelieving

CREO Gk *kreas* flesh. Eg **creophagous** flesh-eating, **creosote** flesh-preserving (substance) – because it has antiseptic properties

CREP Lat *crepare, crepit-* to creak, crackle, sound. Eg **crepitation** a crackling, **discrepancy** a sounding apart – ie a sounding discordantly, a failure to tally

CRESC, CRET Lat *crescere, cret-* to grow. Eg **accretion** a growing to – ie an enlarging, or a growing of separate things into one, or something that has 'grown (on) to' something else, **concrete** grown together – ie formed into a mass, solid, **crescendo** a growing (in loudness), **crescent** (of the moon) growing – hence applied to other things, eg streets, of the same shape as a 'growing' (waxing) moon, **excrescence** outgrowth

CRET Lat *creta* chalk. Eg **cretaceous** chalky

CRET Eg **excreta, secret** – see CERN

CRIM Lat *crimen, crimin-* accusation, guilt, fault. Eg **incriminate** (lay an) accusation on, **recrimination** accusation back – ie counteraccusation

CRIN(I) Lat *crinis* hair. Eg **crinicultural** relating to the growth of the hair, **crinoline** hair (and) thread – see LIN

CRIS, CRIT Gk *krisis* judgement, decision, outcome, hence decisive stage or turning-point (of a disease); *krites* judge. Eg **crisis** turning-point (of a disease etc), **criterion** (standard of)

judgement, **critical** relating to a turning-point (ie crucial) or judgemental

CRUC(I), CRUX Lat *crux, cruc-* cross; *cruciare* to torture (hanging on a cross being a form of torture). Eg **crucial** cross(like) – ie decisive (as at a crossroads – one can go one way or another), essential, **Cruciferae** cross-bearing (plants) – name of a family of plants with cross-shaped flowers, **crucifix** (representation of Christ) fixed (on a) cross, **crucifixion** a fixing on a cross, **cruciform** cross-shaped, **crux** a cross – ie something that torments, a puzzle, knotty point, essential point, **excruciating** (thoroughly) torturing

CRUD Lat *crudus* raw, rough. Eg **crude** raw, rough – ie unsophisticated, coarse, rude, **recrudescent** (becoming) raw again – ie (of a wound) opening again, (in general) breaking out again

CRUST Lat *crusta* rind, shell. Eg **crust** rind, **Crustacea** shelled (creatures) – name of a class of animals (crabs, shrimps etc)

CRUX see CRUC(I)

CRYPH, CRYPT(O) Gk *kryptos* hidden. Eg **apocryphal** hidden away – ie of doubtful authorship or authenticity, **crypt** hidden (chamber) – ie underground chamber, **cryptic** hidden – ie difficult to decipher, **crypto-fascist** hidden (ie secret) fascist, **cryptogram** hidden writing – ie writing in code, **crypton** (or **krypton**) hidden (gas) – a gas present in the air only in very small quantities

CUB, CUMB Lat *cubare, cubit-* lie (down); *-cumbere, -cubit-* to lie. Eg **concubine** (woman who) lies down with (a man) – ie woman who lives with a man without being married to him, **cubicle** (room for) lying down – ie bedroom, cell, compartment, **incubate** lie down upon (eggs, to hatch them), **incumbent** lying upon – ie pressing upon (eg as a duty), **recumbent** lying back, **succumb** lie down under – ie be defeated (by something), give way

CULP Lat *culpa* fault, blame. Eg **culpable** blamable – ie

41

blameworthy, **exculpate** (free) from blame, **inculpate** (lay) blame on

CULT, COL Lat *colere, cult-* to till, farm, dwell in, grow, tend, pay respect to, worship. Eg **agriculture** the tilling of the fields, **cult** a worshipping, **cultivated** farmed – or tended (ie refined), **culture** a growth (of bacteria) – or a tending or refining (of the mind etc), **horticulture** tending of gardens, **piscicolous** dwelling in fish – ie living as a parasite within fish, **pisciculture** fish-farming, **terricolous** earth-dwelling – ie living in or on the soil

CUMB Eg **incumbent, recumbent** – see CUB

CUMUL Lat *cumulus* heap. Eg **accumulate** heap to – ie heap up, **cumulative** heaping (up), **cumulus** heap (of cloud)

CUPI(D) Lat *cupere* to desire, long for; *cupido, cupidin-* (sexual) desire, longing, love. Eg **concupiscence** (thorough) desirousness – ie (usually) sexual desire, **cupidity** longing – ie greed for gain. Lat *cupido* was personified as *Cupido* Cupid – the Roman god of love (identified with the Greek Eros – see ERO(T)). A **cupid** is a winged figure of a boy (especially a baby boy) representing the god; he carries a bow and arrow (with which he shoots darts of love into hearts both divine and human)

CUPR(O) Lat *cyprium (aes)* (metal) of Cyprus – ie copper. Eg **cupreous** of copper, coppery, **cupro-nickel** (alloy of) copper and nickel

CUR Lat *cura* care. Eg **accuracy** (a giving of) care to – ie exactness, **curate** (clergyman having the) care (of souls) – now specifically an assistant to a parish priest, **curator** (person having the) care (of an institution, building etc), **cure** (successful medical) care, **curiosity** a caring – ie a being careful, a paying attention, inquisitiveness, **manicure** hand care, **secure** without care – ie safe, **sinecure** (clergyman's post) without care (of souls) – ie clergyman's post without pastoral duties, or some other appointment not involving any work

42

CUR(R), CURS Lat *currere, curs-* to run; *curriculum* a 'little running' – ie a race, (race-)track, course. Eg **concur** run together – ie agree, **concurrent** running (ie happening, existing etc) together, **currency** (coins etc) running – ie flowing, being passed about, **current** running – ie flowing, in evidence (at a particular time); or (as a noun) a flow (of water etc), **curriculum** a track, course – ie a programme (to be followed, eg, in studies), **curriculum vitae** (summary of the) 'course of (one's) life', **cursor** runner – eg a moving indicator on a VDU screen, **cursory** runner(-like) – ie running quickly over, rapid, **discursive** running apart – ie running off in different directions, moving from one subject to another, **excursion** a run out, **incur** run into – ie fall liable to, **incursion** a running into or against – ie an inroad, invasion, **occur** run in the way of – ie happen, or come to mind, **precursor** forerunner, **recur** run again – ie happen again

CUS Lat *causa* reason, motive, lawsuit, (legal) plaint. Eg **accuse** (bring someone) to a lawsuit – ie charge someone with a wrongdoing, **excuse** (free someone) from plaint – ie free someone from blame, or overlook (a fault), **recusant** (person who makes a) plaint back – ie refuses (to comply with a demand)

CUSS Lat *quatere, quass-* to shake, strike. Eg **concussed** (thoroughly) shaken, **discuss** strike apart – ie break down, analyse, talk about, **percussion** (instruments for) striking (thoroughly) – ie instruments played by striking, **repercussion** a striking (thoroughly) back – ie a striking in return, reaction, consequence

CUT Lat *cutis* skin; *cuticula* little skin. Eg **cuticle** little skin – ie the outer skin (epidermis), or the skin at the edge of the nails, **percutaneous** through the skin, **subcutaneous** under the skin

CYCL(O) Gk *kyklos* circle, wheel. Eg **bicycle** two-wheeled (vehicle), **cycle** (series of events moving in a) circle – ie repeating itself, (etc), **encyclical** (letter) in a circle – ie circular, letter for circulation, **encyclopaedia** (or **encyclopedia**) (work of) circular education – ie work of all-round education, book of information on all subjects, **tricycle** three-wheeled (vehicle)

CYN(O) Gk *kyon, kyn-* dog. Eg **cynosure** the dog's tail – ie Ursa Minor, the constellation containing the North Star; hence, a centre of attention or attraction. The derivative Greek adjective *kynikos* (relating to dogs, dog-like) was also used to name the Cynics, a Greek philosophical sect – either because of a dog-like (or 'currish') quality attributed to them, or from the name of the gymnasium (see GYMN(O)) where they taught (the *Cynosarges,* apparently 'white dog'). The cynics disapproved of material comforts and refined pleasures such as art and learning; this unenthusiastic approach to life led to Eng **cynic** being used of someone unwilling to recognise that there is any good in the world

CYST(O) Gk *kystis* the bladder. Eg **cyst** bladder(-like sac), **cystitis** (inflammation of the) bladder, **cystoscope** bladder-viewer – ie instrument for examining the bladder

CYT(O) Gk *kytos* vessel, hollow. (In English, the word element 'cyt(o)' generally carries the meaning 'cell'.) Eg **cytology** science of cells, **cytotoxic** toxic to cells, **leucocyte** white cell (of the blood etc)

CZAR see CAESAR

D

DACTYL Gk *dactylos* finger or toe. Eg **didactyl** two-fingered or two-toed – or two-clawed, **pterodactyl** wing-fingered (creature) – because of its 'winged' forelimbs

DAMN, DEMN Lat *damnum* loss, damage, harm; *damnare, damnat-* to inflict loss on, find guilty, sentence. Eg **condemn** (thoroughly) find guilty, sentence, **damnation** a sentencing (to Hell), **indemnify** make unharmed – ie recompense for a loss, **indemnity** (provision so that one remains) unharmed – ie secure against loss

DAT Lat *dare, dat-* to give. Eg **date** (day on which a letter etc was) given (ie written) – derives from the Latin formula formerly used for dating letters etc (eg given at Rome on ...), **datum/data** '(thing/s) given'

DE Lat *de* down from, away from, off. (As a prefix *de* may also indicate a reversal or negation, or simply strengthen the word – 'thoroughly'). Eg **decelerate** de-swift – ie make less swift, **decentralise** reversal of centralisation, **declivity** a down-sloping, **decrease** grow down – ie grow less, **deflect** bend (ie turn) away, **dehydrate** (take) water away from, **dejected** thrown down – ie downcast, **deliberate** weigh (options etc) (thoroughly), **demented** away from (ie out of) (one's) mind, **demonstrate** show (thoroughly), **depilatory** (taking) hair away – ie hair-removing, **deposit** place down, **depressed** pressed down, **describe** write from (something) – ie write down, represent in words, **desensitise** reversal of sensitise, **deviate** (turn) off the way – ie leave the straight track, differ from the norm

DEB Lat *debere, debit-* to owe. Eg **debenture** – from *debentur* ('there are owed'), the first word of a statement of debt, **debit** (that which is) owed, **debt** (that which is) owed

DECA Gk *deka* ten. Eg **decade** (group of) ten (years), **decahedron** ten-seated (figure) – ie solid figure with ten faces, **decalitre** ten litres, **Decalogue** the Ten Sayings – ie the Ten Commandments, **Decameron** (Boccaccio's book of tales supposed to have been told during) ten days, **decathlon** ten (-event) contest

DECEN(T) Eg **decent** – see DEC(OR)

DEC(I) Lat *decem* ten, *decimus* tenth. (Note: in names of units, 'deci' is used in English to mean a tenth part.) Eg **December** tenth (month) – our twelfth month was the tenth month of the Roman year, which began in March (see also SEPT(I), OCTAV, NOV), **decibel** tenth of a bel, **decilitre** tenth of a litre, **decimal** relating to tenths, **decimate** (pick out every) tenth (man) (originally, for punishment) – ie reduce by a tenth, (loosely) reduce drastically

DEC(OR) Lat *decere* to be becoming, fitting, seemly; or related Latin words. Eg **decent** seemly, **decorate** make becoming – ie adorn, **decorous** seemly, **decorum** (that which is) seemly

DEI Lat *deus* god. Eg **deify** make (into a) god, **deist** (believer in) god (but rejecting revealed religion), **deity** a god

DELTA Gk *delta* – fourth letter of the Greek alphabet (equivalent to the English 'd'), written Δ as a capital. The **delta** of the Nile was so named because its shape resembled the shape of the letter. The word subsequently came to be used to refer to the alluvial deposit at the mouth of other rivers

DEMI Lat *dimidius* halved, half. Eg **demigod** half-god, **demi-monde** half-world – ie world on the edge of (high) society, **demisemiquaver** half a semiquaver, **demiwave** half-wave

DEMN Eg **condemn, indemnity** – see DAMN

DEM(O) Gk *demos* the people, a people or a district. Eg **demagogue** leader of the people, **democracy** rule by the people, **demography** writing (ie study) of peoples (ie of population), **endemic** (of a disease) (constantly present) in a people or district, **epidemic** (visitation of a disease) upon a people or district, **pandemic** (of a disease) (affecting) all a people or district – ie very widespread in a community

DENDR(O) Gk *dendron* tree. Eg **dendrometer** tree-measure – ie instrument for measuring trees, **rhododendron** rose tree

DENS Lat *densus* thick. Eg **condense** (make) (thoroughly) thick, **dense** thick

DENT(I) Lat *dens, dent-* tooth. Eg **dental** relating to the teeth, **dentiform** tooth- (or teeth-) shaped, **indent** (make a) tooth (or teeth) in – ie make notches in, or (of a line of text) start further in from the margin than the other lines, **indenture** (a making of) teeth in – ie a making of identical notches in all copies of a contract, a contract, **trident** three-toothed (ie three-pronged) (spear)

46

DERM(AT)(O) Gk *derma, dermat-* skin. Eg **dermatitis** (inflammation of) the skin, **dermatology** science of the skin, **epidermis** over-skin – ie the outer skin, **hypodermic** relating to the under-skin (ie the skin under the epidermis), **taxidermist** skin-arranger – ie one who stuffs and mounts animal skins

DEUT(ER)(O) Gk *deuteros* second, secondary. Eg **deuterium** the second (hydrogen) – ie 'heavy hydrogen' (hydrogen with twice the mass of ordinary hydrogen – see PROT(O)), **deuterogamy** second marriage, **Deuteronomy** – fifth book of the Bible, so named because of a reference it contained, in the Greek version, to a 'second law' (later understood to mean 'a copy of this law') (Deut 17:18)

DEXIO Gk *dexios* (on the) right. Eg **dexiotropic** turning (to the) right

DEXTR(O) Lat *dexter* (on the) right. Eg **ambidextrous** right (-handed) both sides – ie having both hands skilful, **dexterity** right(-handedness) – ie skilfulness, **dextrorotatory** rotating (to the) right, **dextrous** right(-handed) – ie skilful

DI Gk *dis* twice, double; *di-* double, two-. Eg **diatomic** two-atomed – ie consisting of two atoms, **dibranchiate** two-gilled, **dilemma** (form of argument in which the adversary is presented with a) double assumption (giving a choice between two unattractive alternatives – the 'horns' of the dilemma), **dimorphous** two-formed (species etc), **dipetalous** two-petalled, **dipthong** double sound – ie two vowel-sounds together

DI Eg **different, digress** – see DIS

DI Eg **diuretic** – see DIA

DIA, DI Gk *dia-, di-* through, between, apart, thoroughly. Eg **diagnose** know apart – ie tell apart, identify (a disease etc), **diagonal** (line) between (opposite) corners (of a figure), **diagram** (figure etc) written through – ie marked out with lines, **dialogue** a speaking between – ie a conversation,

dialysis a loosening apart – ie a separating out (eg of impurities in the blood, by a kidney machine), **diameter** (line) measured through – ie crossing a circle (etc) through its centre, **diaphanous** showing through – ie transparent, **diapositive** a through (ie transparent) (photographic) positive, **diarrhoea** (US **diarrhea**) a through-flowing, **diuretic** (promoting) urine through – ie promoting urination

DIA(N), DIURN Lat *dies* day; *quotidie* every day. Eg **ante meridiem ('am')** before midday, **diary** daily (journal), **dismal** – from *dies mali* ('evil days'), **diurnal** relating to (or lasting, in etc) a day (or) the day(time), **meridian** (sun's position at) midday (and other derivative meanings), **post meridiem ('pm')** after midday, **quotidian** (happening) every day

DICHO Gk *dicha* in two. Eg **dichotomy** a cutting into two

DIC(T) Lat *dicere, dict-* to say, speak; *dictare, dictat-* to say again, say often; *dicare, dicat-* to say forcefully, proclaim. Eg **abdicate** proclaim away – ie renounce, **benediction** a well-saying – ie a blessing, **contradict** speak against – ie deny (a statement), **dictator** (person who) says often – ie gives commands, has absolute authority, **diction** (way of) speaking, **dictionary** (book) relating to sayings (ie words), **dictum** '(thing) said', 'saying', **edict** (thing) said out – ie proclaimed, **jurisdiction** law-saying – ie legal authority, authority, area over which an authority has sway, **malediction** an ill-saying – ie a curse, **predict** say before – ie foretell, **valediction** a saying farewell, **verdict** a true-saying – ie a finding, judgement, **veridical** saying the truth

DIDACT Gk *didaskein* to teach. Eg **autodidact** self-taught (person), **didactic** relating to (ie intended as etc) teaching

DIGIT(I) Lat *digitus* finger, toe. Eg **digit** (number counted on the) finger(s), **digitiform** finger-shaped

DIPLO Gk *diploos* double, twofold. Eg **diploma** doubled (ie folded) (paper), **diplomatic** relating to doubled (ie folded) (papers) – ie the documents through which international

48

relations are conducted, **diplopia** double eyes – ie double vision

DIRGE From the first word of an antiphon in the office for the dead beginning, in Latin, *Dirige, Domine, Deus meus ... viam meam* – Direct, Lord my God ... my path

DIS, DI (or DIF, before 'f') Lat prefix *dis-, di-,* of which the main senses are (1) apart, asunder, (2) a negation or reversal of meaning. Eg **different** bearing apart – ie tending in separate directions, not the same, **difficult** not easy, **diffident** not trusting (oneself) – ie lacking self-assurance, **digress** step apart – ie depart from (a subject etc), **discordant** (with) hearts apart – ie out of harmony, disagreeing, **disinter** to reverse interment – ie dig up, **dislocate** place asunder – ie put out of joint, **dismiss** send apart – ie send away, **disperse** scatter apart, **dispute** a reckoning apart – ie an assessing, a debate, an argument, **disrupt** break apart – ie break up, **dissect** to cut apart – ie cut up, **disseminate** to seed apart – ie scatter around, spread around, **dissident** (person) sitting apart – ie not agreeing, **dissonant** sounding apart – ie out of harmony, **distant** standing apart

DISCIPL Lat *discipulus* pupil. Eg **disciple** pupil, **discipline** (that which is learned by) pupils – or the training given to them, or the means by which the training is inculcated, (etc)

DIURN Eg **diurnal** – see DIA(N)

DIV(IN) Lat *divus* (feminine: *diva*) belonging or relating to a god, godlike. Eg **diva** goddess(-like singer), **divination** godlike (ie god-inspired) (foretelling of the future), **divine** godlike (or belonging or relating to God/a god)

DOC(T) Lat *docere, doct-* to teach; *docilis* teachable. Eg **docile** teachable – ie easily led, easily handled, **doctor** teacher – ie learned person, **doctrine** teaching, **document** teaching – ie lesson, pattern, proof, written instruction, paper, text, **indoctrinate** teach (thoroughly)

DODECA Gk *dodeka* twelve. Eg **dodecahedron** twelve-seated (figure) – ie solid figure with twelve faces

DOGMA, DOX Gk *dokeein* to think; *doxa* opinion; *dogma, dogmat-* opinion, resolution, tenet. Eg **dogma** tenet, **dogmatic** relating to a tenet – or asserting something as though it was an (unchallengeable) tenet, **heterodox** (holding) another opinion (ie other than the conventional opinion), **orthodox** of the straight (ie conventional) opinion, **paradox** (statement etc) against (conventional) opinion – ie contrary to what one would expect

DOL Lat *dolere* to suffer pain, grieve. Eg **condolence** a grieving with (ie in sympathy), **dolorous** grieving or painful, **indolence** painlessness – ie freedom from pain or trouble, unwillingness to put oneself to any trouble, laziness

DOM Lat *domus* house, home. Eg **domestic** relating to the house, **domicile** home – ie place of residence, **major-domo** greater (officer) of the house – ie official responsible for managing a large household

DOMIN Lat *dominus* master, lord. Eg **AD** (abbreviation of **anno domini**) (in the) year of (our) Lord, **condominium** (property etc subject to) lordship with – ie joint control, **dominate** (exercise) lordship (over), **domineering** lording (it) (over others), **dominical** relating to the Lord('s Day), **dominion** (territory etc subject to) lordship

DON Lat *donare, donat-* to give. Eg **condone** give (thoroughly) – ie give away, forgive (a fault), overlook or excuse (a fault), **donate** give, **donor** giver

DORM Lat *dormire, dormit-* to sleep. Eg **dormant** sleeping, **dormitory** (place for) sleeping

DORS(I) Lat *dorsum* the back. Eg **dorsal** relating to the back, **dorsibranchiate** (having) gills (on) the back, **endorse** (write one's signature etc) on the back (of a document) – ie ratify, approve etc

DOS, DOT Gk *dosis* a giving; *-dotos* given. Eg **anecdote** not given out – ie unpublished (thing) – the modern meaning owes much to the seventh-century *Anekdota* ('Things Unpublished') by Procopius, which were a gossipy account of his time, **antidote** (substance etc) given against (poison etc), **dose** a giving – ie a portion

DOX Eg **orthodox, heterodox** – see DOGMA

DRACONIAN Gk *Draco* – name of an Athenian chief magistrate of the seventh century BC renowned for the severity of his code of laws. Hence **draconian** is used to mean very severe or harsh

DROM Gk *dromos* course, running; *dromas, dromad-* running; or related Greek words. Eg **aerodrome** aero(plane) course, **dromedary** running (camel), **hippodrome** horse (race-) course, **palindrome** (word) running back – ie reading the same backwards, **syndrome** a running together – ie a set of symptoms occurring together

DUC(T) Lat *ducere, duct-* to lead. Eg **abduct** lead away – ie carry off, kidnap, **aqueduct** a leading of (ie a channel for) water, **conduct** lead (ie draw) together (an orchestra etc), **deduce** lead away – ie draw out (an inference etc), **deduct** lead away – ie subtract, **duct** a leading – ie a channel, **ductile** leadable – ie malleable etc, **educate** lead (ie draw) out (a person's potential), **induce** lead in – ie draw on, **introduce** lead within – ie bring in, **produce** lead (ie bring) forth, **reduce** lead back – ie lessen, lead aside (ie astray), **seduce** lead apart – ie lead astray, **viaduct** a leading of a way – ie a carrying of a way, a structure to carry a road or railway across (eg) a valley

DU(O) Lat *duo* two. Eg **dual** two, **duet** a little (song etc) (for) two, **duo** a twosome, **duotone** two-toned

DUODEC(I), DUODEN Lat *duodecim* twelve; *duodeni* twelve each. Eg **duodecimo** (book) (in a) twelfth – ie made up of pages twelve of which formed a sheet, **duodenum** – short for medieval Lat *intestinum duodenum digitorum* ('intestine of twelve fingers' – ie intestine twelve fingers' breadth long)

51

DUPL Lat *duplex, duplic-* double, twofold. Eg **duplex** twofold – eg two-floored (apartment), **duplicate** a double – ie a copy, **duplicity** double(-dealing)

DUR Lat *durus* hard. Eg **duration** a hardening – ie time lasted, **duress** hardship, **durum (wheat)** hard (wheat), **endurance** an enhardening – ie staying power, **obdurate** (thoroughly) hardened (against something) – ie stubborn

DYNA(M)(O) Gk *dynamis* power. Eg **dynamic** relating to (or full of) power – or force(s), movement or energy, **dynamite** power (substance), **dynamo** power (generator)

DYS Gk prefix *dys* badly, ill-. Eg **dysentery** ill(ness of the) intestines, **dysfunction** ill-function, **dyslexic** badly (reading) speech (ie words) – ie word-blindness, **dyspepsia** (state of) badly digesting – ie indigestion, **dystrophy** ill-nourishment – or a wasting away (eg of the muscles)

E

E Eg **eject, emit, evoke** – see EX

EC, EX Gk *ek* from, out of, away from (or, as a prefix, forth). Eg **appendectomy** a cutting out of the appendix, **eccentric** out of centre – ie off-centre, deviating from the norm, **eclectic** picking out (bits of philosophy etc) (from different sources), **ecclesiastic** – see ECCLES, **eclipse** a leaving out – ie an omission, a disappearance (of the sun or moon etc), an overshadowing, **ecstasy** a putting out (of place) (of one's mind) – ie a state of distraction, a trance, **eczema** a boiling out – ie a boiling over or breaking out (of the skin), **exegesis** a guiding out – ie an explanation or interpretation (of a text etc), **exodus** a way (ie a going) out

ECCLES Gk *ekklesia* assembly of the citizens summoned by the crier, from *ekkletos* called forth (see EC). Eg **ecclesiastic** relating to the assembly – ie to the church

ECO, ECU Gk *oikos* house; *he oikoumene ge* the inhabited world, the civilised world. Eg **ecology** study of houses (ie habitats), **economy** house(hold) management – ie the management of the material resources of a community (eg a country), or the thrifty or efficient ('economical') use of resources, **ecumenical** relating to the inhabited (world) – ie to the whole (Christian) Church

ECTO Gk *ektos* outside. Eg **ectoderm** outside skin – ie outer layer (of cells in an embryo), **ectoparasite** outside parasite –ie parasite taking nourishment from the skin of its host, **ectoplasm** outside plasm – ie outer layer of the part of a cell called the cytoplasm, or a supposed emanation from a spiritualist medium in a trance

ECTOM(Y) Eg **hysterectomy, tonsillectomy** – see TOM

ECU Eg **ecumenical** – see ECO

EDIF Lat *aedificare, aedificat-* to build. Eg **edifice** building, **edifying** building (up) – ie improving, instructive

EGO Lat *ego* I, I myself. Eg **alter ego** other I – ie one's other self, **ego** the 'I' – or the conscious thinking self, **egocentric** self-centred, **egoism** selfishness, **egotism** (over-concern with) self

EID Eg **kaleidoscope** – see OID

ELECTR(O) Gk *elektron* amber. Eng **electricity** was first applied to the property of attraction observed in amber and other substances when rubbed; it was subsequently applied to the cause of this phenomenon

EM (US) **anemia, leucemia** – see (H)AEM(O)

EM Eg **emblem, empathy** – see EN

EMES, EMET Gk *emein* to vomit. Eg **emetic** (medicine) (causing) vomiting

EMPT Lat *emere, empt-* to take, buy. Eg **exempt** taken out – ie freed from liability, **peremptory** (thoroughly) taking – ie taking entirely, destroying, deadly, final, ruling out opposition, **pre-empt** buy before – eg forestall others by taking up an opportunity first, **redemption** a buying back – or a freeing, salvation

EN, EM Gk *en* in. Eg **emblem** (thing) thrown in (ie inserted) – as a sign or representation of something else, **empathy** an in-feeling – ie a getting 'inside' another person (or, eg, a work of art) so that one feels with him/her, **energy** (power of being) in work – ie at work, active, **enthusiast** (person with) god in – ie who is inspired by a god, is fervent, keen

ENANTIO Gk *enantios* opposite. Eg **enantiomorph** (crystal etc) (with the) opposite shape (to another) – ie that is the mirror-image of another

ENCEPHAL(O) Eg **encephalogram** – see CEPHAL(O)

ENDO Gk *endon* within, (on the) inside. Eg **endocardium** (membrane) on the inside of the heart – ie the lining of the heart, **endocrine** (of glands) separating within – ie secreting internally, **endoderm** inside skin – ie inner layer (of cells in an embryo), **endogamy** (custom of) marriage within (a tribe etc) – or pollination between two flowers on the same plant, **endogenous** produced inside – ie developing internally, having no external origin, **endometrium** (membrane) inside the womb – ie the lining of the womb, **endoscope** inside viewer – ie instrument for looking inside the body

ENN Eg **biennial, millennium** – see ANN

ENNEA Gk *ennea* nine. Eg **enneagon** nine-cornered (ie nine-angled) (figure)

ENT, ESS Lat *esse* to be. Eg **absent** being away, **entity** a being – ie something that is, **essence** (the very) being (of something), **essential** (constituting) (the very) being (of something) – or necessary for the existence of something, **presence** a being before – ie a being in view, a being there

ENTER(O) Gk *enteron* intestine. Eg **dysentery** ill(ness of the) intestines, **enteric** relating to the intestines, **enterovirus** virus (affecting) the intestines, **gastroenteritis** (inflammation of) (the lining of) the stomach and intestines, **gastroenterology** study of the stomach and intestines

ENT(O) Gk *entos* within, inside. Eg **entoptic** within the eye(ball), **entozoon** within animal – ie a parasite living inside its host

ENTOM(O) Gk *entomon* 'cut-into (creature)' – ie 'cut-up creature', 'segmented creature', insect (see TOM). Eg **entomology** science of insects, **entomophagous** insect-eating, **entomophilous** insect-beloved, insect-loving – ie pollinated by insects

EO Gk *eos* dawn Eg **Eocene** – see CENE, **eolith** dawn stone – ie very early stone implement, **eosin** dawn(-red) (dyestuff)

EP(I), EPH Gk *epi* on, upon, over, over and above; (also) near, towards, to (and many other subsidiary meanings). Eg **ephemeral** (lasting only) over (ie for) a day – ie short-lived, **epicentre** (point) over the centre – ie point on the earth's surface directly over the point of origin of an earthquake, **epidemic** (visitation of a disease) upon a people or district, **epidermis** over-skin – ie outer skin, **epiglottis** (flap) over the glottis, **epigram** (thing) written upon (something) – ie an inscription, a pithy saying, (etc), **epigraph** a writing upon – ie an inscription, **epilepsy** (disease characterised by) seizings upon – ie attacks, seizures, **epilogue** speech-upon – ie a speech coming 'on top of' (ie at the end of) a play (or a piece coming at the end of a book), **epiphany** a showing to – ie a manifestation, **episcopal** relating to (or governed by etc) overviewers – ie overseers, bishops, **epitaph** (words) over a tomb – ie (in Greek) a funeral oration, (in English) words written on a tomb, **epithet** (word) placed on (a noun) – ie a word added to a noun (to denote some quality that the thing has), a descriptive term, **eponymous** (having his/her) name upon – ie after whom a book etc was named

EPICUR Gk *Epikouros* Epicurus – a Greek philosopher (c341-

270BC), who taught that the pursuit of 'pleasure' (or, more accurately, the absence of pain – and by absence of pain he meant peace of mind rather than the absence of physical discomfort) is the highest good, a doctrine popularly (but wrongly) taken as sanctioning the exclusive pursuit of sensual gratification. Hence an **epicure** is a person given to refined sensual pleasures, especially as regards food and drink

EQUES, EQUIN, EQUIT Lat *equus* horse; *eques, equit-* horse-rider. Eg **equestrian** relating to horse-riding, **equine** relating to horses, **equitation** horse-riding

EQU(I), INIQUI Lat *aequus* equal. Eg **adequate** made equal (to a purpose) – ie good enough (for a purpose), **equable** equal (-tempered) – ie even(-tempered), **equanimity** equal-mindedness – ie evenness of mind or temper, **equation** an equalling – ie a making equal, **equator** equaliser – so called because day and night are equal when the sun crosses it (ie at the equinoxes – see below), **equidistant** equally distant, **equilibrium** equally balanced (state), **equinox** equal night – ie when the night is equal (in length) to the day, **equity** equalness – ie fairness, **equivalent** (having) equal power, equal worth – ie corresponding, the same, **equivocal** equally named (but capable of meaning different things) – ie of double or doubtful meaning, **equivocate** call equally – ie have the same name (sound) as, use words capable of more than one meaning (in order to mislead), **iniquity** unequalness – ie unfairness, wickedness

EQUIN, EQUIT Eg **equine, equitation** – see EQUES

ERGO Lat *ergo* therefore

ERG(O), URG(Y) Gk *ergon* work. Eg **allergy** other work – ie a different reaction or altered sensitivity (such as is brought about when when one been exposed to a sensitising dose of a substance), **energetic** in work – ie at work, active, **erg** (unit of) work, **ergonomics** (science of) work management – ie study of the best way to organise work, **metallurgy** metal-working – ie including extraction etc, **synergy** a working together

56

ERO(T) Gk *eros, erot-* (sexual) love, desire; *Eros* Eros – the Greek god of love (identified by the Romans with their Cupid – see CUPI(D)). Eg **erogenous** producing love (ie sexual desire or sexual pleasure), **erotic** relating to (sexual) love

ERR Lat *errare, errat-* to wander. Eg **aberrant** wandering away from (the right path, or the usual path), **err** wander – ie stray, make a mistake, **erratic** wandering – ie irregular, unpredictable, **erratum** a wandering – ie a straying, a mistake, **error** a wandering – ie a straying, a mistake

ERT Eg **inert** – see ART

ERYTH(R)(O) Gk *erythros* red. Eg **erythema** redness (of the skin), **erythrocyte** red (blood-)cell, **erythrophyll** red (colouring matter of) leaves

ESOTER Gk *esotero* more within, inner, from *eso* within. Eg **esoteric** relating to (or belonging to) the inner (group) – ie only for the select few

ESS Eg **essence** – see ENT

ESTH Eg **esthetic** (US) – see (A)ESTH

ESTR(O) Eg **estrogen** (US) – see (O)ESTR(O)

ET Lat *et* and. Eg **etc** (abbreviation of **et cetera**) 'and the others', 'and the rest'

ETH(IC) Gk *ethos* custom, usage, character. Eg **ethical** relating (or conforming) to customs – ie to morals, **ethics** (theory or code of) customs – ie of morals, **ethos** character – ie characteristic set of attitudes etc (eg of a group)

ETHN(O) Gk *ethnos* race, nation, people. Eg **ethnic** relating to race – or belonging to a particular race or particular races, or to an exotic race or culture, **ethnography** race writing – ie description of the different races

ETYM(O) Gk *etymos* true. Eg **etymology** discourse on (ie an account of, study of) the true (basis) (of a word) – ie an account of its true sense or origin, or the study of the origins of words

EU Gk *eu-* well-. Eg **eugenics** (science of) producing well – ie of producing fine offspring or improving the racial stock, **eulogy** a speaking well (of someone), **euphemism** a well-speaking – ie substituting a mild term for a blunter one when referring to something unpleasant, **euphonious** well-sounding – ie making a pleasing sound, **euphoria** a well-bearing – ie an exaggerated feeling of wellbeing, **euthanasia** a well-dying – ie a peaceful and painless death, the deliberate bringing about of death (in a painless way) in cases of incurable suffering

EUREKA see HEUR

EV Eg **longevity, medieval** – see (A)EV

EX, E (EF before 'f') Lat *e, ex* from, out of, away from (or, as a prefix, forth). As a prefix, *ex* sometimes has the sense of a changing state ('make...') or completeness ('thoroughly'). In English words and terms, 'ex' also occasionally means 'out of' in the sense 'without'. Eg **educate** lead out (a person's potential), **effeminate** made feminine, **effluent** (matter) flowing out, **effulgent** shining out, **effusion** an out-pouring, **eject** throw out, **eloquent** speaking out – ie speaking well, expressing well, **emaciated** made lean, **emigrate** move out of (a country etc), **emissary** (person) sent forth, **emit** send forth, **eradicate** root out, **erode** gnaw away – ie eat away, **erupt** break out, **evacuate** to empty out – or withdraw from (somewhere), **evoke** call forth – ie summon up, **excite** summon forth – ie rouse, **exclude** shut out, **excrescence** outgrowth, **exculpate** (free) from blame, **excursion** a run out, **exhale** breath out, **exhilarate** make cheerful, **exhort** (thoroughly) encourage or urge, **exit** go out, **ex officio** out of (one's) office – ie by virtue of one's office, **exosmosis** osmosis away (from the solution), **expand** spread out, **expatriate** (person) (in exile) from (his or her) native land, **expel** drive out, **export** carry out (of a country), **ex-president** (person) (coming) from (the rank of) president – ie former president

EX Gk Eg **exegesis, exodus** – see EC

EXO Gk *exo* outside. Eg **exocrine** (of glands) separating outside – ie secreting through a duct, **exogamy** (custom of) marriage outside (a tribe etc), **exogenous** produced outside – ie developing externally, having an external origin, **exoplasm** outside plasm – ie outer layer of the part of a cell called the cytoplasm, **exotic** (from) outside – ie foreign, outlandish

EXTER(N), EXTR(A), EXTREM Lat *exterus* (situated) outside, outward; *exterior* more outward, outer; *extremus* most outward, outermost; *extra* outside; *extraneus* (from) outside. Eg **exterior** outer, **external** relating to the outside, **extra** outside – ie beyond (the ordinary), especially, **extracurricular** outside the (formal) curriculum, **extramarital** outside marriage, **extramural** outside the walls – ie (of a university department) out in the community, serving students not belonging to the university, **extraneous** from outside – ie not belonging, foreign, or not essential, **extraordinary** outside the ordinary, **extrasensory** outside the (normal) senses, **extraterrestrial** (from) outside the earth, **extravagant** wandering outside (the bounds) – ie going beyond reasonable bounds, **extreme** (that which is) outermost – ie at the furthest limit, to the furthest degree, **extrovert** (person) turned outside (ie outwards)

F

FAB Lat *fabulari* to talk; *fabula* talk, story; *fari* to speak. Eg **affable** speakable to – ie easy to talk to, pleasant-mannered, **confab** (short for **confabulation**) a talking together, **fable** story, **fabulous** (like in a) story, **ineffable** not speak-outable – ie unutterable

FACIL, FACULT, FICULT Lat *facilis* easy; *difficilis* not easy. Eg **difficult** not easy, **facile** (over-)easy – ie over-fluent, simplistic, **facilitate** (make) easy (or easier), **facility** easiness – ie fluency, or something (eg sports 'facilities') that makes it 'easy' (ie possible) to do something, **faculty** easiness – ie capacity, (mental) power, or a department of learning at a university

FAC(T), FECT, FIC, FIAT Lat *facere, fact-* to make, do; *fieri, fact-* to be made, to be done; or related Latin words. Eg **abortifacient** making (ie bringing about) abortion, **affect** do to – ie act upon, **affection** a doing-to – ie an acting upon or influencing (the mind) (in favour of another person etc), a (loving) disposition of the mind (towards another person etc), **artificial** made by skill (rather than nature), **benefactor** a well-doer – ie one who does good, **clarification** a making clear, **confection** (thing) made together – ie brought together, mixed, prepared, ready-made, **confectionery** (sweets etc) made together – ie mixed, prepared, **defection** a making-away – ie an abandoning (of one's country, a cause etc), **deficient** (with something) making away – ie missing, **deficit** (that which is) made away – ie missing, **effect** a doing-out, making-out – ie a result, **efficient** doing out, making out – ie accomplishing, **facsimile** a 'make-the-like!' – ie an exact reproduction (eg of handwriting), **fact** (that which has been) done (as in legal contexts – 'accessory after the fact' etc) – or, a reality, **faction** a (group) doing or making – eg a political grouping, **factor** a doer – eg a circumstance etc influencing an outcome, **factory** (place for) making, **factotum** a 'do-all!' – ie a person taken on to do all sorts of tasks, **fiat** a 'let-it-be-done!' – ie a (formal) command or giving of permission, **fortification** a strong-making (structure), **infection** a making-into – ie an imbuing, tainting, corrupting, **magnification** a making great(er) – ie an enlarging (or a praising, extolling), **malefactor** a bad-doer – ie an evil-doer, **manufacture** make by hand – ie work up, produce (especially commercially), **mortification** a making dead – ie humiliation, **nullification** a making (into) nothing – ie a rendering void, **orifice** a mouth-making – ie a mouth-like opening, **pacific** peace-making – or peaceful, **perfect** thoroughly made – ie completely made, finished, faultless, **prolific** making (ie producing) (many) offspring – or having a large output, **putrefacient** making rotten – ie causing rotting, **refectory** (place for) remaking – ie renewing, refreshing oneself, **stupefaction** a making stunned – ie a state of being stunned, **unification** a making (into) one

60

FACULT Eg **faculty** – see FACIL

FALL, FALS Lat *fallere, fals-* to deceive. Eg **fallacious** deceptive, **fallacy** a deception – ie a mistaken belief (or an apparently logical argument which is in fact flawed), **fallible** deceivable – ie capable of making a mistake, **false** deceptive – ie not real, wrong

FAM Lat *fama* talk, rumour, repute. Eg **defamation** (a putting) apart (ie in different directions, about) of (bad) talk (about someone) – ie a spreading of a bad report (of someone), **famous** talked (about) – ie renowned, **infamous** not of repute – ie of ill repute

FAN Eg **infant** – see INFAN

FAN(AT) Lat *fanum* temple; *fanaticus* relating (or belonging) to a temple, inspired by a god. Eg **fan** – short for 'fanatic', **fanatic** inspired by a god – ie obsessed, **profane** before (ie outside) the temple – ie not sacred, unholy

FAN(T), PHAN(T), PHEN Gk *phantazein* to make visible; *phainein* to show. Eg **diaphanous** showing through – ie transparent, **epiphany** a showing to – ie a manifestation, **fantasy** (or **phantasy**) a making visible (of objects to the mind) – ie imagination, an imagined story etc, **fantom** (or **phantom**) a making visible – ie an apparition, **phantasm** a making visible – ie an apparition, **phenomenon** (thing) being shown – ie thing being seen, thing perceived, remarkable thing

FARC(T) Lat *farcire* to stuff, cram. Eg **farce** stuffing – the French word *farce*, through which the English word is derived from Latin, was applied to impromptu interruptions of religious plays to expand on the text; hence the sense derived, in English and French, of buffoonery, a theatrical comedy designed only to provoke laughter, (etc), **infarction** a stuffing-up – ie a portion of tissue in an unhealthy state because the blood supply to it has been obstructed by a blood clot etc

FASC Lat *fascis* bundle (the plural, *fasces*, referred particularly

61

to the bundle of sticks, with an axe sticking out from it, carried in front of the chief Roman magistrates); *fasciculus* little bundle. Eg **fascicle** little bundle (eg of fibres) – or one part of a text issued in parts, **fascist** – from the *Fascisti* in Italy, whose name is taken from the *Fasci di combattimento* ('combat bundles', 'combat groups', perhaps also with the hint of a reference to the *fasces*) founded by Mussolini

FAT Lat *fatum* thing spoken, utterance; hence, an utterance of a god, the expressed will of a god; hence that which has been decreed, destiny, the natural term of life. (The *Fata* or *Parcae*, the Fates, were the three goddesses who, spinning a thread of life for each person, allotted each one's birth, life events and death – see also STAMEN.) Eg **fatal** relating to (or decreed by) destiny – especially relating to (ie bringing about) destined calamity or the final destined event (ie death), **fatalism** (belief that the course of events is governed by) destiny (and so cannot be altered), **fatality** destined (end) – ie death, **fate** destiny, **fatidical** destiny-saying – ie foretelling the future, prophetical

FATU Lat *fatuus* foolish, silly. Eg **fatuous** foolish, silly, **infatuate** en-foolish – ie make foolish, inspire with foolish passion

FAUC, FOC Lat *fauces* throat. Eg **faucal** relating to the throat, **suffocate** (put the hands) under (ie round) the throat – ie deprive of air

FAUN(A) Lat *Faunus* – name of the Roman god or demigod of the countryside (sometimes identified with the Greek Pan – see PANIC), worshipped by shepherds and farmers. Hence the spirits inhabiting the woods were called *fauni* (Eng **faun**). *Fauna*, another rural deity and the sister of *Faunus*, has given English the word **fauna** for the animal life (as opposed to the plant life – see FLOR) of a particular place or time

FEBR(I) Lat *febris* fever. Eg **febrifuge** (medicine) putting fever to flight, **febrile** feverish

FEBRUARY Lat *Februa* – name (from an older word for

purification) of the Roman festival of purification; the festival gave its name to the month in which it occurred. Hence Eng **February**

FECT Eg **affect, infection, perfect** – see FAC(T)

FELIC Lat *felix, felic-* happy. Eg **felicitate** (make) happy – or pronounce oneself happy (ie congratulate), **felicitous** happy – or well chosen, apt, **felicity** happiness

FENEST(R) Lat *fenestra* window; *fenestella* little window (or other opening). Eg **defenestration** a (throwing) from a window, **fenestella** little window – or window-like opening or niche, **fenestrated** windowed – or pierced or perforated

FER Lat *ferre* to bear, carry, bring; or related Latin words. Eg **carboniferous** coal- (or carbon-) bearing, **circumference** a bearing round – ie a boundary line round, **conference** a bearing together – ie a bringing together, a meeting for discussion, **conifer** cone-bearing (tree), **deference** a carrying down – ie a handing over, giving way, treating with respect, **different** bearing apart – ie tending in separate directions, **infer** bear in, bring in (a conclusion etc) – ie draw a conclusion, imply, **offer** bear in the way of – ie bring in front of, hold out, **prefer** bear in front – ie give more prominence to, like better, **proliferate** bear (many) offspring – ie reproduce, multiply, **refer** bear back – ie turn (to) for information etc, hand over for consideration, (etc), **suffer** carry under – ie carry from underneath, support, put up with, **transfer** bear across (from one place to another), **vociferous** voice-carrying – ie uttering (or uttered) in a loud voice

FER, FEROC Lat *ferus* wild; *fera (bestia)* wild animal; *ferox, feroc-* wild, savage. Eg **feral** wild – or like a wild animal, **ferocious** savage

FERR(O), FERRUGO Lat *ferrum* iron; *ferrugo* iron rust, the colour of iron rust. Eg **ferric** and **ferrous** relating to (or containing) iron, **ferro-alloy** alloy of iron, **ferrotype** iron-type – ie photograph on an iron plate, **ferruginous** relating to (ie containing, like, of the colour of) iron rust, **ferrugo** rust (disease of plants)

FERV Lat *fervere* to boil, glow with heat. Eg **effervescent** boiling forth – ie boiling up, frothing up, bubbling, **fervent** boiling, glowing with heat – ie burning with emotion or belief, **fervour** a boiling, a glowing with heat – ie a burning, passion

FESS Lat *fateri, fass-* to declare, avow (guilt etc). Eg **confess** (thoroughly) declare (one's guilt), **profess** declare forth – ie declare publicly, take religious vows, declare oneself expert in, **profession** a declaring forth – ie a public declaration (of faith etc), a calling

FET, FOET Lat *fetus* a giving birth, that which is given birth – ie offspring; *effetus* having given birth, weakened by having given birth. Eg **effete** weakened by having given birth – ie exhausted, worn out, decadent, **fetus** (or **foetus**) offspring (in the womb)

FIAT see FAC(T)

FIBULA Lat *fibula* brooch, clasp, buckle. Eg **fibula** brooch- or clasp-(like bone) – the outer bone stretching from the knee to the ankle, **infibulation** a clasping-up – ie a fastening-up with a clasp, a sewing-up

FIC Eg **clarification, efficient, orifice, pacific** – see FAC(T)

FICT Lat *fingere, fict-* to mould, fashion. Eg **fictile** relating to moulding – ie relating to pottery, made by a potter, or capable of being moulded, plastic, **fiction** a moulding, fashioning – ie invention, an invented story

FICULT Eg **difficult** – see FACIL

FID Lat *fidere* to trust, have faith in; *fides* trust, faith; *fidelis* trustworthy, faithful. Eg **affidavit** 'he/she has (applied) faith to' (ie has stated on faith, declared on oath) – ie statement made on oath, **bona fide** '(in) good faith' – ie genuine, **confide** (thoroughly) trust – ie impart secrets (to someone),

confident (thoroughly) trusting – ie sure, self-assured, **diffident** not trusting (oneself) – ie lacking self-assurance, **fidelity** faithfulness, **Fido** (as a dog's name) Faithful, **fiduciary** relating to (or depending on, held in, etc) trust, **infidel** unfaithful (person) – ie unbeliever, person who does not accept a (particular) (religious) faith

FILI Lat *filius* son; *filia* daughter. Eg **affiliation** (adoption) as a son or daughter – ie as a branch, as a related organisation etc, **filial** relating to (or like, suited to, etc) a son or daughter

FIN Lat *finis* boundary, end. Eg **affinity** a bounding-to – ie a bordering on, a having something in common, **confine** (have a) boundary together – ie to share a boundary, to border, limit, enclose, **define** to (thoroughly) bound – ie to establish the limits of, describe precisely, **definite** (thoroughly) bounded – ie having fixed limits, fixed, **finite** bounded, ended – ie having a boundary, having an end, **infinite** unbounded, unended – ie having no boundary, no end

FISC Lat *fiscus* wicker basket, money-basket, chest, treasury. Eg **confiscate** (take possession of) with (ie for) the treasury – ie seize (by authority), **fiscal** relating to the treasury (or taxes)

FISS(I) Lat *findere, fiss-* to split, cleave. Eg **fissile** splittable, **fissilingual** (having a) cloven tongue, **fission** a splitting (eg of the nucleus of an atom), **fissiparous** bringing forth (by) splitting – ie reproducing by dividing, **fissipede** (creature with) split feet (ie separate digits), **fissure** a split

FLAGELL Lat *flagrum* a whip; *flagellum* a (little) whip. Eg **flagellation** a whipping, **flagellum** little-whip(-like appendage)

FLAGR Lat *flagrare, flagrat-* to blaze, burn. Eg **conflagration** a (thorough) burning – ie a burning-up, blaze, **flagrant** blazing – ie blatant, outrageous, **in flagrante delicto** in 'the offence blazing' – ie in the very act of committing the offence

FLAT Lat *flare, flat-* to blow, breathe. Eg **conflate** blow together – ie fuse, combine, **deflated** de-blown (up) – ie having had the air let out of, **flatulence** (tendency to) blowing (ie producing wind), **inflated** blown into – ie blown up

FLAV Lat *flavus* yellow. Eg **flavescent** yellowish or yellowing, **flavin** yellow (dye)

FLECT, FLEX Lat *flectere, flex-* to bend. Eg **circumflex** bent-round (accent, over a letter), **deflect** bend (ie turn) away, **flex** to bend – or (as a noun) bendable insulated electric wire etc, **flexible** bendable – ie pliable, **genuflect** bend the knee, **inflection** a bending in – ie a modulation (of the voice), **reflect** to bend back – ie to throw back (light, an image etc), or turn one's mind (on to something), **reflex** a bending back – ie an involuntary reaction

FLICT, FLIG Lat *fligere, flict-* to strike (down), dash (down). Eg **afflicted** struck against – ie troubled, suffering, **conflict** a striking together – ie a struggle, clash, **inflict** dash (a blow etc) against (someone) – ie impose harm or trouble (on someone), **profligate** struck down forward – ie struck to the ground, overthrown, ruined, dissolute

FLOR Lat *flos, flor-* flower. Eg **floral** relating to (or consisting of etc) flowers, **floret** little flower, **florid** flowery. Also from Lat *flos, flor-* came *Flora*, the name of the Roman goddess of flowers, adopted as a term (**flora**) for the plant life of a particular place or time (see also FAUN(A))

FLU, FLUX Lat *fluere, flux-* to flow. Eg **affluence** a flowing towards – ie a flowing plentifully, wealth, **confluence** a flowing together, **effluent** (matter) flowing out, **fluent** flowing, **fluid** flowing, **flux** a flowing, **influence** an in-flowing – first used of the supposed flow from the planets of a fluid that had power over humans and their affairs; hence such power exercised by humans themselves, **influx** an in-flowing, **mellifluous** honey-flowing – ie flowing with honey, flowing sweetly, sweet as honey, **superfluous** above-flowing – ie overflowing, present in greater quantity than is needed

FLUCTU Lat *fluctus* a wave. Eg **fluctuate** (move up and down like a) wave

FLUVI(O) Lat *fluvius* river. Eg **fluvial** relating to (ie belonging to etc) rivers, **fluvio-glacial** relating to glacial rivers

FLUX Eg **influx** – see FLU

FOC Lat *focus* hearth. Eg **focus** hearth – ie the centre of activity, **matrifocal** mother-hearthed – ie (of a society, family etc) in which the mother has the leading role

FOC Eg **suffocate** – see FAUC

FOET Eg **foetus** – see FET

FOLI Lat *folium* leaf. Eg **bifoliate** two-leaved, **foliage** leaves, **foliation** leafing (of plants etc), **folic (acid)** leaf (acid) – because folic acid was originally obtained from leaves, **folio** leaf (of paper), **portfolio** leaf-carrier – ie case for carrying papers, collection of papers, the office of a minister of state

FORENSIC see FORUM

FORM Lat *forma* shape; *formula* 'little shape' – ie pattern. Eg **conform** (thoroughly) shape – ie fashion in accordance with an established shape, follow an established pattern, **cruci-form** cross-shaped, **deformed** misshapen, **form** shape, **formal** relating to shape – or following an established 'shape' or mode, **format** shape, **formula** pattern (of words, symbols etc), **inform** enshape – ie give shape to (someone's thoughts, by conveying knowledge), **reform** a reshaping, **transform** to shape across – ie change from one shape to another, change completely, **uniform** of the same shape – ie the same, unvarying

FORM(IC) Lat *formica* ant. Eg **formic (acid)** ant (acid) – because formic acid is found in ants, **formication** ant(-feeling) – ie a sensation of ants crawling over the skin

FORT Lat *fortis* strong. Eg **comforting** (thoroughly) strengthening, **effort** strength (put) forth – ie deployment of strength, exertion, **fort** strong (place), **forte** (person's) strong (point), **fortify** make strong, **fortitude** strength

FORTU(N) Lat *fortuna* chance, luck, personified as *Fortuna*, the goddess of chance (especially of good luck); *forte* by chance. Eg **fortuitous** by chance, **fortunate** lucky, **fortune** chance – or the good or bad luck allotted to an individual, or the gifts of chance (wealth etc)

FORUM, FORENS Lat *forum* market-place, the open space or square in a Roman town where commercial, legal and political business was conducted. Hence Eng **forum**, applied to various kinds of meetings for discussion etc. Lat *forensis* (relating to the forum, hence relating to legal proceedings) gives Eng **forensic** (relating to legal proceedings)

FOSS Lat *fodere, foss-* to dig; *fossa* a ditch, trench. Eg **fosse** ditch, trench, **fossil** diggable – ie (of remains) preserved in the earth, **fossorial** (suited to) digging

FRACT, FRAG, FRING Lat *frangere, fract-* to break; *fragilis* easily broken; *fragmentum* piece broken off. Eg **diffract** break apart – ie break up (light etc), **fraction** a breaking – or the part or piece broken off, **fractious** breaking – ie discordant, quarrelsome, fretful, **fracture** breakage, **fragile** easily broken, **fragment** piece broken off, **frangible** (easily) breakable, **infringe** break into – ie violate, **refract** break back – ie break up, break the straight line of (light etc)

FRANTIC – see PHREN(O)

FRAT(E)R(I) Lat *frater* brother; (plural) *fratri* brothers and sisters. Eg **fraternal** brotherly, **fraternity** brotherhood, **fraternise** (associate as) brothers, **fratricide** killing (or killer) of (one's own) brother

FREN Eg **frenetic, frenzy** – see PHREN(O)

FRI(C) Lat *fricare* to rub; *friare* to rub, crumble. Eg **friable** crumbly, **friction** a rubbing

FRIG Lat *frigus* cold. Eg **frigid** cold, **frigorific** cold-making – ie causing cold, freezing, **refrigerate** to cold back – ie make cold

68

FRING Eg **infringe** – see FRACT

FRONT Lat *frons, front-* forehead. Eg **affront** (insult someone) to the forehead – ie to his/her face, openly, **confront** (bring) foreheads together – ie come face to face, challenge, **effrontery** out-foreheadedness – ie bare-faced behaviour, impudence, **front** forehead – ie the foremost part

FRUCT(I), FRUG(I), FRUI Lat *frui, fruct-* to enjoy; *fructus* enjoyment, fruits of the earth, fruit; *frux, frug-* fruits of the earth, fruit. Eg **fructiferous** or **frugiferous** fruit-bearing, **fructivorous** or **frugivorous** fruit-eating, **fructose** fruit (sugar), **frugal** (using as) fruits of the earth (sparingly) – ie sparing, economical, **fruition** enjoyment – ie the bearing-fruit of plans, measures taken etc, **usufruct** use (and) enjoyment (of a thing) – but without ownership

FUG Lat *fugere, fugit-* to flee; *fugare* put to flight. Eg **centrifugal** fleeing the centre, **febrifuge** (medicine) putting fever to flight, **fugacious** (tending to) flee – ie not lasting long, **fugitive** fleeing (person etc), **refuge** (place for) fleeing back – ie shelter, place of safety, **subterfuge** flight below – ie secret flight, secret escape, device used to escape

FULG Lat *fulgere* to shine. Eg **effulgent** shining out

FULMIN Lat *fulmen, fulmin-* lightning-strike, thunderbolt. Eg **fulminate** to thunder

FUM Lat *fumus* smoke, vapour. Eg **fume** smoke, **fumigate** (treat with) smoke, **perfume** to smoke through – ie to fill with a (sweet-smelling) smoke, to scent

FUNCT Lat *fungi, funct-* to be busy, occupy oneself with, do or discharge (a task etc). Eg **defunct** (thoroughly) discharged – ie dead, **function** a doing, a discharging – ie an activity, purpose, **perfunctory** thoroughly discharged (or discharging) – ie got (or getting) rid of, done (or doing) for form's sake or superficially

FUND Lat *fundus* bottom, base. Eg **fund** base – ie basis, source, supply, stock of money, **fundamental** basic, **profundity** (a going) forward (to the) bottom – ie a going deep down

FUN(IC) Lat *funis* rope; *funiculus* little rope. Eg **funambulist** rope walker, **funicular (railway)** (railway hauled by a) little rope – ie by a cable

FURC Lat *furca* fork. Eg **bifurcate** to two-fork – ie to fork into two branches, **furcate** forked

FUS Lat *fundere, fus-* to pour, melt. Eg **confuse** pour together – ie mix up, **diffuse** pour asunder – ie pour out on all sides, spread about, scatter, publish, **effusion** an out-pouring, **fuse** melt (together) – or, in electrics, to fail as a result of the melting of a fuse, which is a piece of meltable metal (not the same derivation as the 'fuse' of a bomb – see FUS below), **fusible** meltable, **fusion** a melting, **infuse** pour in – ie instil, allow to penetrate, **profusion** a pouring forth – ie an abundance, **suffuse** pour (from) under(neath) – ie pour through, spread over, **transfuse** pour across – ie pour from one place to another, pour through

FUS Lat *fusus* spindle. Eg **fuse** (of a bomb etc) spindle(-shaped container, tube etc) – not the same derivation as an electrical 'fuse' (see FUS above), **fuselage** spindle(-shaped structure) – ie the body of an aeroplane, **fusiform** spindle-shaped

G

GALACT(O), GALAXY Gk *gala, galakt-* milk. Eg **galactometer** milk measure – ie instrument for measuring the specific gravity of milk, **galactopoietic** milk-producing, **galactose** milk sugar – because it is derived from whey, **Galaxy** Milky (Circle) – ie the Milky Way

GAM, GAMET Gk *gamos* marriage; *gamete* wife; *gametes* husband. Eg **bigamous** twice married – ie married to two people at once, **gamete** wife/husband – ie an egg cell or a sperm cell, **gamopetalous** (having) married petals – ie with petals joined, **monogamy** single marriage – ie marriage with only one person at once, **polygamy** many-marriage – ie marriage with more than one person at once

GAMMA, GAMUT Gk *gamma* – third letter of the Greek alphabet (equivalent to the English 'g'). Eg **gamma rays** – name of a type of radiation, **gammadion** or **gammation** – a figure made up of capital gammas, written *Γ*, notably the swastika, **gamut** – the Greek letter was used to name the lowest note of the medieval musical scale, a note added below the A which was the bottom note of the old scale; 'gamut' was then used to refer to the whole of this scale, then to other whole ranges of notes, and finally to a range in general

GAST(E)R(O) Gk *gaster, gastr-* belly, stomach. Eg **Gast(e)ropoda** belly-footed (creatures) – class of molluscs with a 'foot' on the belly, **gastric** relating to the stomach, **gastritis** (inflammation of) the stomach, **gastroenterology** study of the stomach and intestines, **gastronomy** belly management – ie the art or science of good food

GAUD Lat *gaudere* to be joyous. Eg **gaudy** joyous – ie tastelessly showy

GEMIN Lat *geminus* twin. Eg **geminate** to twin – ie to double (in botany), **Gemini** the Twins – sign of the zodiac (a reference to the two bright stars Castor and Pollux – twin brothers of classical mythology)

GEM(M) Lat *gemma* bud, hence precious stone. Eg **gem** precious stone, **gemmate** (having or reproducing by) buds

GEN, GENESIS Gk *genea* birth, descent, race; *genos* race, stock, kind; *genesis* origin, birth; suffix *-genes* -born, -produced (the derivative English suffixes are also used to mean '-producing', '-producer') or of a (particular) kind. Eg **carcinogen** cancer-producer, **endogenous** produced inside – ie developing internally, having no external origin, **eugenics** (science of) producing well – ie of producing fine offspring or improving the racial stock, **exogenous** produced outside – ie developing externally, having an external origin, **gene** producing (factor) (or stock/descent factor) – ie physiological unit responsible for passing on hereditary characteristics, **genealogy** stock-discourse – ie an account of a person's descent, **genesis** origin, birth, **genetic** relating to origin, **genocide** killing of a race, **haematogenesis** (US **hematogenesis**) blood birth – ie the formation of blood, **heterogeneous** of another kind – ie different, made up of differing elements, **homogeneous** of the same kind – ie the same throughout, consistent, **hydrogen** water-producer – because hydrogen in combination with oxygen produces water, **mutagenic** change-producing, **oxygen** sharpness-producer – ie acid-producer (from the belief that oxygen was essential for the formation of acids), **pathogenic** suffering-producing – ie disease-producing

GEN(ER) Lat *genus, gener-* birth, descent, stock, race, class, kind; *Generare, Generat-* to beget (see also GEN(IT), INGEN). Eg **degenerate** (fallen) from the stock – ie having lost the qualities characteristic of the stock, having become debased, **general** relating to a class or kind – ie applying to the whole, not specific, **generate** beget – ie produce, **generation** a begetting – ie those who are begotten, all those who are begotten by one parent or are on the same level in a family tree, all those born at about the same time, **generator** begetter (ie producer) (of electrical power etc), **generic** relating to (ie belonging to) a class or kind – ie not specific, applying to the whole group, **generous** of (high) birth – ie noble, magnanimous, **genus** class, kind, **regeneration** a begetting again – ie rebirth

GENESIS – see GEN

GENI Lat *genius* the guardian spirit of a person or a place. Eg **congenial** guardian (or characteristic) spirits together – ie having the same spirit or temperament, suited to one's temperament, **genial** relating to (a person's) guardian spirit (or characteritic spirit) (as participating in enjoyment) – ie joyous, goodhumoured, **genie** guardian spirit – the meaning of the word 'genie', deriving from Latin, has been influenced by its use to translate the Arabic *jinn*, the name of a type of spirit in Muslim mythology; the jinn can assume animal and human shapes, and the 'genie' summoned by Aladdin with his lamp was in fact a jinni, **genius** guardian spirit – or characteristic spirit, or natural aptitudes, or extraordinary aptitude

GEN(IT) Lat *gignere, genit-* to beget, give birth to; *genitura* a begetting, birth; *progenies* descendants, offspring; all from the same root as *genus* and *generare* – see GEN(ER). Eg **congenital** born with (a person etc) – ie dating from birth, **genitals** begetting (organs), **primogeniture** (state of being) first-born (in a family) or the practice of inheritance by the first-born child, **progenitor** begetter forth – ie founder of a family, ancestor, **progeny** offspring

GENT Lat *gentilis* belonging to a clan or stock, or to the same clan or stock; from *gens, gent-* clan, stock. Eg **genteel** belonging to a (good) stock – ie well-born, well-bred, refined, **gentile** belonging to (or relating to) a clan (or race or nation) – or, as in the Bible, pagan or non-Jewish, **gentle** belonging to a (good) stock – ie well-born, well-bred, mild-mannered

GENU Lat *genu* knee. Eg **genuflect** bend the knee, **genuine** – the word has in the past been attributed the same root as genus etc (see GEN(ER)) but it is now thought that it derives from *genu*, knee, and originally referred to the gesture of recognition of a newborn child by its father: the custom was for him to take it on to his knees

GE(O) Gk *ge* earth; or related Greek words. Eg **apogee** (distance) (far) from the earth – ie the point at which a planet etc is farthest from the earth, the 'high point' of something, **geocentric** earth-centred – ie taking/having the earth as centre; or as viewed from the centre of the earth, **geography** earth writing – ie the description or science of the earth (its physical features etc), **geology** science of the earth, **geometry** (science of) measuring the earth – ie of physical dimensions and their relationships etc, **geophysics** the physics of the earth, **geosphere** earth-sphere – ie the solid part of the earth as opposed to the hydrosphere (see HYDR(O))

GER Eg **belligerent, dentigerous** – see GEST

GERAN Gk *geranos* crane. Eg **geranium** crane (plant) – because the seed-vessels are shaped like a crane's bill

GERM Lat *germen, germin-* bud, sprout. Eg **germ** the bud or sprout (of an illness, of an idea, etc) – from which the whole will grow, **germinal** relating to (or constituting) the bud (ie earliest stage) (of something), **germinate** to sprout

GER(ONTO) Gk *geras* old age; *geron, geront-* old man. Eg **geriatrics** old age doctoring – ie medical care of the old, **gerontocracy** rule by the old, **gerontology** study of the old (ie of old age)

GEST, GER Lat *gerere, gest-* to carry, carry out, wage (war etc); *-ger* carrying; *gestus* carriage (of the body), bodily movement; *gesticulus* little bodily movement. Eg **belligerence** war waging, **congestion** a carrying together – ie a heaping up, over-crowding, **dentigerous** teeth-carrying – ie having teeth, **digest** carry apart – ie break down into its separate parts, break down (in the stomach), **gestation** a carrying (of young in the womb), **gesture** carriage (of the body) – ie bodily movement, **gesticulate** (make) little bodily movements, **ingest** carry in – ie take in, **suggest** carry (from) under-(neath) – ie bring forward, put forward (eg into the mind)

GIGA, GIGANT Lat *gigas, gigant-* a giant; Gk *gigas, gigant-* a giant. (Note: in names of units, 'giga' is used in English to mean ten to the ninth power – a thousand million.) Eg **gigantic** giant (-like), giant(-sized), **giganticide** a giant-killing, **gigawatt** a thousand million watts

GIRO – see GYR(O)

GLACI(O) Lat *glacies* ice. Eg **glacial** icy – or relating to, or made of, ice; or (in chemistry) normally or easily solidified, **glacier** (mass of) ice

GLADI Lat *gladius* sword; *gladiolus* little sword. Eg **gladiate** sword(-shaped), **gladiator** swords(man), **gladiolus** little sword (plant) – because the leaves are sword-shaped

74

GLAUC Gk *glaukos* bluish-green, grey. Eg **glaucoma** (eye disease marked by) grey-green (cloud over the eye), **glaucous** greyish-green or greyish-blue – or covered with a greenish or bluish bloom

GLOM(ER) Lat *glomus, glomer-* ball (of thread or yarn). Eg **agglomerate** (gather) to a ball – ie gather into a mass, **conglomerate** ball together – ie mass together, **glomerulus** little ball (or cluster) (of small organisms in the body)

GLOSS, GLOT Gk *glossa* or *glotta* tongue; Lat *glossa* word needing explanation – or the explanation itself. Eg **gloss** explanation of a word etc, **glossary** (collection of) explanations of words etc, **glossectomy** a cutting out of the tongue, **glottis** tongue (opening) – ie the opening at the top of the windpipe, **idioglossia** one's own tongue – ie condition in which pronunciation is so bad that it cannot be understood, **monoglot** one-tongued person – ie one who speaks only one language, **polyglot** many-tongued (person) – ie one who speaks many languages

GLUC Eg **glucose** – see GLYC

GLUTEN, GLUTIN Lat *gluten, glutin-* glue. Eg **gluten** glue – ie the element in flour that makes it sticky when water is added, **glutinous** gluey

GLYC, GLUC Gk *glykys* sweet; *glykeros* sweet; *gleukos* sweet new wine, unfermented or only partially fermented grape-juice. Eg **glucose** sweet(ness of) wine – ie grape-sugar, **glycerine** sweet (substance), **glycosuria** sweetness (ie sugar) (in the) urine, **hyperglycaemia** (US **hyperglycemia**) over-sweetness (in the) blood – ie an abnormally high blood sugar level

GLYPH Gk *glyphein* to carve; *glyphe* carving. Eg **anaglyph** a carving-back – ie an embossed ornament, an ornament in low relief, **anaglypta** carving-back – ie embossed wallpaper, **hieroglyphics** sacred carvings – ie the picture-writing of the ancient Egyptians etc, **petroglyph** rock-carving

GNAT Eg **cognate** – see second NAT

GNOM Gk *gnomon* one who knows, an interpreter, a judge; *gnome* means of knowing, judgement, opinion (both related to *gnosis* knowledge – see GNOS). Eg **gnomic** relating to (or amounting to) an opinion (ie a general principle, a maxim), **physiognomy** interpreting from nature (ie from bodily characteristics) – ie the art of judging people's characters from their physical characteristics (especially those of the face); or the face itself

GNOS, GNOST, GNOTO Gk *gnosis* knowledge, the seeking of knowledge; *gnotos* known; *gignoskein* to know (see also GNOM). Eg **agnostic** (person) without knowledge – ie who does not believe that we have knowledge of any spiritual reality behind the material world, **diagnose** know apart – ie tell apart, identify (a disease etc), **gnosis** knowledge – especially spiritual knowledge, **gnostic** relating to (or having) knowledge – or (as a noun) a person claiming to have special spiritual knowledge, **gnotobiology** study of known life – ie study of life under germ-free conditions, **prognosis** a knowing before – ie a forecast (of the course of a disease etc)

GOG Eg **demagogy, pedagogue, synagogue** – see AGOG

GON, GONIO Gk *gonia* corner, angle. Eg **diagonal** (line) between (opposite) corners (of a figure), **goniometer** angle-measure – ie an instrument for measuring angles, **hexagon** six-cornered (figure), **octagon** eight-cornered (figure), **pentagon** five-cornered (figure), **polygon** many-cornered (figure)

GON(O) Gk *gonos* or *gone* begetting, birth, offspring, seed. Eg **geogony** (or **geogeny**) (an account or theory of) the begetting (ie the formation) of the earth, **gonad** begetting (organ) – ie an organ producing sex-cells, **gonocyte** begetting cell – ie sex-cell (egg-cell or sperm), **gonorrhoea** (US **gonorrhea**) seed flow – from the belief once held that the discharge characterising the disease was semen

GORGON Gk *Gorgo, Gorgon-* Gorgon; from *gorgos* terrible. The three Gorgons were female monsters of classical mythology. They were winged and had live snakes for hair. The most famous of the Gorgons is Medusa (see also MEDUSA); anyone who looked at her head turned to stone. Thus a **gorgon** is a monstrous or terrifying person (especially a woman)

GRAD, GRED, GRESS Lat *gradus* step; *gradi, gress-* to step, walk. Eg **aggressive** stepping against – ie on the attack, **centigrade** (relating to a system with) a hundred steps (ie degrees – between the freezing and boiling points of water), **congress** a walking together – ie a get-together, **degrade** down-step – ie reduce in rank or dignity etc, **digitigrade** walking on the toes, **digress** step apart – ie depart from (a subject etc), **grade** step – ie stage, classification etc, **gradual** step by step, **ingredient** (thing) stepping into (ie going into) (a mixture etc), **progress** a stepping forward, **regress** step back – ie go back (to an earlier stage), **retrograde** stepping backwards, **retrogress** step backwards, **transgress** step across – ie go beyond (the bounds), commit a fault

GRAM Gk *gramma, grammat-* thing written, writing, letter, line, from *graphein* to write (see also GRAPH). Eg **anagram** (new word formed by writing the) letters (of a word) back(wards) – or mixing them up, **cryptogram** hidden writing – ie writing in code, **diagram** (figure etc) written through – ie marked out with lines, **epigram** thing written upon (something) – ie an inscription, a pithy saying, (etc), **grammar** (the science of) letters (ie language – its structures etc), **hologram** a whole-writing – ie a three-dimensional image (produced by laser), **monogram** (two or more letters interwoven to make a) single letter – ie to make one symbol, **program(me)** a writing forth – ie a public notice, a schedule of events, a sequence of instructions for a computer, (etc), **telegram** a far-writing – ie a message sent over a long distance

GRAMIN(I) Lat *gramen, gramin-* grass. Eg **graminaceous** grassy – or belonging to the grass family, **graminivorous** grass-eating

GRAPH Gk *graphein* to write (see also GRAM). Eg **autograph** self writing – ie a person's own handwriting (especially his/her signature), **bibliography** writing relating to books – ie a list of books, writing about books, **biography** a life-writing – ie the story of someone's life, **calligraphy** beautiful writing, **choreography** dance writing – ie the notation or composition of dance, **epigraph** a writing upon – ie an inscription, **ethnography** race writing – ie description of the different races, **geography** earth writing – ie the description or science of the earth, **graph** written (ie drawn) (representation) (of relative proportions etc), **graphic** relating to writing (or drawing, painting etc) – or vivid like vivid writing or drawing, **graphite** writing (substance) – so called because it is used in pencils, **graphology** study of (hand)writing – and how character can be judged by it, **monograph** a single(-subject) writing – ie a treatise on a single subject, **orthographic** relating to straight (ie correct) writing – ie spelling, **paragraph** – see PAR(A), **photograph** light writing – ie production of an image by the action of light on a special surface, **pornography** writing relating to prostitutes – ie obscene writing (or pictures etc), **tachograph** speed-writer – ie instrument in a vehicle for recording its speed, distanced travelled etc, **telegraph** far-writer

GRAT Lat *gratia* favour; *gratus* welcome, pleasing, deserving thanks, thankful. Eg **congratulate** (thoroughly) (show that one finds something) pleasing, **gratify** make pleasing to – ie do a favour to, indulge, **gratis** '(by) favours' – ie for nothing, **gratitude** thankfulness, **gratuitous** (by) favour – ie for nothing, voluntary, uncalled for, **gratuity** favour – ie gift, **ingrate** unthankful (person), **ingratiate** (bring oneself) into favour

GRAV Lat *gravis* heavy. Eg **graveolent** heavy-smelling – ie strong-smelling, foul-smelling, **gravid** heavy (with child) – ie pregnant, **gravity** heaviness – ie weightiness, seriousness, or the force attracting an object towards the centre of the earth, **primigravida** (woman) first (time) heavy (with child) – ie a woman pregnant for the first time

GRED Eg **ingredient** – see GRAD

GREG Lat *grex, greg-* flock, herd. Eg **aggregate** made (into a) flock – ie brought together, made into one mass, **congregate** flock together, **egregious** (standing) out from the flock – ie

78

notable, outrageous, **gregarious** (associating in) flocks – or liking a flock, sociable, **segregate** (move) apart (from) the flock – ie separate from the flock, set apart

GRESS Eg **congress, progress** – see GRAD

GYMN(O) Gk *gymnos* naked; *gymnasion* place where physical training took place (men in ancient Greece used to exercise naked), as well as discussion and general social intercourse; *gymnastes* trainer of athletes. Eg **gymnasium** place for physical training, **gymnast** trainer of athletes – or simply an athlete, **gymnosperm** naked-seeded (plant) – ie a plant the seeds of which are not enclosed in an ovary

GYN Gk *gyne, gynaik-* woman; *gynaikeion* women's quarters. Eg **androgynous** man-woman – ie having the characteristics of both sexes, **gynaeceum** women's quarters – or the female organs of a flower, **gynaecology** (US **gynecology**) study of (the diseases of) women, **misogynist** woman-hater, **monogynous** (having) one woman – ie having one wife, or having one style (part of the female organs of a plant)

GYR(O), GIRO Lat *gyrus* ring, circle; Gk *gyros* ring, circle. Eg **giro** (method of money transfer moving in a) ring – ie in which the money is moved direct from one person's bank (etc) account to that of another, **gyrate** (move in a) circle (or spiral), **gyrocompass** circling (or spinning) compass (ie involving a spinning wheel the axis of which is free to turn in any direction)

H

HAB, HIBIT Lat *habere, habit-* to have, hold. Eg **exhibit** hold out – ie display, **habeas corpus** 'you shall have (ie cause) the body (to be brought)' – the opening words of a writ to a jailer requiring a prisoner to be produced in court for an investigation of the legality of the detention, **inhibit** hold in – ie restrain, suppress, **prohibit** hold in front – ie hold back, prevent, forbid

HABIT Lat *habitare* to dwell, live. Eg **cohabit** live together, **habitat** 'it lives' – the word was used to introduce a description (in Latin) of where a particular plant etc tended to grow etc, **habitation** dwelling (place), **inhabit** live in

HABIT Lat *habitus* condition of the body, appearance, dress, disposition etc. Eg **habit** dress (rider's, monk's etc); or (customary) disposition – or customary action etc

(H)AEM(O), (H)EM(O) Gk *haima, haimat-* blood. Eg **anaemia** (US **anemia**) bloodlessness – ie lack of blood, **haematite** (US **hematite**) blood(-red) (stone), **haematuria** (US **hematuria**) blood (in the) urine, **haemophiliac** (US **hemophiliac**) blood-loving – ie bleeding-loving, having a tendency to excessive bleeding, **haemorrhage** (US **hemorrhage**) a bursting forth of blood – ie a discharge of blood from the blood-vessels, **haemorrhoids** (US **hemorrhoids**) blood-flowing (veins) – ie a swelling of the veins of the anus (sometimes with bleeding), piles, **hypercalcaemia** (US **hypercalcemia**) over (ie too much) calcium (in the) blood, **leucaemia** (US **leucemia**) white blood – ie a disease involving an excess of white blood-cells, **septicaemia** (US **septicemia**) rotten blood – ie infection of the blood with bacteria

HAGI(O) Gk *hagios* holy. Eg **hagiography** holy (ie saint) writing – ie biography of a saint, adoring biography, **hagiolatry** worship of holies (ie saints), **hagioscope** holy viewer – ie a small opening, in a wall inside a church, through which the high altar can be seen

HAL Lat *halare* to breathe; *halitus* breath. Eg **exhale** breathe out, **halitosis** (bad) breath, **inhale** breathe in

HAL(O) Gk *hals* salt. Eg **halobiont** salt-living (organism) – ie organism found in a salty environment, **halogen** salt-producer – ie element forming salts by combining directly with metals, **halophyte** salt plant – ie plant able to live in salty soil or water

HARPY Gk *harpyiai* 'the snatchers', creatures of Greek mythology. The harpies were originally personifications of winds; later they were pictured as filthy winged monsters, part woman part bird, who snatched people and things. Hence a **harpy** is a grabbing or grasping person (especially a woman)

HAUST Lat *haurire, haust-* to draw (water etc). Eg **exhaust** (of a pipe) drawing-out – ie draining, discharging waste, **exhausted** drawn out – ie drained, used up

HEBDOMAD Eg **hebdomadal** – see HEPTA

HECT(O), HECAT Gk *hekaton* a hundred. Eg **hecatomb** a hundred oxen – ie a mass sacrifice, a large number of victims, **hectare** a hundred ares (an are is 100 square metres), **hectogram** a hundred grams, **hectolitre** a hundred litres

HECTOR Gk *Hektor* ('he who holds firm') – name of a Trojan hero of the Trojan War. His name was at one time used in English to refer to a noble-minded warrior or, in a debasement of the hero's memory, a bully or blusterer. The latter of these senses provided the verb **hector** meaning to bully or bluster

HEDR(ON) Gk *hedra* seat; *kathedra* seat. Eg **cathedral** (church containing a bishop's) seat (or throne) – ie the principal church of a diocese, **octahedron** eight-seated (figure) – ie a solid figure with eight faces, **polyhedron** many-seated (figure) – ie a solid figure with many faces, **tetrahedron** four-seated (figure) – ie a solid figure with four faces

HELICO, HELIX Gk *helix, helik-* anything twisted, a spiral or screw shape. Eg **helicoid** spiral or screw-shaped, **helicopter** screw-winged (machine) – ie flying-machine with flying blades arranged in a screw shape, **helix** spiral (or screw shape)

HELI(O) Gk *helios* the sun. Eg **heliocentric** sun-centred – ie taking/having the sun as centre; or as viewed from the centre of the sun, **helioscope** sun-viewer – ie apparatus allowing one to observe the sun without damaging the eye, **heliotropy** sun-turning – ie (in plants) property of turning under the influence of light (either towards it or away from it), **helium** sun

81

(element) – so named because it was first discovered in the sun's atmosphere

HELIX see HELICO

HEMER, AMER Gk *hemera* day. Eg **Decameron** (title of Boccaccio's book of tales supposed to have been told during) ten days, **ephemeral** (lasting only) over (ie for) a day – ie short-lived

HEMI Gk *hemi-* half-. Eg **hemidemisemiquaver** half a demisemiquaver, **hemiplegia** a half-striking – ie paralysis of one side of the body only, **hemisphere** half-sphere, **hemistich** half-line (of verse)

(H)EM(O) (US) Eg **anemia, hemophilia, hemorrhage** – see (H)AEM(O)

HENDECA Gk *hendeka* eleven. Eg **hendecagon** eleven-cornered (ie eleven-angled) (figure), **hendecahedron** eleven-seated (figure) – ie a solid figure with eleven faces, **hendecasyllable** eleven-syllabled (rhythmic line of verse)

HEPAR, HEPAT(O) Gk *hepar, hepat-* liver. Eg **heparin** (substance formed in the) liver, **hepatic** relating to (or acting on the) liver, **hepatitis** (inflammation of the) liver, **hepatology** study of the liver

HEPTA, HEBDOMAD Gk *hepta* seven; *hebdomas, hebdomad-* set of seven, a week. Eg **hebdomadal** weekly, **heptagon** seven-cornered (ie seven-angled) (figure), **heptatonic** seven-toned – ie (of a musical scale) having seven notes

HER, HES Lat *haerere, haes-* to stick; *haesitare, haesitat-* to stick fast. Eg **adhere** stick to, **adherent** a sticker-to – ie a supporter, **adhesive** sticking to, **cohere** stick together, a **cohesion** sticking together, **hesitate** stick fast – ie stammer, be in doubt, delay making a decision, **inherent** sticking in – ie vested in, constituting an inseparable part

HERB(I) Lat *herba* grass, plant with stalks. Eg **herbicide** plant-killer – ie weedkiller, **herbivore** grass (etc) eater

HERCULEAN Gk *Herakles* Hercules – a hero of classical mythology, famous for his strength, about whose exploits there were many legends. The 'twelve labours of Hercules' were tasks imposed on him after he had murdered his children in a fit of madness visited on him by the goddess Hera. Hence the word **herculean** is used to describe tasks and achievements involving great strength, effort or endurance. (One of the labours of Hercules was to kill the hydra of Lerna – see HYDR(O)).

HERM Gk *Hermes* – name of a Greek god, who served as the messenger of the gods and was the equivalent of the Roman Mercury (see MERCUR). (See also HERMENEUT.) Together with Aphrodite, goddess of love (see APHROD), Hermes had a son named *Hermaphroditos*, who has given English the word **hermaphrodite** (a person, animal or plant with the organs or characteristics of both sexes). (While bathing, *Hermaphroditos* grew together with a nymph into a body that was both male and female.) Also deriving (somewhat indirectly) from Hermes is **hermetic**. The Egyptian god Thoth came to be identified with the Greek Hermes and was called in Greek *Hermes Trismegistus* ('Hermes thrice greatest'); he was the god of science and was regarded as the founder of the occult sciences such as alchemy. Thus the word 'hermetic' is used to mean relating to occult science, especially alchemy, and a 'hermetic' seal is the airtight closure of a container by fusion etc, as practised by alchemists

HERMENEUT Gk *hermeneus* interpreter, perhaps derived from *Hermes*, name of the messenger of the gods (see HERM). Eg **hermeneutic** relating to interpretation (eg of a text)

HERO Gk *heros* hero. A Greek **hero** was a man with strength or ability beyond the ordinary; indeed heroes came to be regarded as having superhuman abilities and occupying a rank between humans and gods. Sometimes they were born of a union between a god and a mortal; in other cases their heroic status arose from the performance of great feats in the service of humanity. The name of the drug **heroin** is also said

83

to be derived from *heros* – because it supposedly makes the user feel like a hero or demigod

HERP, HERPETO Gk *herpein* to creep; *herpeton* a creeping thing, reptile, snake. Eg **herpes** a creeping (of the skin) – name of a skin disease, **herpetology** study of reptiles (and amphibians)

HES Eg **adhesive, cohesion** – see HER

HETERO Gk *heteros* other. Eg **heterodox** (holding) another opinion (ie other than the conventional opinion), **heterogeneous** of another kind – ie different, made up of differing elements, **heterosexual** sexual (towards) the other (sex) – ie sexually attracted by members of the other sex rather than one's own

(H)EUR Gk *heuriskein* to find, find out. **Eureka!** 'I have found (the answer)!' is supposed to have been the cry of the Greek scientist Archimedes when he suddenly realised the answer to a problem which had been put before him: how to test whether a crown was made of real or adulterated gold. The story tells how, getting into his bath, he was struck by the realisation that a body immersed in water must displace a bulk of water equal to its own bulk; and therefore that the same weight of two different materials one of which is a heavier material than the other (such as gold and an alloy) will displace different amounts of water (because the same weight of the two materials would differ in bulk). Eng **heuristic** means relating to (or facilitating) finding out (for oneself, or by considering past experience, etc)

HEX(A) Gk *hex* six. Eg **hexagon** six-angled (figure), **hexameter** six-measured (line) – ie line of verse with six measures or 'feet'

HIBERN Lat *hibernus* wintry. Eg **hibernate** to winter – or to spend the winter sleeping or resting

HIBIT Eg **exhibit, prohibit** – see HAB

HIER(O) Gk *hieros* sacred; *hiereus* priest. Eg **hierarchy** (ranked body of) sacred rulers (ie rulers in sacred matters – priests or angels) – or any body of individuals organised in ranks with differing degrees of power, **hieratic** priestly – or relating to a particular type of ancient Egyptian hieroglyphics, **hiero-glyphics** sacred carvings – ie the picture-writing of the ancient Egyptians

HILAR Lat *hilaris* cheerful. Eg **exhilarate** make cheerful, **hilarity** cheerfulness

HIPP(O) Gk *hippos* horse. Eg **hippic** relating to horses, **hippodrome** horse (race-)course, **hippopotamus** river-horse

HIST(O) Gk *histion* thing woven, woven cloth, sail; *histos* ship's mast, web-beam (of a loom – ie a roller, vertical in ancient looms, on which the cloth is wound as it is woven), woven cloth. (In English, 'hist(o)-' generally refers to tissue). Eg **histogenesis** birth (ie formation) of (organic) tissues, **histogram** ship's mast (or web-beam) writing – ie a graph using rectangles drawn against a vertical and horizontal axis, **histology** study of (organic) tissue

(H)OD(O) Gk *hodos* way. Eg **anode** – see ION, **cathode** – see ION, **electrode** electric way – ie a pole by which a current enters or leaves a substance in electrolysis, **episode** a way in over-and-above – ie a coming in besides, an entrance, a story or passage introduced into a work (of literature, music etc) giving relief from the main subject, a self-contained set of events, **exodus** a way (ie a going) out, **hodometer** (or **odometer**) way measure – ie instrument for measuring distance travelled, **method** a way after – ie a following after, an enquiry into, a system of enquiry, a way of doing, **period** a way round – ie a going round, a circuit, cycle of years, stretch of time, **synod** a way together – ie a coming together, an assembly (eg of bishops)

HOI POLLOI Gk 'the many' – ie the majority, the common people

HOL(O) Gk *holos* whole. Eg **holistic** relating to the whole – ie (of medicine) attending to the whole person (body and mind),

holocaust whole burnt(-offering) – ie complete or wholesale destruction, **hologram** a whole-writing – ie a three-dimensional image (produced by laser)

HOM(O) Lat *homo, homin-* human being, man (in sense: human being). Eg **homicide** killing (or killer) of a human, **Homo sapiens** – see SAPIEN

(H)OM(O) Gk *homos* same; *homalos* even, level; *homoios* similar, like. Eg **anomaly** unevenness – ie irregularity, inconsistency, **hom(o)eopathy** – see PATH(O), **homogeneous** of the same kind – ie the same throughout, consistent, **homologous** speaking the same – ie saying the same, agreeing, corresponding, **homonym** same name (but with a different meaning) – ie word sounding the same as another but having a different meaning, **homosexual** sexual (towards) the same (sex) – ie sexually attracted by members of the same sex

HORM Gk *hormaein* to stir up. Eg **hormone** stirring-up (substance) – ie a secretion inside the body producing a specific physiological reaction

HOR(O) Gk *hora* (period of) time, hour. Eg **horologist** (maker of) time-speakers (ie clocks), **horoscope** a time-viewing – ie a charting of the heavens at a particular time, eg the time of a person's birth; hence a prediction from the stars of a person's future

HORR Lat *horrere* to bristle, (of hair) to stand on end; to shudder (eg with fear). Eg **abhor** shudder away from, **abhorrent** (prompting a) shuddering away from, **horrendous** shudder(-causing), **horrible** shudder(-causing), **horrid** bristly – ie savage, unpleasant, **horrifying** shudder-making, **horripilation** bristling of the hair – ie a contraction of the skin so that the hair stands up, 'gooseflesh', **horror** a bristling or shuddering (with fear etc)

HORT Lat *hortus* garden. Eg **horticulture** cultivation of gardens

HORT Lat *hortari* to encourage (someone to do something),

86

urge. Eg **exhort** (thoroughly) encourage or urge, **hortatory** urging, encouraging

HOSP(IT) Lat *hospes, hospit-* stranger, guest, host. Eg **hospice** (lodging for) strangers or guests (eg travellers, the needy, the dying), **hospital** (lodging for) strangers or guests (eg travellers, the needy, the sick), **hospitality** (receiving of) guests

HOST Lat *hostis* enemy. Eg **host** enemy (army) – hence, army, great number (of people etc), **hostile** enemy(-like)

HUM Lat *(h)umere* to be moist; *humor* moisture, liquid, fluid. Eg **humectant** (substance that) moistens, **humid** moist, **humidify** make moist, **humour** fluid – in medieval physiology, the temperament was supposed to be determined by four fluids or 'humours' identified as blood, phlegm, bile and black bile (or 'melancholy'); thus 'humour' came to mean mental disposition or mood, and later mirth etc (see CHOL(ER), SANGUI(N))

HUM Lat *humus* the ground, earth, soil; *humilis* near the ground, low. Eg **exhume** (take) from the ground – ie dig up, **humiliated** lowered, **humility** lowness – ie meekness, **humus** soil (rich with decomposed organic matter), **transhume** (move) across ground – ie move livestock from summer to winter pastures or vice versa. Note: Eng **posthumous** derives not from the Lat *humus* but from Lat *postumus* (last, last-born, applied particularly to a child born after his/her father's will or death). Lat *postumus* later came to be associated with Lat *humus* (soil) and *humare* (to bury), and thus an 'h' found its way into the English word, used of a work published after the author's death, etc.

HYBRID Lat *hibrida* or *hybrida* half-breed – originally applied to the offspring of a domestic sow and a wild boar, or to that of a Roman man and a non-Roman woman, or a freeman and a slave. Hence Eng **hybrid** (half-breed)

HYDR(O) Gk *hydor* water; *hydra* water-snake. Eg **anhydrous** waterless, **dehydrate** (take) water away from, **hydra** – a reference to the hydra of Lerna of Greek mythology, a water-monster with many serpent heads, two of which grew to replace every one cut off (see HERCULEAN); hence the word is applied to an evil with many manifestations or one difficult to root out, **hydrangea** water-vessel (plant) – so named because of the cup-like seed-capsules, **hydrant** water (connection) – ie connection for drawing water from the mains, **hydraulic** (involving) water-pipes – ie involving water carried in pipes, **hydroelectricity** electricity (produced by) water(-power), **hydrogen** water-producer – because hydrogen in combination with oxygen produces water, **hydrolysis** loosening (by) water – ie chemical decomposition brought about by water, **hydrophilic** water-beloved, water-loving – ie attracting water, **hydrophobia** fear or hatred of water – or (because an aversion to water is a symptom of rabies in humans) rabies, **hydrophobic** water-hating – ie repelling water, **hydrosphere** water-sphere – ie the areas of water on the surface of the earth

HYGR(O) Gk *hygros* wet, moist. Eg **hygrometer** moisture-measure – ie instrument for measuring humidity, **hygroscopic** (enabling) moisture-viewing – ie (of a substance) readily absorbing or reacting to moisture and therefore serving to indicate how much moisture is present

HYL(O) Eg **hylophyte** – see YL

HYMEN(O) Gk *hymen* membrane, virginal membrane; *hymenaios* wedding-song; Lat *Hymen* – name of the god of marriage. Eg **hymen** virginal membrane, **hymeneal** relating to marriage, **Hymenoptera** membrane-winged (insects) – name of an order of insects with four transparent wings

HYPER Gk *hyper* over. Eg **hyperactive** overactive, **hyperbole** a throwing over – ie a throwing beyond, overstatement, rhetorical exaggeration, **hypercalcaemia** (US **hypercalcemia**) over (ie too much) calcium (in the) blood, **hypercritical** overcritical, **hypersensitive** oversensitive, **hypertension** over-tension – ie high blood pressure, great emotional strain. (Note: for **hype** see HYPO)

HYPN(O) Gk *hypnos* sleep. Eg **hypnagogic** sleep-leading – ie sleep-bringing, or relating to the process of falling asleep, **hypnosis** sleep(-like state) – in which the mind responds to external suggestion

HYPO Gk *hypo* under. Eg **hypochondria** (areas) under the (rib) cartilage – ie part of the abdomen under the ribs, once thought to be the site where black bile or 'melancholy' (see CHOL(ER)) and unhealthy 'vapours' would gather, causing depression and unfounded fears (eg about illness), **hypo-dermic** under the skin, **hypotension** under-tension – ie low blood pressure, **hypotenuse** (side of a right-angled triangle) stretching under – ie opposite the right angle, **hypothermia** under-heat – ie low body temperature, **hypothesis** a placing under – ie a foundation, basic assumption, assumption for the purposes of discussion, or a theory put forward to explain something. Note: the word **hype** apparently derives from 'hypodermic' as in the injection of drugs by hypodermic syringe; ie the idea is one of artificial stimulation – eg of sales, by a very vigorous publicity campaign

HYSTER Gk *hystera* womb. Eg **hysterectomy** a cutting out of the womb, **hysteria** womb (sickness) – hysteria was thought to be caused by malfunction of the womb

I

IATR(O) Gk *iatros* physician, healer. Eg **geriatrics** old-age healing – ie medical care of the old, **iatrogenic** healing-produced – ie (of a disease) caused by treatment (of another disease), **paediatrician** (or **pediatrician**) child-healer – ie specialist in children's diseases, **psychiatry** mind-healing – ie treatment of mental disease

ICHTHY(O) Gk *ichthys* fish. Eg **ichthyology** study of fish, **ichthyosaur** fish-lizard – a fishlike reptile

ICON Gk *eikon* image. Eg **icon** image, **iconoclast** breaker of images – ie person who challenges cherished beliefs, **icon-ography** the writing of images – ie pictorial representation (or the study or description of this or of images used in art)

ID Lat *id* it, that (one). Eg **ie** (abbreviation of *id est*) that is

IDIO Gk *idios* one's own, personal, private; *idiotes* a private person (eg as opposed to one holding public office), hence an ordinary person, a non-expert, an ignorant person. Eg **idiom** one's own (way of saying) – ie mode of expression peculiar to or characteristic of a language, to a particular group etc, **idiot** ignorant person – ie a fool, **idiosyncrasy** personal mixing-together – ie a blend (or characteristic etc) peculiar to oneself

IDOL Gk *eidolon* image or representation (eg of a god). Eg **idol** image (of a god) – or other object of worship, **idolatry** worship of images (of gods) – or of false gods

IENT Eg **ambient, transient** – see IT

IGN Lat *ignis* fire. Eg **gelignite** gel(atin) fire – a gelatin-like explosive substance, **igneous** relating to fire, fiery – or produced by volcanic action, **ignite** (set on) fire, **ignition** (a setting on) fire

IGNOR Lat *ignorare* not to know. Eg **ignoramus** 'we do not know (it)' – ie we do not acknowledge (it): formerly written on an indictment when it was rejected by a grand jury; hence came to be used as a name for the ordinary, undistinguished lawyer, and for an uninformed person in general, **ignorant** not knowing, **ignore** (to act as though) not knowing (of something's existence etc) – or to disregard

IM Eg **impose, impotent** – see IN

IMIC Eg **inimical** – see AMIC

IMPER Lat *imperare, imperat-* to order; *imperium* command, sovereignty. Eg **imperative** commanding – ie expressing command (in grammar), or necessary, essential, **imperious** commanding – ie authoritative, overbearing

IN, IM, I (or IL, IR before 'l', 'r') Lat prefix *in-* with various senses, including (1) in, into, on, onto, upon, towards, against, (2) un- (ie negating that which follows); or it may (3) simply have a vague strengthening effect on the word, or the sense of an action or change completed. Eg **illicit** not licit, **illuminate** enlighten, light (up), **immure** wall in, **impose** place (a burden etc) on, **impotent** powerless, **incarnate** (made) into flesh, **incise** cut into, **include** shut in – ie take in, encompass, **indubitable** not doubtable – ie that cannot be doubted, **innate** inborn, **inscribe** write in or on, **insomnia** sleeplessness, **invincible** unconquerable, **irrevocable** not able to be called back – ie not able to be anulled or cancelled

INFAN Lat *infans, infant-* dumb, unable to speak (from *in-* not, and *fari* to speak); hence, one too young to speak, a young child. Eg **infant** young child, **infantry** young (men) – ie foot-soldiers

INFER Lat *inferus* below, low(er); *inferior* lower; *infernus* below, low(er). Eg **inferior** lower – or less good, **infernal** relating to (or belonging to) the lower (world) – ie hellish, **inferno** the lower (world) – ie hell, a hell-like fire

INFER Eg **infer** – see FER

INFRA Lat *infra* below. Eg **infracostal** below the ribs, **infra dig(nitatem)** 'below (one's) dignity', **infra-red** below (ie beyond) the red (end of the spectrum), **infrastructure** below-structure – ie underlying structure, basic structure

INGEN Lat *ingenuus* native, inborn, or free-born, frank, noble; *ingenium* inborn disposition, natural ability, talent, cleverness; (both from same root as *genus* birth, and *generare* to beget – see GEN(ER)). Eg **disingenuous** not frank, **ingenious** clever – or inventive, **ingenuous** frank

INSUL Lat *insula* island. Eg **insular** relating to an island – or island(-like), **insulate** (make into) an island – ie cut off from its surroundings, put a barrier covering round (for the purpose of keeping heat in etc), **insulin** island (substance) – ie a substance produced by certain cell-groups in the pancreas called the 'islands' of Langerhans, **peninsula** an almost-island – ie a piece of land almost surrounded by water

INTEG Lat *integer, integr-* whole, intact. Eg **disintegrate** de-make-into-a-whole – ie break up, **integer** whole (number), **integral** whole – or constituting part of the whole, or essential to the whole, **integrate** make into a whole, **integrity** wholeness – or soundness, uprightness

INTER Lat *inter* between, among; *interim* in the meantime. Eg **inter alia** 'among other (things)', **intercession** a going between – ie a pleading with one person on behalf of another, **intercommunicating** between-communicating – ie mutually communicating, **intercontinental** between continents, **interdependence** between-dependence – ie mutual dependence, **interim** the meantime – or (as an adjective) temporary, **interject** throw between – ie throw in, break in, **international** between nations, **interpose** place between, **interregnum** (period) between reigns, **interrupt** break between – ie break into, **intersperse** scatter among or between – or diversify, **interval** (space) between ramparts – ie space beween two events etc, **intervene** come between – or act to alter the course of events

INTERIOR, INTERN, INTIM Lat *interior* inner; *intimus* inmost; *internus* inward, inner. Eg **interior** inner, **internal** inner, **internment** (confinement) inward – ie within a set area, **intimate** inmost – private, close

INTRA Lat *intra* within. Eg **intra-urban** within a city, **intra-uterine** within the uterus, **intravenous** within a vein

INTRO Lat *intro* inwards, within. Eg **introduce** lead within – ie bring in, **introspection** a looking within (oneself), **introvert** (person) turned inwards

IO(D) Gk *ion* a violet; *ioeides* violet-coloured. Eg **iodine** (element forming a) violet-coloured (vapour), **iolith** violet (-coloured) stone

ION Gk *ion* going, from *ienai* to go. Eg **ion** going (particle) – ie an electrically charged particle, such as are produced when an electric current is passed through some substances; negatively charged ions (**anions**) are attracted to to the anode (the 'way up' – the pole by which the current enters the substance), while positively charged ions (**cations**) go to the cathode (the 'way down' – the pole by which the current leaves the substance). See AN(A), CAT(A), (H)OD(O)

IOTA, JOT Gk *iota* – ninth letter of the Greek alphabet (equivalent to the English 'i'); it is the smallest Greek letter and thus in English **iota** has come to mean a tiny part or tiny bit. Eng **jot** (tiny amount) also derives from Gk *iota*

IR(A) Lat *ira* anger. Eg **irascible** angerable – ie easily angered, **irate** angered, angry, **ire** anger

IRID, IRIS Gk *iris, irid-* rainbow. Eg **iridescent** (coloured like a) rainbow, **iridium** rainbow (metal) – so named because of the rainbow-like colours produced when it is dissolved in hydrochloric acid, **iris** rainbow(-like part of the eye) or rainbow (-like flower)

ISO, ANISO Gk *isos* equal, the same; *anisos* unequal. Eg **anisophyllous** unequal-leaved – ie (of a plant) having different types of leaf, **isobar** (line connecting places of) equal weight (ie pressure), **isosceles** equal-legged – ie (of a triangle) having two sides equal, **isotope** (one of two or more forms of an element occupying the) same place (in the periodic table) – ie with the same atomic number; but differing in atomic weight

IT, IENT Lat *ire, it-* to go. Eg **ambient** going round – ie surrounding, **ambit** a going round – ie an encompassing, the area encompassed, the scope of something, **ambition** a going round – ie (in ancient Rome), a going round to canvass votes; hence, a desire for office etc, **circuit** a going round, **coitus** a going together – ie sexual intercourse, **exit** a going out, **initial** relating to a going into – ie belonging to the entering into, the beginning, **initiate** go into – ie enter into, begin, **sedition** a going apart – ie a quarrel, a rebellion, fermenting of rebellion, **transient** going across – ie passing over, short-lived, **transit** a going across (from one place to another), **transition** a going

93

across – ie a change, **transitory** going across – ie passing over, short-lived

ITIN Lat *iter, itiner-* journey. Eg **itinerant** journeying – ie travelling, **itinerary** (record, route etc of a) journey

J

JAC Lat *jacere,* to lie. Eg **adjacent** lying towards – ie lying beside or near, **circumjacent** lying round, **subjacent** underlying, **superjacent** lying above

JAN Lat *janua* door; *Janus* – name of an ancient Italian god, depicted with two faces (one facing forward and one back) and associated with doorways. Eg **janitor** door(-keeper), **January** Janus' (month)

JECT Lat *jacere, jact-* to throw. Eg **abject** thrown away – ie thrown down, base, miserable, **adjective** (word) thrown to (a noun) – ie a word added to a noun (to say something more about it), **conjecture** (an opinion) thrown together – ie a view based on incomplete evidence, guesswork, **dejected** thrown down – ie downcast, **eject** throw out, **inject** throw in – ie drive in, **interject** throw between – ie throw in, break in, **object** (thing) thrown in front of – ie presented (to one's attention, one's senses), **objection** a throwing in front of, in the way of – ie a challenge, protest, **project** (thing) thrown forward – ie a plan, scheme, **reject** throw back – ie turn away, deem unacceptable, **subject** (person etc) thrown under – ie person under the sway of a monarch etc, or a matter under discussion, (etc), **trajectory** (path of a body) thrown across – ie path of a body sent through the air

JOT – see IOTA

JOV Lat *Jovis* Jove – name of the chief god of the Romans (corresponding to Zeus, king of the Greek gods). The old-fashioned expression **by Jove** referred to him. Another name for Jove was Jupiter, and the planet **Jupiter** was named after him. Those born under the influence of this planet are supposed to be of a goodhumoured disposition – hence Eng **jovial**

JUD, JUR, JUST Lat *jus, jur-* law, that which is right; *judex, judic-* 'law-sayer' – ie judge; *judicare, judicat-* to 'law-say' – ie to judge; see also JUR. Eg **adjudicate** law-say towards – ie decide as a judge, **injury** unrightfulness – ie a wrong, harm, **juridical** relating to law-saying – ie to legal proceedings, **jurisdiction** law-saying – ie legal authority, authority, area over which an authority has sway, **jurisprudence** knowledge of the law, **just** (conforming to) the law, or that which is right – ie fair, right, **justice** (behaviour conforming to) the law, or that which is right – ie fairness, rightfulness, **sub judice** 'under a judge' – ie currently being dealt with by a court, under consideration

JUG, JUNCT, JUNG Lat *jungere, junct-* to join; *jugum* yoke (joining two oxen); *jugulum* 'little yoking (bone)' – ie collar-bone; *conjux, conjug-* spouse (ie one of a 'joined together' pair). Eg **adjunct** (thing) joined to (another) – ie something accompanying but subordinate to another, **conjugal** relating to spouses – ie to marriage, **conjunction** a joining together – ie a word joining other words or clauses etc; or a simultaneous occurrence (of events), **conjunctiva** joining-together (membrane) – ie membrane joining the inner eyelid and the cornea, **injunction** a joining into (ie to) – ie an attaching, an imposing (of an order etc), an order, **jugular** collar-bone (vein) – ie one of the large veins either side of the neck, **junction** a joining, **juncture** joining(-point) – or crucial moment, point in time, **subjugate** (bring) under the yoke – ie conquer, bring under control

JULY The month of **July** derives its name from the Roman month *Julius*, named after Julius Caesar (see CAESAR), who was born in this month

JUNE The month of **June** derives its name from the Roman month *Junius*, which appears to have been named after either the goddess Juno or the Junius clan

JUNIOR – see JUVEN

95

JUR Lat *jurare* to swear, from *jus, jur-* law (see JUD). Eg **abjure** swear away – ie renounce, **conjure** swear together – ie join together by oath, call on by oath or by a sacred name, summon up (a spirit etc), accomplish something by summoning up magic powers, perform magic tricks, **jury** (body of people) sworn (in) (to deliver a verdict), **perjury** a swearing thorough (ie to destruction) – ie a swearing falsely

JUR Eg **juridical, jurisdiction, injury** – see JUD

JUST Eg **justice** – see JUD

JUVEN, JUNIOR Lat *juvenis* young; *junior* younger. Eg **junior** younger – or lesser, **juvenile** young (person), **rejuvenate** (make) young again

JUXTA Lat *juxta* close. Eg **juxtapose** place close (together)

K

KAISER see CAESAR

KAL Eg **kaleidoscope** – see CALL(I)

KILO Gk *chilioi* a thousand. Eg **kilogram** a thousand grams, **kilometre** a thousand metres, **kilowatt** a thousand watts

KIN(E), CINE Gk *kinein* to move; *kinema* movement; *kinesis* movement. Eg **akinesia** (state of being) without (voluntary) movement, **cinema** (originally short for **cinematograph**:) movement writer – ie apparatus for representing movement, apparatus showing motion pictures, **kinesis** movement, **kinetic** relating to (or caused by) movement, **photokinesis** light movement – ie movement brought about by changes in light

KRYPTON see CRYPH

L

LAB, LAPS Lat *labi, laps-* to slip, glide, slide, fall. Eg **collapse** fall together – ie fall in, fall down, **elapse** slip away, **labile** slippery – ie liable to slip or change, **lapse** a slip, **prolapse** slip forward – ie slip out of place, **relapse** slip back

LABIA Lat *labium* lip. Eg **labial** relating to (or pronounced with) the lips, **labia majora** 'larger lips' (of the vagina), **labia minora** 'smaller lips' (of the vagina), **labiate** lipped

LABOR Lat *labor* work. Eg **collaborate** work together, **elaborate** (produced) out of work – ie produced by hard work, highly worked, complicated, **laboratory** work (place), **laborious** (full of) work – ie working hard, demanding hard work

LACONIC Gk *Lakonikos* Laconian. The people of Laconia, or Lacedaemonia, an ancient state in the south of the Pelponnese, were renowned for using few words; hence Eng **laconic**. (See also SPARTAN – Sparta was the capital city of Laconia)

LACRIM (or LACHRYM) Lat *lacrima* tear. Eg **lacrimal** (or **lachrymal**) relating to tears, **lacrimation** (or **lachrymation**) (the weeping of) tears, **lacrimose** (or **lachrymose**) tear(ful)

LACT(O) Lat *lac, lact-* milk. Eg **lactation** milk(-production) (ie by a nursing mother), **lactic** relating to milk (or produced from milk), **lactoprotein** milk-protein – ie a protein found in milk, **lactose** milk(-sugar) – a sugar produced from milk

LALIA Gk *lalia* talk. Eg **echolalia** echo-talk – ie the senseless echoing of words heard (in mental illness), **rhinolalia** nose talk – ie nasal speech

LAN(I) Lat *lana* wool. Eg **lanate** woolly, **laniferous** wool-bearing, **lanolin(e)** wool-oil – ie fat obtained from sheep's wool

LAPID, LAPIS Lat *lapis, lapid-* stone. Eg **dilapidated** (having its) stones apart – ie (eg of a building) with its stones scattered, tumble-down, falling to pieces, **lapidarist** stone

(-expert) – ie an expert on gems, **lapidary** relating to stones (or to inscription on stone), **lapis lazuli** azure stone

LAPS Eg **collapse, elapse** – see LAB

LAT Lat *latus* borne, carried, brought – used as past participle of *ferre* to bear, carry, bring (see FER). Eg **collate** bear together – ie bring together, **dilatory** bearing apart – ie tending in another direction, delaying, **elated** borne away – ie carried away, excited, exultant, **legislation** law-bearing – ie law-proposing, law-making, **relate** bear back – ie make a connection, be connected, recount (a story etc), **superlative** borne beyond – ie surpassing all others, taken to the highest degree, **translate** bear across (from one place to another, from one language into another)

LATER Lat *latus, later-* side. Eg **bilateral** two-sided – ie affecting two sides (or parties), **collateral** (something in a position with) sides together (with something else) – ie something side by side with (or parallel to) something else, someone descended from the same ancestor but by a parallel line on the family tree rather than the same one, or something linked up (at the side, as it were) as security for a loan, **lateral** relating to the side (or sideways, at the side etc), **multilateral** many-sided – ie affecting many sides (or parties), **unilateral** one-sided – ie affecting one side (or party) only

LAT(I) Lat *latus* broad. Eg **dilate** broaden apart – ie spread out, expand, **latifoliate** broad-leaved, **latirostral** broad-beaked, **latitude** breadth (or looseness) (of interpretation etc) – or position on the globe measured in relation to a particular 'breadth'(-wise circle)

LATIN Lat *Latium* – name of the region of Italy in which Rome was situated

LAT(R) Gk *-latreia* -worship; *latreuein* to serve, worship. Eg **geolatry** earth-worship, **heliolater** sun-worshipper, **idolatrous** worshipping images (of gods) – or false gods, **Mariolatry** worship of (the Virgin) Mary, **pyrolatry** fire-worship

LAUD Lat *laus, laud-* praise. Eg **laud** to praise, **laudable** praisable – ie praiseworthy, **laudatory** praising

LAVA, LATRINE, LAVISH Lat *lavare* to wash; *latrina* (short for *lavatrina*) bath, privy. Eg **latrine** privy, **lavabo** 'I shall wash' – used for the ritual washing of his hands by a priest saying mass (it is the first word of the verses of psalm 26 recited during the action); also used for a washbasin, **lavatory** wash (-place) – now used for WC, **lavish** washing (down – like a deluge of rain) – ie extravagant, generous

LAX Lat *laxus* loose. Eg **lax** loose, **laxative** loosening (substance) (for the bowels), **relax** loosen back – ie loosen up, slacken

LECT, LEG, LIG Lat *legere, lect-* to gather, pick, choose (also, to read – see next entry). Eg **collect** gather together, **college** a gathering together – ie an association (or institution) (especially with an educational purpose), **diligent** choosing apart – ie choosing out, taking particular notice, taking great care, conscientious, **elect** pick out – ie choose, **eligible** pick-out-able – ie choosable, fit to be chosen, fulfilling the qualifications (for something), **intellect** (faculty of) picking between – ie picking out, perceiving with the mind, **intelligent** (good at) picking between – ie good at picking out, perceiving with the mind, **neglect** not pick (out) – ie fail to notice, fail to take notice of, fail to take care of, **negligence** a not picking (out) – ie a failure to take notice, a failure to take care of (something), **negligible** able not to be picked (out) – ie not needing to be taken notice of, **predilection** a choosing apart before – a choosing out in preference to others, a preference, **recollect** gather together again – ie recall, remember, **sacrilege** a gathering (up) of sacred things – ie theft of sacred things, violation of something sacred, **select** choose apart – ie choose out

LECT, LEG Lat *legere, lect-* to read (also, to gather, pick, choose – see preceding entry). Eg **lectern** reading(-desk), **lectionary** (collection of) readings – ie of lessons to be read in church,

lecture a reading – or a talk, **legend** (story etc) to be read – originally referred, in English, to the story of a saint's life; later used of a traditional story, a story passed down or passed around with a dubious foundation in fact, a person about whom many stories are told, etc, **legible** readable

LECT, LOG Gk *legein* to gather, pick, choose; also, to speak (see also LOG). Eg **anthology** a gathering of flowers – ie a collection of choice pieces (of writing), **dialect** a speaking between – ie conversation, the particular conversation (way of speaking) of an area, **dialectic** speaking between – ie conversation, discussion, logical argument, **eclectic** picking out (bits of philosophy etc) (from different sources)

LEG Lat *lex, leg-* law; *legitimus* lawful. Eg **legal** relating to the law – or lawful, **legislation** law-bearing – ie law-proposing, law-making, **legitimate** lawful, **privilege** private law – ie a law relating to one person only, right(s) belonging to one person or group, favour or advantage enjoyed by an individual or group

LEG Eg **college, sacrilege** – see LECT

LEGAC, LEGAT Lat *legare, legat-* to send as ambassador, to send, or to bequeath. Eg **delegate** to send (someone) away as ambassador – ie to entrust someone with a task, **legacy** bequest, **legate** (person) sent as ambassador, **legatee** (person to whom) a bequest (is made), **legation** (a person, body of people) sent as ambassador(s), **legator** (person making) a bequest, **relegate** send back – ie send away (into exile), demote

LEGION Lat *legio, legion-* legion – a division of the Roman army consisting of ten cohorts (see COHORT) and numbering up to about six thousand men. Hence Eng **legion** (a military force, or simply a great number)

LEMMA Gk *lemma* something taken or received, an assumption. Eg **dilemma** (originally: form of argument in which the adversary is presented with a) double assumption (giving a choice between two unattractive alternatives – the 'horns' of

100

the dilemma), **lemma** assumption (in mathematics)

LEN Lat *lenis* soft. Eg **lenient** soft – ie not strict

LENS, LENT Lat *lens, lent-* lentil; *lenticula* little lentil. Eg **lens** lentil(-shaped) (structure in the eye, in a camera, etc), **lenticular** little-lentil(-shaped) – ie lentil-shaped or lens-shaped

LEO(N) Lat *leo, leon-* lion; Gk *leon, lenont-* lion. Eg **chameleon** on-the-ground lion – a type of lizard, **Leo** the Lion – sign of the zodiac, **leonine** relating to lions – or lion-like, **leopard** lion-pard – the leopard was thought to be a cross between the lion and an animal called the 'pard'

LEP, LEPID(O) Gk *lepis, lepid-* scale; *lepros* scaly. Eg **Lepidoptera** scale-winged (creatures) – name of the order of insects with four scale-covered wings (ie butterflies and moths), **leprosy** (disease characterised by) scaly (skin)

LEPS, LEPT Gk *-lepsis* and *-lepsia* a taking, seizure; *lambanein* to take, seize. Eg **catalepsy** seizure down – ie trance, seizure (or a disease involving this), **epileptic** relating to (a disease characterised by) seizures upon – ie attacks, seizures

LEPT(O) Gk *leptos* slender, slight. Eg **leptocephalic** slender-headed – ie narrow-skulled, **leptodactyl** slender-toed (creature), **lepton** slight (subatomic particle)

LESBIAN Gk *Lesbos* – name of an island (part of Greece) off the coast of Turkey. It was the birthplace of the female poet Sappho (c600BC), who was reputed to be homosexual; thus **lesbian** came to mean a female homosexual (and 'sapphism' is an old-fashioned term for female homosexuality)

LEUC(O) Gk *leukos* white. Eg **leucaemia** (US **leucemia**) white blood – ie a disease involving an excess of white blood-cells, **leucocyte** white cell (of the blood etc), **leucorrhoea** white flow – ie an abnormal white discharge from the vagina

LEV Lat *levis* light (see also next entry). Eg **alleviate** make light – ie lighten, lessen, make less bad, **levitate** (rise by reason of being) light – or (of a person) float in the air as though the body was light, **levity** lightness

LEV Lat *levare, levat-* to raise (from *levis* light – see preceding entry). Eg **elevate** raise forth – ie raise up, uplift, **the Levant** (land of the) rising (sun) – ie the East (later restricted to the eastern Mediterranean and the countries on its shores), **lever** (bar etc used to) raise (something heavy etc), **levy** raising (of money etc) – or the money etc raised

LEX Gk *lexis* speech, word(s). Eg **dyslexia** ill-speech – ie word-blindness, **lexicography** word-writing – ie dictionary-making, **lexicology** study of words, **lexicon** word-book – ie dictionary

LIB **ad lib** – see AD

LIBAT Lat *libare, libat-* to pour out (wine etc) as an offering (to a god). Eg **libation** the pouring of wine etc as an offering to a god – or the liquid poured (now generally used facetiously for drink poured out for less solemn purposes...)

LIBEL see LIBR

LIBER Lat *liber* free; *liberalis* relating to freedom, or befitting a freeman (or woman) (ie as opposed to a slave); *libertinus* freedman (ie former slave). Eg **liberal** befitting a freeman (or woman) – ie noble, generous, broad-minded, etc (a 'liberal education' is one befitting a 'freeman': ie one that cultivates the mind as an end in itself, not just for narrow technical or vocational purposes), **liberality** (behaviour) befitting a free-man – ie nobility of character, generosity, **liberate** (set) free, **libertine** freedman – ie free-thinker, person of loose morals, **liberty** freedom

LIB(E)R Lat *libra* a balance, scales. Eg **deliberate** (thoroughly) balanced – ie weighed carefully, considered carefully, intentional, **deliberation** a (thorough) balancing – ie careful weighing (of pros and cons etc), careful consideration, **equilibrium** equally balanced (state), **Libra** the Balance – ie the Scales (sign of the zodiac)

102

LIBR, LIBEL Lat *liber, libr-* book; *libellus* little book. Eg **libel** little book – ie leaflet, defamatory leaflet etc, written defamation, **library** book(-place)

LIC(IT) Lat *licere, licit-* to be allowed, to be allowable. Eg **illicit** not-allowed, **licence** (US **license**) an allowing – ie a (written) permission, or freedom from restraint, **licentious** allowing – ie permissive, **licit** allowed

LIC(T) Eg **relic, derelict** – see LINQ

LIG Lat *ligare, ligat-* to bind. Eg **ligament** (thing that) binds – eg band of tissue joining bones, **ligature** (thing that) binds, or (the action of) binding – eg the printing of two letters joined together (æ etc), **obligation** a binding against – ie a binding up, something one is tied to doing

LIG Eg **eligible, negligence** – see first LECT

LIGN(I) Lat *lignum* wood. Eg **ligneous** woody, **lignin** wood (substance) – substance found in woody plant fibre, **lignite** wood (coal) – ie 'brown' coal (vegetable matter at a certain stage of conversion into coal, at which it still has a woody texture), **lignivorous** wood-eating

LIMBO Lat *limbus* border, hem, fringe. Eng **limbo** was originally used of the place on the borders of Hell to which unbaptised infants and those who had led good lives but died before the coming of Christ were supposed to be consigned. Thus to be 'in limbo' is now to be in an uncomfortably halfway or indefinite state

LIMIN Lat *limen, limin-* threshold. Eg **eliminate** (put) out of (ie over) the threshold – ie throw out, get rid of, **preliminary** before (crossing) the threshold – ie introductory, preparatory, **subliminal** under the threshold – ie subconscious

LIN Lat *linum* flax, linen, thread. Eg **crinoline** hair (and) thread – 'crinoline' was originally a stiff fabric made of horsehair and thread, **linoleic (acid)** (acid obtained from) flax(-seed) oil (ie linseed oil), **linoleum** flax(-seed) oil (cloth)

– 'linoleum' was originally a cloth coated with flax-seed oil (ie linseed oil) used as a floor-covering

LINGU(I) Lat *lingua* tongue. Eg **bilingual** two-tongued – ie in (or speaking) two languages, **linguiform** tongue-shaped, **linguistic** relating to tongues – ie to language(s), **multilingual** many-tongued – ie in (or speaking) many languages

LINQ, LIC(T) Lat *linquere, lict-* to leave; or related Latin words. Eg **delinquent** (thoroughly) leaving (one's duty) – ie failing in one's duty, offending against social morality, **derelict** (thoroughly) left back – ie thoroughly left behind, abandoned, neglected, **relic** (thing) left back – ie thing left behind, piece of a saint's bodily remains or belongings, remnant, **relinquish** leave back – ie leave behind, abandon

LIP(O) Gk *lipos* fat. Eg **lipid** a fat, **lipoma** fatty (tumour), **lipoprotein** fat-protein – a protein containing cholesterol found in the blood

LIPS, LIPT Gk *leipein* to leave. Eg **eclipse** a leaving out – ie an omission, a disappearance (of the sun or moon etc), an overshadowing, **ellipsis** a leaving in – ie a leaving behind, a missing out (of words in a sentence); or a series of dots indicating this omission

LIT(E) Eg **phonolite** – see LITH(O)

LITER Lat *lit(t)era* letter (of the alphabet). Eg **literal** relating to letters – or accurate 'to the letter', **literate** lettered – ie able to read and write, educated, **obliterate** to against-letter – ie to strike out (a letter etc), blot out, efface, **transliteration** a (writing) letters across (from one language to another) – ie a writing of the sounds of one language in the way they would be written if they belonged to another

LITH(O), LIT(E) Gk *lithos* stone. Eg **lithium** stone (element) – so called because it is found in various minerals, **lithography** stone-writing – ie printing in which impressions are made using a stone to which ink has been applied (or modern versions of this), **lithology** science of stones – ie the branch of medicine concerned with 'stones' forming in the body, or the science of stones and rocks, **megalith** big stone – especially in reference to prehistoric monuments, **Mesolithic** (belonging to the) Middle Stone (Age) – between the Palaeolithic and the Neolithic (see below), **monolith** (block or pillar of a) single stone, **monolithic** (like a block or pillar of a) single stone – ie massive, the same throughout, or difficult to shift or influence, **Neolithic** (belonging to the) New Stone (Age), **Palaeolithic** (belonging to the) Old Stone (Age), **phonolite** sound-stone – ie clinkstone (which rings when struck)

LITIG Lat *litigare, litigat-* quarrel, go to law; *litigium* a quarrel, a going to law. Eg **litigation** a going to law – ie legal action, **litigious** relating to going to law – or fond of going to law

LOC Lat *locus* place. Eg **allocate** place to – ie assign to a place, **dislocate** place asunder – ie put out of place, disjoint, **local** relating to place – or belonging to a particular place, **location** placement, **locomotion** a moving of place – ie (power of) moving from place to place, **locum** (short for **locum tenens**) (doctor etc) (temporarily) 'taking the place' (of another)

LOC, LOQ Lat *loqui, locut-* to speak. Eg **circumlocution** a speaking round (instead of going straight to the point), **colloquial** relating to speaking together – ie belonging to everyday conversational speech, **colloquy** a speaking-together – ie a conversation, **elocution** (art of) speaking out – ie art of good delivery, **eloquent** speaking out – ie speaking well, expressing (something) well, **grandiloquent** great-speaking – ie speaking (or spoken) grandly or pompously, **locution** a speaking – ie an utterance, or a way of speaking, **loquacious** speechy – ie talkative, **soliloquy** a lone-speaking – ie a talking to oneself, a speech made to oneself, **ventri-loquism** a belly-speaking – ie a speaking from the belly (as it were) rather than through the mouth (as it were) so that the sound appears to be coming from some source other than the speaker

LOG Gk *logos* a speaking, speech, saying, word, discourse, thought, reasoning, reckoning, ratio; *legein* to speak (see also third LECT); *-logia* a ... speaking, or discourse on ... (ie the science or study of ...) – or related Greek suffixes. Eg **analogy** (originally, in mathematics, a case of) (the same) ratio over again – ie an equality of ratios or proportions, a correspondence, a corresponding case, **anthology** – see the third LECT, **arch(a)eology** study of ancient (things), **dialogue** a speaking between – ie a conversation, **epilogue** speech-upon – ie a speech coming 'on top of' (ie at the end of) a play (or a piece coming at the end of a book), **eulogy** a speaking well (of someone), **homologous** speaking the same – ie saying the same, agreeing, corresponding, **horologist** (maker of) time-speakers (ie clocks), **ideology** discourse on ideas – ie a system of ideas, **logarithm** ratio number, **logic** (the art of) reasoning – ie rational thought and argument, **logistic** relating to reckoning – ie relating to calculation (or to the practical arrangements needed to achieve something), **monologue** a speaking alone – ie speech by one person only (as opposed to a conversation), **neologism** new speech – ie a new word or phrase, or the introduction of new applications for words and phrases, **obloquy** a speaking against – ie a speaking ill of, a being spoken ill of, disgrace, **ornithology** study of birds, **prologue** before-speech – ie a speech made before a play, **philology** love of words – ie the science of language, **psychologist** (person who) studies the mind, **syllogism** a reasoning together – a form of argument in which a conclusion is derived from two propositions taken as premises, **trilogy** (series of) three discourses – ie series of three plays, novels etc

LOQ Eg **colloquial, eloquent, loquacious** – see LOC

LUBRIC Lat *lubricus* slippery. Eg **lubricate** (make) slippery, **lubricity** slipperiness – or 'dirty'-mindedness

LUC Lat *lux, luc-* light; *lucere* to be light, to shine; *lucidus* full of light, shining, clear. Eg **elucidate** make clear, **lucid** clear, **Lucifer** Light-bearer – this was the name given by the Romans to the planet Venus as a morning star; the name was later given to the archangel who was once 'bright' but then rebelled against God and fell from heaven (ie Satan), **lucifugous** fleeing light, **pellucid** shining through – ie transparent, **translucent** shining across – ie shining through, letting light through

LUD, LUS Lat *ludere, lus-* to play; *ludus* game, play. Eg **allude** play towards – ie play with, sport with, touch playfully on, refer indirectly (to), **collusion** a playing together – ie a secret acting-in-concert or agreement (especially for the purpose of deception), **delude** play away (from the right way) – ie play falsely, cheat, deceive, **elusive** playing away from – ie parrying a blow, evading, difficult to pin down, **illusion** a playing against – ie a mocking, a deceptive appearance, a deceptive belief, **interlude** a play between – ie a short performance between the acts of the main piece, an interval, **ludicrous** playful – ie not serious, ridiculous, **ludo** 'I play' – name of a board game, **prelude** a playing before – ie an introductory performance or piece

LUMB Lat *lumbus* loin. Eg **lumbago** (pain in the) loins, **lumbar** relating to the loins

LUMEN, LUMIN Lat *lumen, lumin-* light. Eg **illuminate** enlighten, light (up), **luminary** (source of) light, **luminous** (full of) light – or relating to light, **phillumenist** lover of light(-box labels) – ie collector of matchbox labels

LUNA Lat *luna* the moon. Eg **lunar** relating to the moon, **lunatic** moon(-struck person) – from the belief that bouts of insanity were brought on in some people by the changes of the moon, **semilunate** half-moon (shaped), **translunar** relating to beyond the moon – ie relating to the region beyond the moon's orbit round the earth

LUS Eg **collusion, elusive** – see LUD

LUSTR Lat *lustrare, lustrat-* to light up. Eg **illustrate** (thoroughly) light up – ie throw light on (or make clear) by means of pictures; or by giving an example, **illustrious** (thoroughly) lit-up – ie highly distinguished, renowned, **lustre** a lighting-up – ie a sheen, gloss, **lustrous** lit-up – ie shining

LUT, LUV Lat *-luere, -lut-* to wash; *diluvium* a 'washing apart', 'washing away' – ie a flood. Eg **ablution** a washing away (of dirt), **alluvial** relating to (matter) washed-to (ie washed up) (by the sea or a river), **antediluvian** before the Flood, **dilute**

107

wash apart – ie wash away, dissolve, weaken by adding water

LYCEUM Lat *Lyceum*, Gk *Lykeion* – the name of the 'gymnasium' (see GYMN(O)) in Athens where Aristotle taught. Hence a **lyceum** is a lecture-hall, educational institution, etc

LYR(IC) Gk *lyra* lyre – a musical instrument rather like a harp, used by the Greeks to accompany the singing of poetry. Thus **lyric** poetry was originally that suitable for singing to the lyre; now the term is used of poems in which the poet expresses personal thoughts and emotions

LYS, LYT Gk *lyein* to loose, loosen. Eg **analytical** loosing up – ie unloosing, separating out into different elements, **bacteriolysis** loosening of bacteria – ie destruction of bacteria by an antibody, **catalyst** (substance bringing about a) loosening down – ie a dissolving, breaking down, chemical reaction, **dialysis** a loosening asunder – ie a separating out (eg of impurities in the blood, by a kidney machine), **electrolysis** loosening (by) electricity – ie chemical decomposition brought about by an electric current, **hydrolysis** loosening (by) water – ie chemical decomposition brought about by water, **paralysis** a loosening at the side – ie disablement on one side, loss of the power of movement or feeling

M

MACH(Y) Gk *-machia* a fight, battle. Eg **gigantomachy** a battle of giants (especially the war, in Greek mythology, waged by the Giants against the gods), **logomachy** a fight (ie dispute) (about) words

MACRO Gk *makros* long, big. Eg **macrobiotic** (promoting) long life – applied to foods grown without chemical fertilisers, **macrocosm** big world – see COSM(O), **macrodactylic** long-fingered, or long-toed, **macroeconomics** big(-scale) economics – ie study of the economics of large units (eg whole national economies) as opposed to microeconomics (see MICRO), **macromolecule** big molecule

MACULA Lat *macula* spot. Eg **immaculate** spotless, **macula** spot (of different-coloured skin etc)

MAECENAS Lat *Maecenas* – name of a wealthy Roman (c70-8BC) who was famous for his patronage of the arts (he helped the poets Virgil and Horace among others). Thus **Maecenas** is now a term for any wealthy supporter of the arts

MAGIST(E)R Lat *magister, magistr-* master, teacher, chief. Eg **MA** (abbreviation of *Magister Artium*) Master of Arts, **magisterial** relating to (or in the manner of) a master or a teacher – or a magistrate, **magistrate** master – ie an official with power to enforce the law. (In ancient Rome, and formerly in English, the term applied to a wider range of offices than in today's usage)

MAGNES, MAGNET, MANGANESE Gk *Magnesia* – name of a district of Thessaly in central Greece. There were supposed to be large quantities of the lodestone in Magnesia, as a result of which the stone was known as *ho Magnes lithos* (or *ho Magnetes lithos* or other variations) – the Magnesian stone. Hence derives Eng **magnet** (the lodestone is the natural magnet). Hence also derived the medieval Lat *magnesia*, which was used to refer both to the lodestone and other types of stone and from which derive Eng **manganese, magnesia** and **magnesium**

MAGN(I) Lat *magnus* big, great. Eg **Magna Carta** the 'Great Charter', **magnanimous** great-minded – ie noble-minded, generous, **magnate** great (person), **magnificent** great-making – ie doing great things, making a great show, resplendent, glorious, **magnify** make great(er) – ie enlarge (or praise, extol), **magnitude** greatness – ie size, importance, **magnum** big (bottle) – eg a bottle (of wine or champagne) twice the ordinary size, **magnum opus** 'great work' – especially the chief work of, eg, an artist or author

MAJOR, MAYOR Lat *major* bigger, greater. Eg **major** greater – or more important, important (or an officer of 'greater' rank), **major-domo** greater (officer) of the house – ie official responsible for managing a large household, steward in a house, **majority** greater (part or number) – or (as in 'the age

109

of majority') the legal state of adulthood, **mayor** greater (officer) (of a town etc)

MAL(E) Lat *male* badly, ill; *malus* bad, evil. Eg **malaria** (fever once believed to be caused by) bad air (rising from marshy ground), **malediction** an ill-saying – ie a curse, **malefactor** an ill-doer – ie one who does evil, **malevolent** ill-wishing – ie ill-willed towards others, **malfunction** to function badly – or a faulty functioning, **malice** badness – ie ill-will, spitefulness, **malign** to (do) bad (by speaking unjustified ill of someone) – or (as an adjective) bearing ill-will, harmful, **malignant** bad (-doing) – ie bearing ill-will, harmful, **malodorous** smelling ill – ie having an unpleasant smell, **malpractice** a practising-badly – ie incorrect professional practice, wrong-doing, **maltreat** treat badly

MALLE(I) Lat *malleus* hammer. Eg **malleable** hammerable – ie capable of being shaped by hammering (or by education etc), **malleiform** hammer-shaped, **mallet** (wooden-headed) hammer

MAMMA, MAM(M)ILL Lat *mamma* breast, nipple; *mamilla* 'little breast' – ie nipple, breast. Eg **mammal** breasted (animal) – ie one that suckles its young, **mammary** relating to the breast(s), **mammiform** breast-shaped, **mam(m)illary** relating to the breast(s) – or nipple-shaped, or having nipple-shaped protuberances

MAN, MANS Lat *manere, mans-* to remain, stay. Eg **immanence** a remaining in – ie an indwelling, inherence, the pervasion of the universe by God (or a divine principle), **mansion** (place for) staying – ie a dwelling, a manor-house, a large house, **permanent** remaining thoroughly – ie remaining to the end, lasting, meant to last

MANC, MANT Gk *manteia* divination, foretelling the future; *mantis* diviner, seer, prophet. Eg **geomancy** divination by earth – ie divination by interpreting the patterns formed by earth thrown down, **hydromantic** relating to divination by (consulting) water, **mantis** (eg the **praying mantis**) prophet (insect), **necromancy** divination by (communicating with) the dead

110

MAND Lat *mandare, mandat-* to entrust, commission, order. Eg **command** (thoroughly) order, **countermand** order against – ie issue an order cancelling a previous one, **demand** (thoroughly) commission – ie claim, ask for (with authority or as though with authority), **mandate** an order or commission (to do something) – or authority given (eg authority given to one country to govern another), **mandatory** (of the nature of) an order – ie compulsory, **remand** an ordering back – ie a sending back (eg of a prisoner into custody or on bail while further investigations are made)

MANGANESE see MAGNES

MAN(I), MANU Lat *manus* hand; *manipulus* a handful. Eg **amanuensis** (slave) 'at hand' – ie (originally) a slave serving as a secretary or clerk who took down dictation, (more generally) someone who takes down dictation, **manage** (control by) hand – ie handle, **manicure** hand care, **manipulate** (to deal with) handfuls – ie to handle, to shape (someone's behaviour etc) to one's own ends, **manual** a 'hand'(-book) (ie a book of instructions etc to be kept 'at hand') – or, relating to (or done with) the hands (and not by a machine), **manufacture** make by hand – ie work up, produce (especially commercially), **manuscript** (thing) written by hand

MANI(A) Gk *mania* madness. Eg **dipsomania** thirst madness – ie cravings for alcohol amounting to an illness, **kleptomania** thief madness – ie stealing as a manifestation of psychological illness, **mania** madness, **maniac** mad (person), **manic** mad, **megalomania** great(ness) madness – ie a passion for big things, or the delusion that one is great, **monomania** single (-subject) madness – ie madness on one subject only, or an obsession with one thing, **pyromania** fire madness – an obsessive desire to set fire to things (a manifestation of psychological illness)

MANS Eg **mansion** – see MAN

MANT, MANTIS Eg **hydromantic, praying mantis** – see MANC

111

MANU Eg **manufacture, manuscript** – see MAN(I)

MARATHON Gk *Marathon* – name of a plain where the Greeks defeated the Persians in the Battle of Marathon in 490BC. News of the victory is traditionally supposed to have been brought to Athens by a messenger who ran the 20 miles or so from Marathon. When the modern Olympic games (see OLYMP) were founded in 1896, the placename **marathon** was adopted as the name of a foot-race of similar distance (about 26 miles) – and it was later also applied to other long-distance races

MARCH, MARS, MARTIAL Lat *Mars, Mart-* – name of the Roman god of war. Both the planet **Mars** and the month of **March** were named after this god; and **martial** means relating to Mars – ie relating to war or to the military. (Note, however, that the verb 'to march' does not come from this root)

MAR(IN) Lat *mare* the sea; *marinus* of or relating to the sea. Eg **aquamarine** (name of a precious stone the colour of) sea-water – or the colour itself (blue-green), **marinade** sea (-water) – ie brine (salt water) or some other liquid in which meat etc is steeped, **marine** of or relating to the sea, **mariner** sea(man), **maritime** relating to the sea, **submarine** under-sea – or (as a noun) a vessel going under the sea

MARS, MARTIAL – see MARCH

MAST Gk *mastos* nipple, breast. Eg **mastectomy** a cutting-out of the breast – ie surgical removal of a breast, **mastitis** (inflammation of) the breast – ie of the milk gland, **mastoid** breast-shaped or nipple-shaped – also the name of a projection of bone behind the ear, **mastodon** breast-toothed (creature) – an extinct elephant-like creature with nipple-shaped protuberances on some of its teeth, **polymasty** (condition of having) many (ie more than the usual number of) breasts or nipples

MATER(N), MATRI Lat *mater, matr-* mother. Eg **alma mater** 'bountiful mother' – a school or university is said to be the 'alma mater' of its students and ex-students, **maternal** relating to a mother, motherly, **maternity** motherhood, **matriarch** mother ruler (of a family etc), **matricide** killing (or killer) of (one's own) mother, **matrilineal** (traced through the) mother line – ie (when tracing ancestry) going back through the female line, **matrimony** mother (status) – ie marriage

MATH Gk *mathema* that which is learnt, learning, knowledge; or related Greek words. Eg **mathematics** learning, **philomath** lover of learning, **polymath** (person) having learnt much – ie person versed in several fields of learning

MATIN Lat *matutinus* relating to the morning, early-morning; from *Matuta* – name of the goddess of the early morning. Eg **matinal** relating to (or happening in) the morning, **matinee** (performance taking place in the) morning – ie early in the day, in the afternoon rather than the evening, **matins** (or **mattins**) early-morning or morning (worship)

MATRI Eg **matriarch, matricide** – see MATER(N)

MAUSOLEUM Gk *Mausolos* – name of a ruler of Caria (a Persian province, now part of Turkey). After he died in 353BC his widow had a magnificent tomb built, called the *mausoleion*. It was regarded as one of the 'seven wonders' of the ancient world and gave English the word **mausoleum** – an edifice, especially a grand one, built as a tomb and monument

MAXIM Lat *maximus* biggest, greatest. Eg **maxim** greatest (proposition) – ie self-evident proposition, general principle or rule of conduct (especially when briefly and cleverly expressed), **maximum** greatest – or (as a noun) the greatest amount etc

MAY Lat *Maius (mensis)* (the month of) **May** – (probably) the month of Maia, an ancient Italian goddess

MAYOR see MAJOR

MEAND(E)R Gk *Maiandros* – name of a river (now called Menderes and situated in Turkey) which was famous for its

113

winding course; hence *maiandros* a winding. Hence to **meander** is to follow a wandering or winding course, and **meandrous** means winding

MEDI Lat *medius* middle, mid; *mediocris* of/at middle height. Eg **immediate** unmiddled – ie with nothing in the middle, with nothing in the way, direct, without delay, **intermediary** (person going in) the middle between (two parties) – ie a go-between, **intermediate** (in) the middle between – ie in a position (or at a level etc) between two others, **medi(a)eval** relating to (or belonging to etc) the middle ages, **median** (in, or passing through) the middle – or the middle value in a range, etc, **mediate** (go in the) middle (of two parties) – ie act as a go-between with the aim of bringing about reconciliation, **mediocre** of middle height – ie of only middling quality, not remarkable, **medium** middling – or (as a noun) something 'going in the middle' (ie acting as a vehicle for, or means of, communication etc)

MEDUS(A) Gk *Medousa* – name of one of the Gorgons (see GORGON). She had live snakes for hair; **medusa** is used as a name for a jellyfish because some species resemble a head with snake hair

MEGA(LO) Gk *megas, megal-* big, great. (Note: in names of units 'mega' is used in English to mean a million, and 'megamega' means a million million, though for the latter the term 'tera' is now preferred – see TERA(TO).) Eg **megabyte** a million bytes, **megalith** big stone – especially in reference to prehistoric monuments, **megalomania** great(ness) madness – a passion for big things, or the delusion that one is great, **megalosaurus** great lizard – an enormous reptile, **megaphone** (instrument for making a) big sound – ie instrument for amplifying sound, **megaton** a million tons – or the explosive power of a million tons of TNT, **megavolt** a million volts, **megawatt** a million watts

MELA, MELAN(O) Gk *melas, melan-* black. Eg **melancholy** (condition of having too much) black bile – see CHOL(ER), **Melanesia** Black Islands – this group of islands in the Pacific was so named because of its dark-skinned population,

114

melanin black (pigment) (in the skin, hair, etc)

MELIOR Lat *melior* better. Eg **ameliorate** make better, **meliorist** (person who believes that the world can be made) better – an attitude midway between optimism (see OPTIM) and pessimism (see PESSIM)

MEL(L)(I) Lat *mel, mell-* honey; Gk *meli* honey. Eg **meliphagous** honey-eating, **melliferous** honey-bearing – ie producing honey, **mellifluous** honey-flowing – ie flowing with honey, flowing sweetly, sweet as honey

MELO(D) Gk *melos* song; *meloidia* a singing. Eg **melodrama** song (with) action – ie (originally) a play with musical accompaniment, **melody** a singing – ie a tune

MEN(O) Gk *men* month. Eg **amenorrhoea** (US **amenorrhea**) no monthly flow – ie non-occurrence of menstruation, **dysmenorrhoea** (US **dysmenorrhea**) badly monthly-flowing – ie painful menstruation, **menarche** beginning of the monthly – ie the onset of menstruation for the first time, **menopause** stopping of the monthly – ie the time of life in which menstruation ceases, **menorrhagia** bursting of the monthly – ie excessive menstrual flow

MENS Lat *mensis* month. Eg **mensal** and **mensual** monthly, **menstruation** monthly (discharging) (from the womb)

MENS Lat *metiri, mens-* to measure. Eg **commensurate** (of a) measure together – ie with the same measure, of the same (or proportional) measurements, **dimension** a measuring apart – ie a measuring out, a measurement, **immense** immeasurable – ie very large, **mensuration** (act or science of) measurement

MENT Lat *mens, ment-* mind. Eg **compos mentis** 'in control of (one's) mind' – ie of sound mind, **demented** away from (ie out of) (one's) mind, **mental** relating to (or done in) the mind, **mentality** (attitude of) mind

MENTOR Gk *Mentor* – name of a friend of the Greek hero Odysseus (see ODYSSEY). When, after the Trojan War,

115

Odysseus' son Telemachus went in search of his father, he was guided by Mentor (or rather by the goddess Athene who had taken on Mentor's shape). Thus a **mentor** is someone who gives help and guidance

MERCUR Lat *Mercurius* – name of the Roman equivalent of the Greek god Hermes (see HERM). As well as being the messenger of the gods, Mercury was the god of eloquence, and of theft and commerce, and conducted the souls of the dead to the Underworld. The planet **Mercury** was named after him, and later the planet gave its name to the liquid metal now found in thermometers (also known as 'quicksilver'). Originally when people were described as **mercurial** they were being attributed the characteristics supposedly belonging to those born under the planet Mercury (eg eloquence, enterprise), but later the meaning of 'mercurial' was influenced by the connection with the metal mercury – a 'mercurial' person is a lively, volatile one

MERETRIC Lat *meretrix, meretric-* prostitute. Eg **meretricious** of (or as though of) a prostitute – ie gaudy, flashy

MERG, MERS Lat *mergere, mers-* to plunge, dip, dive. Eg **emerge** plunge out – ie rise out, come to light, reappear, **emergency** (something) plunging out – ie appearing suddenly (and needing urgent action), **immersed** plunged into – eg plunged into water (or into an activity etc), **merganser** diver-goose, **merge** to plunge (into something else) – ie lose separate identity by becoming part of, or joining with, something else, **submerged** plunged under – ie covered or hidden by a liquid etc, or overwhelmed by something, **submersed** plunged under – ie (of plants) growing under water

MER(O) Gk *meros* part. Eg **dimerous** (having) two parts, **merogenesis** part production – ie segmentation, **polymer** (compound consisting of) many parts – ie compound of which the molecules are in effect a molecule of a simpler substance many times over

MERS Eg **immersed, submersed** – see MERG

116

MES(O) Gk *mesos* middle. Eg **Mesolithic** (belonging to the) Middle Stone (Age) – ie between the Old Stone (Palaeolithic) Age and the New Stone (Neolithic) Age, **meson** middle (thing) – ie one of a group of subatomic particles classified (in terms of mass) between the leptons ('slight') and the baryons ('heavy'): see LEPT(O) and BAR(O), **Mesozoic** middle-life – see ZO(O)

MET(A), METH Gk *meta* (many meanings, including) among, with, beside, after; or 'across' – with a sense of change from one state, place etc to another. Eg **metabolism** a throwing across – ie change, the chemical changes undergone by food in the body (etc), **metamathematics** after-mathematics – ie analysis going 'beyond' or 'behind' mathematics (and examining the very concepts of mathematics), **metamorphosis** an across-form – ie a change of form, a changing into something else, **metaphor** a bearing across (from one place to another) – ie the use of a word (or phrase) to describe or refer to something to which it does not literally apply, **metaphysics** – see note at end of entry, **metatarsal** after (ie beyond) the tarsus – ie between the tarsus (a group of bones at the ankle) and the toes, **method** a way after – ie a following after, an enquiry into, system of enquiry, way of doing. (Note: it might at first appear that the branch of philosophy known as 'metaphysics' is so called because it deals with matters 'after' or 'beyond' the physical, and indeed the word does derive from the title, *Metaphysics*, given to a group of treatises of Aristotle on various fundamental philosophical questions, but this group of works was in fact so named simply because – in the usual arrangement of Aristotle's works – it came 'after' the '*Physics*', the works dealing with natural science)

METEOR Gk *meteoros* high in the air, aloft. Eg **meteor** (thing) high in the air, **meteorology** study of (things) high in the air (ie the weather)

METER, METR(O) Gk *metron* measure. Eg **barometer** weight measure – ie instrument for measuring pressure, **diameter** (line) measured through – ie crossing a circle (etc) through its centre, **geometry** (science of) measuring the earth – ie of physical dimensions and their relationships etc, **meter**

117

measure – ie measuring device, **metre** (US **meter**) measure – ie a unit of length (or the rhythm of verse, or a particular pattern of it), **metronome** measure rule – ie instrument for marking a 'measure' (ie beat), **parameter** a measure beside – ie (loosely – there are various technical meanings) a point of reference, or a boundary or limit within which an activity etc takes place, **pentameter** five-measured (line) – ie line of verse with five measures or 'feet', **perimeter** a measure around – ie a boundary line round, boundary, **symmetrical** (of a) measure together – ie of the same measure, of corresponding proportions, divisible into parts corresponding exactly either side of the dividing line, **thermometer** heat measure – ie instrument for measuring temperature

METH Eg **method** – see MET(A)

METR(O) Gk *meter, metr-* mother. Eg **metropolis** mother-city – ie (in ancient Greece) the parent city or state from which colonies were sent out; (now also) capital city, chief cathedral city

METR(O) Eg **metre** (US **meter**), **metronome, symmetrical** – see METER

METR(O) Gk *metra* womb. Eg **endometrium** (membrane) inside the womb – ie the lining of the womb, **metritis** (inflammation of the) womb, **metrorrhagia** womb bursting – ie bleeding from the womb between monthly periods

MICRO Gk *mikros* small. (Note: in names of units, 'micro' is used in English to mean a millionth.) Eg **microampere** a millionth of an ampere, **microbe** small life – ie small living thing, **microbiology** small biology – ie the biology of very small organisms, **microcomputer** (very) small computer, **microcosm** small world – see COSM(O), **microeconomics** small(-scale) economics – ie study of the economics of small units (eg individual companies) as opposed to 'macro-economics' (see MACRO), **microgram** a millionth of a gram, **micro-organism** (very) small organism, **microphone** small-sound (instrument) – ie instrument for amplifying small sounds, **microscope** small-viewer – ie instrument for looking at small things,

MIGR Lat *migrare, migrat-* to move (from one place to another). Eg **emigrant** (person) moving out of (a country), **immigrant** (person) moving into (a country), **migration** a moving (from one place to another), **transmigration** a moving across – ie (of a soul) a moving into another body

MILE, MILL(I) Lat *mille* a thousand. (Note: in names of units, 'milli' is used in English to mean a thousandth.) Eg **mile** a thousand (paces) – the Roman 'mile' was some 150yd shorter than the modern mile, **millennium** a thousand years, **millilitre** a thousandth of a litre, **millimetre** (US **millimeter**) a thousandth of a metre (US meter), **million** a thousand (thousands)

MIN(OR) Lat *minor* smaller, less(er); *minutus* made smaller, small, very small. Eg **minor** lesser – or less important, not very important (or someone who is under the age of legal adulthood), **minority** smaller (part or number) – or the state of being below the age of legal adulthood, **minus** less, **minutiae** very small (details)

MINIM Lat *minimus* smallest, least. Eg **minim** smallest (note) – though the minim is no longer the shortest note, **minimum** least – or (as a noun) the smallest amount etc

MIO Gk *meion* smaller, less(er). Eg **Miocene** – see CENE

MIR, MIRAC Lat *mirari* to wonder (at). Eg **admire** to wonder at, **miracle** (something provoking) wonder

MISC Lat *miscere* to mix. Eg **miscegenation** mixed-race (breeding), **miscellaneous** mixed – ie of various kinds, **miscible** mixable, **promiscuous** (thoroughly) mixed – ie of different kinds 'jumbled up' together, indiscriminate, practising indiscriminate sexual intercourse

MISER Lat *miser* wretched; *miserari, miserat-* to pity (someone), to bewail (something). Eg **commiserate** (thoroughly) bewail – ie express one's sympathy for someone who has suffered misfortune, **miser** wretched (person) – specifically a mean person, **misery** wretchedness

119

MIS(O) Gk *mis(o)*- -hater, -hatred etc. Eg **misanthropist** human-hater – ie hater of humankind, **misogynist** woman-hater

MIS(S), MIT Lat *mittere, miss*- to send. Eg **admit** send to – ie let near, let in, **commit** send together – ie put together, engage oneself, carry out (a crime etc); or send (to prison etc), **demise** a sending away – ie a death (or the transfer of an estate etc), **dismiss** send apart – ie send away, **emissary** (person) sent forth (with a task to do), **emit** send forth, **intermission** a sending between – ie a break, an interval, **missile** (object for) sending – ie weapon etc for throwing or otherwise projecting through the air, **mission** a sending – ie something one is sent to do, or a group of persons who have been sent somewhere (with a task to do), **missive** (letter etc) sent, **premise** (statement) sent before – ie an assumption on which an argument etc is based, **promise** send forward – ie engage oneself to do something in the future, **remission** a sending back – ie forgiveness (of sins), a lessening (of a prison sentence etc), **submission** a sending under (of oneself) – ie an acceptance of outside control, **transmit** send across – ie send out (eg over the airwaves), pass on

MOL Lat *moles* heap, mass (especially a large mass of stone – a dam or a pier). Eg **molecule** little heap, or little mass

MOL Lat *mola* millstone, meal (especially the meal that, mixed with salt, was sprinkled on sacrificial victims before the sacrifice). Eg **immolate** (sprinkle) (sacrificial) meal on – ie to sacrifice, **molar** relating to a mill – ie relating to grinding, (of teeth) used for grinding

MOLL(I) Lat *mollis* soft; *molluscus* soft. Eg **emollient** softening – or (as a noun) something applied to soften or soothe inflammation etc, **mollify** make soft – ie appease, calm down, **mollusc** soft(-bodied) (creature)

MON Lat *monere, monit*- to warn, remind, advise. Eg **admonition** a (thorough) reminding – ie a reminding of one's duty etc, a rebuke, **monitor** to warn or advise – ie to keep a watch on, **monitory** (giving) warning, **monument** a reminder – ie a memorial, **premonition** a forewarning. Also, Eng **money, monetary**, etc, derive indirectly from this root – by way of Lat *moneta* (the mint – in Rome). The Roman mint was called *moneta* because it was housed in a temple dedicated to the goddess Juno, entitled in this instance *Juno Moneta* – Juno the Reminder

MON(O) Gk *mono-* alone, single, sole, one. Eg **monarch** sole ruler, **monastery** (place for) (living) alone – ie a place in which monks etc live withdrawn from the world, **monocle** single eye(-glass), **monogamy** single marriage – ie marriage with only one person at once, **monogram** (two or more letters interwoven to make a) single letter – ie one symbol, **monograph** a single(-subject) writing – ie a treatise on a single subject, **monolith** (block or pillar of a) single stone, **monologue** a speaking alone – ie speech by one person only (as opposed to a conversation), **monomania** single(-subject) madness – ie madness on one subject only, or an obsession with one thing, **monopoly** a selling alone – ie a situation in which there is only one seller of a particular product, so that this seller has all the market, **monosyllable** (word of a) single syllable, **monotonous** single-toned – ie having only one tone, unvarying, boring

MONSTR Lat *monstrare, monstrat-* to show. Eg **demonstrate** show (thoroughly) (how something is done etc), **remonstrate** show back – ie point out back, argue back, protest

MONS VENERIS – see VENER

MOR Lat *mos, mor-* custom (plural *mores* – customs, ways, manners, character). Eg **moral** relating to character – ie to right and wrong conduct (or, conforming to right conduct), **morale** character – ie disposition, state of heart, **mores** the customs or ways (of a particular place or group)

MORB(I) Lat *morbus* disease, sickness. Eg **morbid** relating to disease, sickly, diseased – or unwholesome, dwelling on unwholesome thoughts (of horrible disaster, death etc), **morbific** disease-making – ie disease-causing

121

MORD, MORS Lat *mordere, mors-* to bite. Eg **mordant** biting, **morsel** a little bite, **remorse** a biting back – ie a biting afterwards, a troubling of the conscience, feelings of repentance

MORPH Gk *morphe* form, shape, figure (see also next entry). Eg **amorphous** shapeless, **anthropomorphism** (the attribution of) human form (or characteristics) (to something that is not human), **isomorphic** (exhibiting) sameness of form – technical term in biology, chemistry, mathematics, **metamorphosis** an across-form – ie a change of form, a changing into something else, **polymorph** (substance that can take) many forms – or one of the forms themselves

MORPH Lat *Morpheus* ('the Shaper', from Gk *morphe* – see previous entry) the name given by the Roman poet Ovid to the god of dreams. Hence Eng **morphia** – because it brings sleep

MORS Eg **morsel, remorse** – see MORD

MOR(T) Lat *mors, mort-* death; *mori, mortu-* to die. Eg **immortal** not (subject to) death – ie living for ever, **moribund** about to die, **mortal** relating to death – ie deadly (of a wound etc), or subject to death, human, **mortify** make dead – ie humiliate, **mortuary** (place) relating to the dead – ie for temporarily storing dead bodies, **postmortem** (examination of a body) 'after death', **rigor mortis** 'stiffness of death'

MOT, MOV Lat *movere, mot-* to move. Eg **commotion** a (thorough) moving – ie a disturbance, tumult, **demotion** a moving down – ie a reduction in status, **emotion** a moving out of (oneself) – ie a being moved, a feeling, **locomotive** (engine) moving place – ie able to move from place to place (under its own power), **motive** that which moves (a person to do something) – ie a person's reason for doing something, **motor** mover, **promotion** a moving forward – ie an increase in status, or an attempt to bring a product etc to the attention of the market, **remote** moved back – ie moved away, out-of-the-way, far away

MULT(I) Lat *multus* (plural *multi*) much, many; *multiplicare* to increase many times. Eg **multicoloured** many-coloured, **multilateral** many-sided – ie affecting many sides (or parties), **multinational** (involving) many nations, **multiple** many (ie more than one), or (having) many (parts) – or (as a noun) a number that contains another number an exact number of times, **multiply** increase many times, **multistorey** (having) many storeys

MUNDAN Lat *mundus* the world. Eg **mundane** of the world – ie worldly, belonging to this world (as opposed to the other world – the realm of the spirit), ordinary, commonplace, **ultramundane** beyond the word – or beyond the solar system

MUN(I) Lat *munus, muner-* office, duty (see also MUNICIPAL), or gift. Eg **munificent** gift-making – ie very generous, **re-munerate** to gift back – ie to give something in return for services etc

MUNICIPAL Lat *municipium* a town whose citizens enjoyed Roman citizenship with its attendant privileges but which was self-governing; literally, civic-function-taking (town), from *munia* (plural of *munus* – see entry above) duties, official duties, civic functions, and *capere* to take (see CAP). Thus *municipalis* meant relating (or belonging) to a *municipium*, and the modern **municipal** means relating to (or run by, etc) local government

MUR Lat *murus* wall. Eg **extramural** outside the walls – ie (of a university department) out in the community, serving students not belonging to the university, **immure** enwall – ie wall in, imprison, shut oneself up (somewhere), **mural** wall(-painting)

MUSE, MUSEUM, MUSIC Gk *Mousa* Muse. The Muses were the goddesses of the arts. There were nine of them, including Euterpe (the Muse of music and lyric poetry), Terpsichore (see CHOR(EO)) and Polyhymnia (the muse of sacred song). A temple or resort of the Muses was a *mouseion*; hence Eng **museum**. From Gk *mousikos* (relating to the Muses) derives Eng **music**

MUT Lat *mutare, mutat-* to change. Eg **commute** (thoroughly) change – ie change altogether, change for something else (eg alter a punishment to a lesser punishment), change place (daily, for work), **immutable** unchangeable, **mutation** a changing – ie (in biology) (broadly) a departure from the hereditary type, **mutatis mutanda** 'those things having been changed that need to be changed' – ie with the appropriate changes, **permutation** a (thorough) changing – ie the arrangent of a set of things in all the different ways possible, or one way of combining a set of things (eg a set of circumstances) out of all the possible ways

MYCET, MYC(O) Gk *myces, mycet-* mushroom, fungus. Eg **Eumycetes** well mushrooms – the higher fungi, **mycology** the study of fungi, **mycosis** (disease caused by a) fungus

MY(O) Gk *mys* mouse, muscle. Eg **myalgia** muscle pain, **myasthenia** muscle weakness, **myocardium** heart muscle, **myosotis** mouse-ear (plant) – because the leaves resemble mouse ears

MYRIA(D) Gk *myrios* numberless, countless; plural *myrioi* ten thousand. Eg **myriad** countless – or, a very large number, **myriapod** (member of the class of) countless-footed (creatures) – eg centipedes

N

NANO Gk *nanos* a dwarf. (Note: in names of units, 'nano' is used in English to mean a thousand-millionth.) Eg **nanogram** a thousand-millionth of a gram, **nanosecond** a thousand-millionth of a second

NARCISS Gk *Narkissos* – name of a beautiful youth in Greek mythology who fell in love with his own reflection in a fountain, thinking it to be a nymph (see NYMPH(O)) inhabiting the water, and killed himself in despair. Hence **narcissism** is an excessive regard for one's own body or one's appearance

NARCO Gk *narke* numbness, torpor. Eg **narcolepsy** torpor-

124

seizure – ie a condition characterised by attacks of an overwhelming desire to sleep, **narcotic** (substance inducing) torpor

NASC Eg **nascent** – see NAT

NAS(O) Lat *nasus* nose. Eg **nasal** relating to (or sounded through etc) the nose, **nasofrontal** relating to the nose and frontal (bone), **nasturtium** (apparently means:) nose-twister – because of the pungent taste, which affects the nose, of the original 'Nasturtiums' (the water-cress genus)

NAT Lat *natare, natat-* to swim. Eg **natant** swimming – or floating, **natation** swimming, **natatorium** swimming (place) – ie swimming-pool

NAT, NATIV, NASC, GNAT Lat *nasci, nat-* (earlier, *gnat-*) to be born; *nativus* born. Eg **antenatal** before the birth, **cognate** born together – ie having a common ancestor, related, **innate** inborn, **nascent** being born – ie in the process of coming into being, **natal** relating to birth, **native** (person etc) born (in a place) – rather than having come in from outside, **nativity** birth, **neonatal** relating to newborn (babies), **perinatal** around the birth – ie relating to a period starting shortly before the birth and ending shortly after it, **postnatal** after the birth, **renascent** being born again – ie coming to life again, getting a new lease of life

NAUS, NAUT Gk *naus* ship; *nautes* sailor; *nausia* (or *nautia*) sea-sickness. Eg **aeronautics** air-sailing – ie travel in the air, **astronaut** star-sailor – ie space-traveller, **nausea** sea-sickness – or sickness in general, **nautical** relating to ships or sailors

NAV, NAVIG Lat *navis* ship; *navigare, navigat-* to sail. Eg **nave** ship (of a church) – ie the (shiplike) main part of a church, **navigation** sailing – or the tracing of one's position and course when at sea, **navy** (fleet of) ships

NE, NEG Lat *ne-, nec-, neg-* not; *negare, negat-* to say no, to deny. Eg **negation** a saying no, a denying, **negotiation** not leisure –

ie business, bargaining, **nescient** not knowing – ie lacking knowledge, **neuter** not either – ie neither one nor the other, neither masculine nor feminine (see also NEUT(R))

NEBUL Lat *nebula* mist. Eg **nebulise** (make into a) mist – ie make into a spray, **nebulous** misty – ie cloudy, vague

NECRO Gk *nekros* dead body (in plural, the dead). Eg **necromancy** divination by (communicating with) the dead, **necrophilia** love of dead bodies, **necropolis** city of the dead – ie cemetery, **necrosis** death (of an area of bone or body tissue)

NECT Eg **connection** – see NEX

NECTAR Gk *nektar* – name of the drink of the gods (see also AMBROSIA). Hence Eng **nectar** is applied to a delicious drink, and to the sweet fluid produced by the glands of plants. The **nectarine** fruit also derives its name from the drink of the gods

NEG Eg **negation, negotiation** – see NE

NEGRO, NIGR Lat *niger, nigr-* black. Eg **denigrate** (thoroughly) blacken – ie defame, decry, **Negro** black (person), **nigrescent** blackening – ie turning black

NEMESIS Gk *nemesis* justified anger (at wrongdoing), personified as *Nemesis*, goddess of retribution. Hence Eng **nemesis** means retribution

NEO Gk *neos* new. Eg **neofascist** new fascist – ie belonging to a revival of support for fascism, **neolithic** (belonging to the) New Stone (Age), **neologism** new speech – ie a new word or phrase, or the introduction of new applications for words and phrases, **neon** new (substance) – the name given to this gaseous element on its discovery in 1898, **neonatal** relating to newborn (babies), **neophyte** newly planted (person) – ie new convert, novice

NEPHELO, NEPHO Gk *nephos* cloud; *nephele* cloud. Eg **nephelo-**

meter cloud measure – ie instrument for measuring the cloudiness of the sky, or one for measuring the cloudiness of liquids etc, **nephology** study or science of clouds

NEPHR(O) Gk *nephros* kidney. Eg **nephralgia** kidney pain, **nephrology** science of the kidneys

NEPOT Lat *nepos, nepot-* grandchild, nephew or niece, descendant. Hence **nepotism** is the practice of unfairly favouring one's relations, eg when allocating jobs. (The word originally applied specifically to the favouring by popes, and other clerics in powerful positions, of their nephews and other relatives)

NESIA Gk *nesos* island. Eg **Indonesia** (East) Indian Islands, **Melanesia** Black Islands – see MELA, **Polynesia** Many Islands

NEUR(O) Gk *neuron* sinew, tendon, nerve. Eg **neural** relating to the nerves, **neuralgia** nerve pain, **neurosis** (malfunction caused by) nervous (disorder) – or (loosely) an irrational anxious preoccupation with something, **neurotransmitter** nerve transmitter – ie a substance that transmits messages between nerve-cells

NEUT(R) Lat *neuter, neutr-* 'not either' – ie neither. Eg **neuter** neither (masculine nor feminine) – or sexless, castrated, etc, **neutral** neither (on one side nor the other), **neutron** (particle) (with) neither (a negative electrical charge nor a positive one)

NEX, NECT Lat *nectere, nex-* to tie. Eg **annex** (building etc) tied to (another) – ie added, joined on, **connection** a tying together, **nexus** a tying – ie a bond, or a group bound together

NID(I) Lat *nidus* nest. Eg **nidification** nest-making – ie nest-building, **nidifugous** nest-fleeing – ie leaving the nest soon after birth

NIGR Eg **denigrate, nigrescent** – see NEGRO

127

NIHIL, NIL Lat *nihil* (or *nil*) nothing. Eg **annihilate** make (into) nothing – ie destroy completely, **nihilism** (belief in) nothing – applied to various specific beliefs, eg the belief that all existing institutions should be overturned, **nil** nothing

NISI Lat *nisi* unless. The word **nisi** is used in English in legal contexts to indicate that something (eg a divorce) will take effect after a specified time 'unless' there is a new development in the matter

NOC, NOX Lat *nocere* to hurt, harm; *noxius* hurtful, harmful. Eg **innocent** not hurtful, harmless – ie not guilty, blameless, ignorant of evil, **innocuous** harmless, **noxious** hurtful, harmful

NOCT(I), NOX Lat *nox, noct-* night. Eg **equinox** equal night – ie when the night is equal (in length) to the day, **noctambulist** night walker – ie sleep-walker, **noctiflorous** flowering at night, **noctivagous** night-wandering – ie wandering at night, **nocturnal** relating to (or done or active in etc) the night, **nocturne** (dreamy or contemplative musical piece appropriate for) the night

NOD, NODUL Lat *nodus* knot; *nodulus* little knot. Eg **node** knot – ie knob (eg on a branch), lump (eg of hard tissue), point on a stem from which leaves sprout, point of intersection, a complication in a story, **nodule** little knot – ie little rounded lump

NOI(A), NOO, NOUS Gk *noos* (or *nous*) mind. Eg **noology** science of the mind – ie of the intellect, **nous** mind – ie intelligence, commonsense, **paranoia** (state of being) beside (one's) mind – ie out of one's mind, subject to delusions or irrational anxieties

NOM(IC) Gk *-nomia* arrangement, management, regulation; related to *nemein* to distribute and *nomos* law – see NOM(O). Eg **agronomics** field management – ie the science of land management, **astronomy** the arranging of the stars – ie the classification of the stars, the science of heavenly bodies, **autonomy** self-regulation – ie independence, **economy** house(hold) management – ie the management of the material resources of a community (eg a country), or the thrifty or efficient use of resources, **ergonomics** (science of) work management – ie study of the best way to organise work, **gastronomy** belly management – ie the art or science of good food

NOM(IN) Lat *nomen, nomin-* name. Eg **denomination** a (thorough) naming – ie the act of naming, a name, a set or class (eg of monetary units) or a sect, **ignominy** (state of being) not named – ie state of being without a good name or reputation, disgrace, **misnomer** a misnaming – ie a wrong or inappropriate name, **nomenclature** a calling by name – ie a set of names or terms, **nominal** (in) name (only), **nominate** to name (a person etc) – eg to propose someone for office etc

NOM(O) Gk *nomos* law, rule (see also NOM(IC)). Eg **anomie** (or **anomy**) lawlessness – ie a condition (of an individual or a society) in which there are no accepted rules of conduct, **metronome** measure rule – ie instrument for marking a 'measure' (ie beat), **nomology** the science of law

NONA Eg **nonagenarian, nonagon** – see NOV

NOO Eg **noology** – see NOI(A)

NOSO Gk *nosos* disease. Eg **nosography** disease writing – ie description of diseases, **nosology** science of diseases – ie the classification of diseases

NOST(O) Gk *nostos* return (home). Eg **nostalgia** return-home pain – ie home-sickness or longing for the past, **nostology** the study of the return (to childhood) – ie the study of senility

NOUS see NOI(A)

NOV Lat *novus* new. Eg **innovate** (make) new – ie renew, introduce something new, **novel** new, or a new (story), **novelty** newness, or new (thing), **novice** new (ie inexperienced) (person), **renovate** renew

NOV, NONA Lat *novem* nine; *novenus* (or *nonus*) ninth; *nonaginta* ninety; *nonagenarius* containing ninety. Eg **nonagenarian** (person) containing ninety (years) – ie person in his or her nineties, **nonagon** nine-cornered (ie nine-angled) (figure), **nonary** (based on) nine, **November** ninth (month) – our eleventh month was the ninth month of the Roman year, which began in March (see also SEPT(I), OCTAV, DEC(I)), **novena** (devotion consisting of specific prayers etc on) nine (days)

NOX Eg **noxious** – see NOC

NOX Eg **equinox** – see NOCT(I)

NUB, NUPT Lat *nubere, nupt-* to marry. Eg **connubial** relating to marriage together – ie relating to marriage, **nubile** marriage-able – ie sexually mature, sexually attractive, **nuptials** marriage – or the wedding ceremony

NUCL, NUX Lat *nux, nuc-* nut; *nucleus* kernel. Eg **nucleus** kernel – or central part of something (eg of an atom), around which the rest operates, or around which the rest will develop, **nux vomica** 'vomit nut' – a seed from which strychnine (which is very poisonous) is obtained

NUL, NULL(I) Lat *nullus* no, none; *nullum* nothing. Eg **anul** (bring) to nothing – ie make invalid, **null** none – ie invalid, **nullify** make none – ie make invalid, **nulliparous** bringing forth none – ie (of a woman) not having had any children

NUNCI Lat *nuntius* messenger, message; *nuntiare* to bring news, announce. Eg **denunciation** a (thorough) announcing – ie an official announcing, an accusing, **enunciate** announce forth – ie utter, utter distinctly, **nuncio** messenger – especially a messenger (ie ambassador) from the pope, **pronunciation** an announcing forward – ie an announcing publicly, an uttering, a way of uttering, **renunciation** an announcing back – ie a disclaiming, a giving up

NUPT Eg **nuptials** – see NUB

130

NUX Eg **nux vomica** – see NUCL

NYMPH(O) Gk *nymphe* bride. In Greek, the word for bride was also used to refer to a member of a class of minor female divinities, the Nymphs, who were pictured as beautiful young women. They were the spirits of nature, inhabiting the trees, rocks, rivers, fountains etc. It is presumably the 'bride' meaning that gives English, eg, **nymphomania** (uncontrollable sexual desire in a woman)

O

OB, O (or OC, OF, OP before 'c', 'f', 'p') Lat *ob* towards, against, in the way of, down – or (as a prefix) it may serve mainly to strengthen the force of the word ('thoroughly'). (In addition, in some English words, mainly scientific ones, 'ob' has the sense 'inversely', 'in the opposite direction'). Eg **obconical** inversely conical – ie (in botany) conical but attached by the point of the cone rather than the base, **obdurate** (thoroughly) hardened (against something) – ie stubborn, **objection** a throwing in front of, in the way of – ie a challenge, protest, **obloquy** a speaking against – ie a speaking ill of, a being spoken ill of, disgrace, **obstruct** build against – ie block, **occident** (place of) the falling-down (sun) – ie place of the setting sun, the west, **occur** run in the way of – ie happen, or come to mind, **offer** bear in the way of – ie bring in front of, hold out, **opposition** a placing against – ie a fighting against

OCTAV, OCT(O) Lat *octo* eight; *octavus* eighth; *octogenarius* containing eighty; Gk *okto* eight. Eg **octagon** eight-angled (figure), **octahedron** eight-seated (figure) – ie solid figure with eight faces, **octant** an eighth (of the circumference of a circle) – or an angle-measuring instrument using this arc, **octave** (range of notes between a note and its) 'eighth' (ie the eighth note above or below it), **October** eighth (month) – our tenth month was the eighth month of the Roman year, which began in March (see also SEPT(I), NOV, DEC(I)), **octogenarian** (person) containing eighty (years) – ie person in his or her eighties, **octopus** eight-footed (ie eight-tentacled) (creature)

OC(U)L Lat *oculus* eye, bud. Eg **binoculars** (lenses for the) two eyes together, **inoculate** enbud – ie insert a bud or graft from one plant into another, or implant the germ or virus of a disease to produce immunity, **monocle** single eye(-glass), **ocular** relating to the eyes

ODI Lat *odium* hatred. Eg **odious** hateful, **odium** hatred

OD(O) Eg **electrode, exodus, odometer** – see (H)OD(O)

ODONT(O) Gk *odous, ondont-* tooth. Eg **odontalgia** tooth pain, **odontology** science of the teeth, **orthodontics** tooth-straightening, **periodontal** relating to (that which is) around a tooth or the teeth – ie the gums etc

ODYSSEY Gk *Odysseus* (Lat *Ulysses*) – in Greek legend, name of a Greek prince, a hero of the Trojan War. His long and eventful journey back from the war is the subject of Homer's epic poem *The Odyssey*, which is named after him. Thus an **odyssey** is a long wandering or an adventurous journey (see also MENTOR)

OEDIP Gk *Oidipous* (Lat *Oedipus*) – in Greek legend, name of a king of the Greek city of Thebes who (not knowing who they were) killed his father and married his mother. Thus an **Oedipal** relationship is an attachment of a son to his mother involving jealousy of his father, or (loosely) an over-close relationship between mother and son

(O)ESTR(O) Gk *oistros* gadfly (and, hence, sting; and also frenzy – something one is 'stung' into). Eg **(o)estrogen** frenzy-producer – ie female sex hormone, **(o)estrus** (or **(o)estrum**) gadfly, or frenzy – or sexual heat

OID, EID Gk *eidos* form, shape. Eg **android** man-shaped (robot), **anthropoid** human-shaped – ie humanlike, **asteroid** star-shaped (body) – ie star-like tiny planet, **kaleidoscope** beautiful-shape viewer, **schizoid** schizo(phrenic)-shaped – ie schizophrenic-like, displaying schizophrenic-like behaviour (without positively suffering from the disorder)

OL Lat *olere* to emit an odour, smell. Eg **olfactory** relating to

132

smell-doing – ie relating to smelling out, relating to smelling, **redolent** (thoroughly) smelling – ie smelling strongly (of something), suggesting (something)

OL(EO) Lat *oleum* oil; *oleaginus* oily. Eg **lanolin(e)** wool-oil – ie fat obtained from sheep's wool, **linoleum** flax(-seed) oil (cloth) – 'linoleum' was originally a cloth coated with flax-seed oil (ie linseed oil) used as a floor-covering, **oleaginous** oily, **oleic** relating to (or obtained from) oil, **oleophilic** oil-loving – ie having an affinity for oil, **petroleum** rock oil – because it is found in rocks (and **petrol** is refined petroleum)

OLIG(O) Gk *oligos* few, little. Eg **oligarchy** rule by the few, **Oligocene** – see CENE, **oligaemia** little blood – ie a deficiency of blood, **oligopoly** (situation of) few selling – ie situation in which there are only a few traders selling a particular product

OLYMP Gk *Olympos* – name of a mountain (which actually exists) on which Zeus (see JOV) and the other major Greek gods were supposed to live. Thus **olympian** means godlike. Every four years games were held in honour of 'Olympian Zeus' (in a place named after him – Olympia) – these were the original Olympic games. (See also MARATHON)

OMEN, OMIN Lat *omen, omin-* sign foretelling or foreshadowing the future (see also AUGUR, AV); *abominari, abominat-* deprecate as a bad omen. Eg **abominate** deprecate as a bad omen – ie be disgusted by, detest, **omen** sign foretelling or foreshadowing the future, **ominous** foretelling or foreshadowing (something bad)

OMNI Lat *omnis* all. Eg **omnibus** (carriage) for all – or a book containing 'all' (or several) of a group of works (eg all the works by one author) (and **bus** is a shortened form of 'omnibus'), **omnipotent** all-powerful, **omniscient** all-knowing, **omnivorous** all-eating – ie eating all kinds of food

ONER, ONUS Lat *onus, oner-* burden. Eg **exonerate** (to free) from burden – ie to free from blame, **onerous** burdensome, **onus** burden (of responsibility)

ONOMAST, ONOMATO Eg **onomastic, onomatopoeia** – see ONYM

ONTO Gk *on, ont-* being. Eg **ontology** the study of being – ie the philosophy of the essence of things and the nature of being, **palaeontology** the study of ancient beings (ie fossils)

ONUS – see ONER

ONYM, ONOMAST, ONOMATO Gk *onoma* (or *onyma*), *onomat-* name. Eg **acronym** name (formed by the) outermost (letters of other words) – ie word made up of the initial letters of a series of other words, **anonymous** nameless – ie unsigned, with no named author, **antonym** opposite name – ie opposite word, word with opposite meaning, **eponymous** (having his/her) name upon – ie after whom a book etc was named, **homonym** same name (but with a different meaning) – ie word sounding the same as another but having a different meaning, **onomastic** relating to a name or names, **onomatopoeia** name-making – ie word-making, the formation of words from the sounds made by the things meant, **patronymic** father name – ie name derived from that of one's father, or indicating one's ancestry, **pseudonym** false name, **synonym** (word that is a) name together (with another one) – ie that is like another one (in that it has the same meaning)

oo Gk *oion* egg. (In English, 'oo' frequently means ovum.) Eg **oocyte** egg cell – ie immature ovum, **ooidal** egg-shaped, **oology** the study of (bird's) eggs

op Eg **myopia** – see OPT(O)

OPER, OPUS Lat *opus, oper-* a work; *opusculum* a little work; *opera* work, a work. Eg **cooperate** work together, **magnum opus** 'great work' – especially the chief work of, eg, an artist or author, **modus operandi** 'way of working', **opera** a work (of musical drama), **operate** to work, **opus** a work, **opuscule** a little work

OPHTHALM(O) Gk *ophthalmos* eye. Eg **ophthalmic** relating to the eye, **ophthalmology** science of the eye

OPS Eg **achromatopsia, autopsy, synopsis** – see OPT(O)

OPT Lat *optare* to choose. Eg **adopt** choose to (oneself) – ie choose for oneself, take on, **co-opt** choose together – ie (of a committee etc) choose to take on as a member, **opt** choose, **option** choice

OPTIM Lat *optimus* best. Eg **optimist** (one who believes that all is ordered for the) best – or who expects the best to happen rather than the worst, **optimum** best

OPT(O), OPS, OP Gk *ops, op-* eye; *opsis* sight, a seeing; *optikos* relating to sight. Eg **achromatopsia** (condition of) no colour sight – ie colour-blindness, **autopsy** a seeing-for-oneself – ie an examination (of a corpse), **myopia** (condition of) shut eyes – ie short-sightedness, **optical** relating to sight, **optics** the science of sight (and of light), **optometer** (or **opsiometer**) sight measure – ie instrument for sight testing, **synopsis** a seeing together – ie an overall view, a summary

OPUS, OPUSCULE – see OPER

OR(AT) Lat *orare, orat-* to speak, make a speech, plead, pray. Eg **adore** speak to, pray to – ie worship, **inexorable** not able to be (thoroughly) pleaded (with) – ie not movable by pleading, relentless, **oracle** a (divine) speaking – or the person through whom a god speaks, **orator** speech-maker, **oratory** (art of) making speeches – or (place for) praying, **peroration** a speaking-throughout – ie a speaking right through to the end, the concluding part of a speech

ORB(IT) Lat *orb* circle, anything round; *orbita* rut made by a wheel, track. Eg **exorbitant** away from the track – ie off the path, excessive, **orb** circle – ie sphere, eyeball, etc, **orbit** track (of a planet etc) – or eye-socket, or sphere of operation

ORCHES(TR) Gk *orcheesthai* to dance; *orchestra* the semicircular space, on which the 'chorus' (see CHOR(EO)) of a Greek drama danced, in front of the stage. Eg **orchesography** dance writing – ie the notation of dancing, **orchestra** – from its original meaning of the space where the chorus danced and sang, in English the word came to be applied to the band of musicians themselves

ORCHI(D) Gk *orchis* (or *orchios* or *orcheos*) testicle. Eg **orchid** testicle (plant) – from the shape of the root tubers of some species, **orchitis** (inflammation of a) testicle

OR(I), OSCUL Lat *os, or-* mouth; *osculum* little mouth, kiss. Eg **oral** relating to the mouth, **orifice** a mouth-making – ie a mouth-like opening, **orotund** round-mouthed – ie round-voiced, full and rounded of speech, pompous-sounding, **osculate** to kiss – or have points of contact

ORI(EN), ORIG Lat *oriri* to rise; *origo, origin-* source (ie from where something has arisen). Eg **orient** (place of) the rising (sun) – ie the east, **orientate** (set facing the) (place of) the rising (sun) – ie set facing the east; or, of a church, to build so that the chancel lies towards the east; or to arrange something in relation to particular bearings, or to ascertain the bearings of something, **origin** source

ORNITH(O) Gk *ornis, ornith-* bird. Eg **ornithology** the study of birds, **ornithophilous** bird-beloved, bird-loving – ie bird-pollinated

ORTH(O) Gk *orthos* straight, right. Eg **orthodontics** tooth-straightening, **orthodox** of the straight (ie conventional) opinion, **orthography** right writing – ie correct spelling, **orthopaedics** (or **orthopedics**) straight child-rearing – ie the rearing of straight children, the curing of deformities arising from bone abnormalities etc in children (and also adults)

OSCUL Eg **osculate** – see OR(I)

OSS(I) Lat *os, oss-* bone. Eg **osseous** bony, **ossify** make (into) bone – ie turn into bone, become rigid, **ossuary** (place for) bones – ie charnel-house etc

OSTE(O) Gk *osteon* bone. Eg **osteo-arthritis** bone arthritis (in which the bones of a joint are worn away), **osteopathy** bone disease-treatment – ie treatment by manipulation of the bones etc

OSTRAC Gk *ostrakon* shell, tile, the eathenware tablet or broken piece of earthenware used for voting. In ancient Greece the citizens would vote to send someone into banishment by writing the person's name on an earthenware tablet or broken piece of pottery. Thus **ostracism** is exclusion from society or from a group

OTI Lat *otium* idleness, leisure. Eg **negotiation** not leisure – ie business, bargaining, **otiose** idle – ie without anything to do, superfluous

OT(O) Gk *ous, ot-* ear. Eg **otalgia** ear pain – ie earache, **otorhinolaryngology** study (etc) of the ear, nose and larynx ('ear, nose and throat')

OV(I) Lat *ovum* egg. Eg **oval** egg(-shaped), **oviparous** bringing forth eggs – ie egg-laying, **ovum** egg

OX(Y) Gk *oxys* sharp. Eg **oxygen** sharpness-producer – ie acid-producer (from the belief that oxygen was essential for the formation of acids), **paroxysm** a sharpening beyond – ie a further sharpening (of a disease etc), a fit, an attack

P

PACHY Gk *pachys* thick. Eg **pachyderm** thick-skinned (creature) – eg an elephant or rhinoceros, **pachymeter** thickness measure – ie instrument for measuring small thicknesses

PAC(I), PAX Lat *pax, pac-* peace. Eg **pace** 'by peace (of)' – ie by leave of, with all due respect to (used when one is 'begging leave' to differ), **pacific** peace-making – or peaceful, **pacifism** (advocacy of) peace-making – ie of non-violent means of settling disputes, **pacify** make peaceful – ie calm down, **'pax!'** (cried out in children's games) 'peace!'

PAED(O) or PED(O) Lat *pais, paid-* child, boy, girl; *paideia* child-rearing, education. Eg **encyclopaedia** (or **encyclopedia**) (work of) circular education – ie work of all-round education, book of information on all subjects, **orthopaedics** (or

orthopedics) straight child-rearing – ie the rearing of straight children, the curing of deformities arising from bone abnormalities etc in children (and also adults), **paediatrician** (or **pediatrician**) child-healer – ie specialist in children's diseases, **paedophile** (or **pedophile**) child-lover – ie person who desires children sexually, **pedagogue** (or **paedagogue**) boy-leader – ie (in ancient Greece) the slave who took a boy to and from school and back; hence, a tutor or teacher, **pederast** (or **paederast**) lover of boys – ie man who has sexual relations with other males (especially boys)

PALACE, PALAT Lat *Palatium* – name of one of the seven hills on which Rome was built. The residence of the Roman emperors was built on the Palatine Hill, and thus *palatium* came to mean an imperial or royal residence and gave rise to Eng **palace**. Eng **palatine** (having royal privileges or jurisdiction) etc derive from *palatinus* (relating to the Palatine Hill or to the imperial palace – or, as a noun, an officer of the imperial palace)

PAL(A)E(O) Gk *palaios* old, ancient. Eg **palaeanthropology** (or **paleanthropology**) the study of ancient humanity – ie the study of the earliest humans, **Palaeolithic** (or **Paleolithic**) (belonging to the) Old Stone (Age), **palaeontology** (or **paleontology**) the study of ancient beings (ie fossils), **Palaeozoic** (or **Paleozoic**) – see ZO(O)

PALAT Eg **palatine** – see PALACE

PAN Lat *panis* bread. Eg **companion** (person with whom one takes) bread together – ie an associate, friend, mate, **pannier** bread(-basket), **pantry** bread(-store)

PAN, PANT(O) Gk *pas, pant-* all. Eg **panacea** all-healer – ie a cure-all, **pan-African** all-African – ie relating to all Africa, or to a policy of unity amongst African states, **pand(a)emonium** (home of) all the devils – introduced by Milton as the name of the capital of Hell in his Paradise Lost; hence 'pandemonium' means uproar or chaos, **pandemic** (of a disease) (affecting) all a people or district – ie very widespread in a community, **panoply** all arms – ie full armour, full array, **panorama** all

138

(-embracing) view, **pantechnicon** (building for) all the arts –
originally a building in London in which it was planned to sell
artefacts of all sorts; the building subsequently became a
furniture warehouse, and thus 'pantechnicon' came to mean a
furniture-van, **pantheism** all-God (belief) – ie belief that
everything is God, that God and the universe are the same
thing, **pantheon** all the gods – ie the complete set of gods (of,
eg, a particular religion); or a temple to all the gods (and now
also applied to various buildings resembling the Pantheon in
Rome), **pantograph** (instrument for) all writing – ie all
drawing, drawing to all scales, copying a drawing to any scale

PANIC Gk *Pan* – name of a Greek god (for the Roman
equivalent see FAUN(A)). Pan was half-man and half-goat. He
was the god of shepherds, but was also supposed to be the
source of sudden feelings of fright felt when out in the
countryside; hence the word **panic** for sudden terror

PANT(O) Eg **pantograph** – see PAN

PAR Lat *parere* to bring forth. Eg **fissiparous** bringing forth
(by) fission – ie reproducing by dividing, **nulliparous**
bringing forth none – ie (of a woman) not having had any
children, **oviparous** bringing forth eggs – ie egg-laying,
parent (person) bringing forth (young), **primipara** (woman)
first (time) bringing forth – ie a woman giving birth for the
first time, **viviparous** bringing forth living (young) – rather
than eggs

PAR Lat *parare, parat-* to make ready. Eg **preparation** a
making ready before, **reparation** a making ready again – ie a
making good (of damage), a making up (for something),
separation a making ready apart – ie a putting apart

PAR(A) Gk *para* beside, beyond. (In English, 'par(a)' is also
used in various derivative technical senses.) Eg **paragraph**
(sign) written beside – originally referred to a mark made at
the side of a piece of text to indicate a change of sense; the
word was then applied to the sections of text thus divided off
from each other, **paragraphia** a beside writing – ie the writing
of letters and words that are 'beside' the ones one wants to

139

write (ie they are wrong) as a result of mental disorder, **paramedic** a beside medic – ie person who is not a doctor but is 'beside' or as though one (ie helps, or carries out some of the functions of, one), **paramilitary** beside (the) military – ie as though military, or intended to supplement the military proper, **paranormal** beyond the normal – ie outside the normal, **paraphernalia** (things) beside the dowry – originally referred to items in the control of a married woman besides her dowry; hence the word came to be applied to personal belongings or trappings, or 'bits and pieces' in general, **paraphrase** a speaking beside – ie saying the same thing in different words, **parasite** (person etc who eats) food beside (another) – ie one who takes food at another's table, one who lives off another, **paratyphoid** beside typhoid – name of a disease which is not typhoid but is 'beside' (ie resembles) it, **paroxysm** a sharpening beyond – ie a further sharpening (of a disease etc), a fit, an attack

PAR(I) Lat *par* equal. Eg **comparison** (a making two things) equal together – ie a making them equal one to the other, a placing them side by side, a measuring one against the other, **disparity** inequality, **par** equal (state) – ie equal footing, normal state, normal number of strokes (in golf), (etc), **parisyllabic** equal-syllabled – ie having the same number of syllables, **parity** equality

PASS, PAT Lat *pati, pass-* to suffer, experience. Eg **compassion** a suffering with (another) – ie fellow-feeling for someone who is suffering, **compatible** capable of being suffered together or experienced together – ie capable of existing together, suited to each other, **impassive** not suffering, not experiencing – ie not being moved by feeling, not showing any reaction, **passion** a suffering (as in the 'passion' of Christ); or an experiencing – ie a being acted upon (by emotion etc), a strong impulse towards something, **passive** suffering, experiencing – ie being acted upon (as opposed to acting), **patience** a suffering (without protest), **patient** (in a hospital etc) a sufferer

PAST(OR) Lat *pastor* person in charge of a herd of animals, shepherd; *pascere, past-* to feed animals, to lead animals to where they can feed, to feed. Eg **pastor** shepherd (of souls), **pastoral** relating to shepherds (or rural life in general), or to shepherding (of souls), **pasture** (land to which animals are led for) feeding, **repast** a feeding back – ie a feeding-up, a meal

PAT Eg **compatible, patient** – see PASS

PATER(N), PATR(I) Lat *pater, patr-* father (see also PATRI, PATRICIAN); Gk *pater, patr-* father. Eg **paterfamilias** 'father of a family (or household)', **paternal** fatherly, **paternity** fatherhood, **patriarch** – see under ARCH, **patrilineal** (traced through the) father line – ie (when tracing ancestry) going back through the male line, **patrimony** father (inheritance) – ie property inherited from one's father (or ancestors), **patronymic** father name – ie name derived from that of one's father, or indicating one's ancestry

PATH(O) Gk *pathos* suffering, experience, feeling; or related Greek words. (In English, the 'suffering' or 'disease' sense has developed so that 'path' often carries the sense of 'treatment' of disease.) Eg **allopathy** disease-treatment (on the principle of) otherness – ie treatment in which drugs etc are used that have the opposite effect on the body to the disease (allopathy is the opposite of homeopathy – see below), **antipathy** feeling against (something or someone), **apathy** feelinglessness – ie failure to be stirred by something (or by things in general), **empathy** an in-feeling – ie a getting 'inside' another person (or, eg, a work of art) so that one feels with him/her, **hom(o)eopathy** disease-treatment (on the principle of) sameness – ie treatment based on the principle that like cures like, using drugs etc that would normally (in a well person) produce the same symptoms as the disease (homeopathy is the opposite of allopathy – see above), **osteopathy** bone disease-treatment – ie treatment by manipulation of the bones etc, **pathetic** relating to the feelings – or, specifically, giving rise to feelings of pity, **pathogenic** suffering-producing – ie disease-producing, **pathology** the study of suffering – ie the study of disease, **pathos** (quality that gives rise to a) feeling (of pity), **psychopath** mind-sufferer – ie (loosely) person ill in the mind, **sympathy** a suffering or feeling together with (another)

141

– ie fellow-feeling, **telepathy** far-feeling – ie far-perception, communication not through the medium of the senses but directly mind to mind (and therefore supposedly possible over a long distance)

PATRI Lat *patria* native land, fatherland (from Lat *pater* – see PATER(N)); Gk *patris* native land, fatherland (from Gk *pater* – see PATER(N)). Eg **compatriot** (person) of a native land together (with another person) – ie of the same native land, **expatriate** (person who lives) away from his/her native land, **patrial** relating to one's native land, **patriotism** (devotion to) one's native land, **repatriate** (send) (a person) back (to) his/her native land

PATR(I) Eg **patriarch, patrilineal** – see PATER(N)

PATRICIAN Lat *patricius* (plural *patricii*), from *pater* – see PATER(N). In Roman society, the *patricii* were the upper class, distinguished from the *plebs*, the common people (see PLEB(I)). A person was a patrician by virtue of being born, or adopted, into one of the old families or clans that had originally made up the citizenry of Rome. Thus **patrician** is used, loosely, in English to mean aristocratic

PAX see PAC(I)

PECCA Lat *peccare* to sin. Eg **impeccable** not sinful – ie faultless, **peccadillo** little sin

PECTOR Lat *pectus, pector-* breast, chest. Eg **expectorant** (medicine for bringing phelgm) out of the chest, **pectoral** relating to (found in, worn on etc) the breast or chest

PED(I), PED(O) Lat *pes, ped-* foot. Eg **biped** two-footed (creature), **centipede** hundred-footed (creature), **expedite** to 'feet-out' – ie disentangle one's feet, remove hindrances, speed up, **impede** to 'enfoot' (a person) – ie entangle his/her feet, hinder his/her progress, **pedal** (lever etc worked by the) foot, **pedestrian** (person going) on foot, **pedicure** foot care – ie the treatment of corns etc on the feet, **pedometer** foot-measure – ie instrument for counting paces (and thus estimating distance walked), **quadruped** four-footed (creature)

PED(O) Eg **encyclopedia, orthopedics, pediatrician, pedophile** – see PAED(O)

PEL, PULS Lat *pellere, puls-* to strike, beat, drive; *pulsus* a beating. Eg **compel** (thoroughly) drive – ie oblige (someone to do something), **compulsion** a (thorough) driving – an obliging (of someone to do something), or an irresistible urge (to do something), **dispel** drive apart – ie scatter, drive away, **expel** drive out, **impel** drive on, **impulse** a driving on – ie a sudden urge (to do something), **propel** drive forward, **pulse** a beating (eg of the arteries), **repel** drive back, **repulsive** driving back – ie disgusting

PELAG Gk *pelagos* sea, the open sea. Eg **Archipelago** chief sea – ie the Aegean Sea; hence any sea with many islands (like the Aegean), or a group of islands, **pelagic** relating to (ie living in etc) the open sea

PELVI(S) Lat *pelvis* basin. Eg **pelviform** basin-shaped, **pelvis** basin(-shaped) (part of the body)

PEN Eg **penultimate** – see PEN(E)

PENCIL, PENICILL(I), PENI(S) Lat *penis* tail, penis; *peniculus* 'little tail' – ie brush; *penicillum* 'little little tail' – ie 'little brush', paintbrush, pencil. Eg **penicillin** (drug made from a) paintbrush(-like) mould – ie mould of which the spore-cases resemble brushes. Also, **pencil, penis**

PEND, PENS Lat *pendēre, pens-* to hang (related to, but not the same as, *pendĕre* to cause to hang, weigh, pay – see next entry). Eg **appendage** (something) hanging to (something else) – ie attached to it, **appendix** (something) hanging to (something else) – ie attached to it (eg, the vermiform appendix, commonly called simply 'the appendix', is an outgrowth of the intestine), **dependant** (person) hanging down (from another) – ie relying on the other (for upkeep etc), **impending** hanging into – ie hanging over, threatening, about to happen, **pendant** hanging (thing) – eg an ornament to be hung round the neck,

pendent hanging, **pending** hanging – ie about to be dealt with, or not finished with yet, **pendulous** hanging, **pendulum** hanging (body) – ie swinging weight in a clock etc, **propensity** a hanging forward – ie a leaning towards, a tendency to, **suspend** hang under – ie hang up, or bring to a temporary halt, postpone, or debar someone temporarily (from school, work etc), **suspense** (state of being) hung under – ie hung up, in a state of tense and uncertain anticipation

PEND, PENS Lat *pendĕre, pens-* to cause to hang; hence to weigh; hence to pay (as money was originally reckoned by weight); (related to, but not the same as, *pendēre* to hang – see previous entry). Eg **compensate** weigh (two things) together – ie weigh one thing against another, use one thing to counterbalance another, **dispense** weigh apart – ie weigh out, distribute, dispose of, **expend** pay out, **expense** a paying out, **pension** (regular) payment

PEN(E) Lat *paene* almost. Eg **peneplain** an almost-plain – ie area where rocks have been so worn down that the land is almost a plain, **peninsula** an almost-island – ie a piece of land almost surrounded by water, **penultimate** almost last – ie last but one, **penumbra** almost shadow – ie partial shadow

PENICILL(I) Eg **penicillin** – see PENCIL

PENIS see PENCIL

PEN(N), PIN(N) Lat *penna* feather, wing; *pinna* feather, wing. Eg **pen** feather – because pens were originally made from quills, **pennate** winged – or wing-shaped, or feathered or feather-shaped, **pinnacle** little feather – ie spire-shaped turret or mountain etc, highest point, **pinnate** (of a leaf etc) (having the form of a) feather – ie with a row of leaflets each side of the leaf-stalk

PEN(O), POENO, PUN Lat *poena* punishment; Gk *poine* punishment. Eg **impunity** unpunishment – ie freedom from punishment, **penal** relating to punishment, **penalty** punishment, **penology** (or **poenology**) the study of punishment – eg the study of prison management, **punitive** that punishes, **sub-**

poena 'under a punishment' – ie under a penalty (formerly the first words of a writ ordering someone to appear in court)

PENS Eg **expense, propensity, suspense** – see PEND entries

PENT(A) Gk *pente* five; *pentekonta* fifty; *pentekostos* fiftieth. Eg **pentagon** five-angled (figure), **pentagram** five-lined (figure) – ie five-pointed star, **pentameter** five-measured (line) – ie line of verse with five measures or 'feet', **Pentateuch** (first) Five Books (of the Bible), **pentathlon** five(-event) contest, **Pentecost** Fiftieth (Day) – name of the Jewish feast on the fiftieth day after the second day of the Passover, and of the Christian feast on the seventh Sunday after Easter

PEPS, PEPT Gk *pepsis* digestion; *peptein* to digest. Eg **dyspepsia** (state of) badly digesting – ie indigestion, **eupepsia** (quality of) well digesting – ie good digestion, **pepsin** digestive (enzyme), **peptic** digestive, relating to digestion (or to the digestive system)

PER Lat *per* through, by; as a prefix *per* can also mean 'thoroughly', 'throughout', 'through and through' or even 'through to destruction'. Eg **perambulate** walk through (a place) – ie walk around (a place), walk around, go from place to place, **per capita** 'by heads' – ie for every head, for every person, **per cent** by the hundred – ie in every hundred, **perception** (power of) seizing thoroughly – ie power of 'grasping' things, of becoming aware of things, **percolate** strain through, **perennial** (lasting) through the year(s), **perfect** thoroughly made – ie completely made, finished, faultless, **perfidious** (taking) faith through (to destruction) – ie breaching faith, treacherous, **perforate** pierce through, **perfume** to smoke through – ie to fill with a (sweet-smelling) smoke, to scent (or the scent itself), **perjury** a swearing through (to destruction) – ie a swearing falsely, **permanent** remaining through – ie remaining to the end, lasting, meant to last, **per se** 'through itself' – ie in itself, **perspective** (the art of) thoroughly looking – ie seeing correctly, drawing things so that they look three-dimensional and the right size in relation to other things, (etc)

PERI Gk *peri* around. Eg **pericranium** (membrane) around

the cranium, **perimeter** a measure around – ie a boundary line round, boundary, **perinatal** around the birth – ie relating to a period starting shortly before a baby's birth and ending shortly after it, **periodontal** relating to (that which is) around a tooth or the teeth – ie the gums etc, **peripatetic** walking around – ie moving from place to place, **periphery** a bearing round – ie a boundary line round, boundary, **periphrasis** a speaking around – ie a roundabout way of expressing oneself, **periscope** around-viewer – ie instrument for looking around (eg above the surface of the water, when in a submarine), **peristyle** pillars round – ie a colonnade round a building or courtyard etc

PESSARY Gk *pessos* an oval-shaped stone used in a game resembling draughts. Hence a **pessary** is a medicated plug, or a surgical device inserted in the vagina

PESSIM Lat *pessimus* worst. Eg **pessimism** (one who believes that all is ordered for the) worst – or who expects the worst to happen rather than the best

PET(IT) Lat *petere, petit-* to seek, strive (for). Eg **appetite** a striving towards – ie a desire (for food etc), **competition** a striving together – ie a striving against one another, **impetuous** (thoroughly) striving against (or towards) – ie moving forcefully against or towards something, acting in a burst of energy, **impetus** a (thorough) striving against (or towards) – ie a forceful movement against or towards something, a setting in motion, a moving force, **petition** a seeking – ie a request, **repetition** a seeking again – ie an asking again, a saying again (or doing again etc)

PETR(I), PETR(O) Lat *petra* rock; Gk *petra* rock; Gk *petros* stone. Eg **petrified** made (into) rock – ie turned into stone, either literally or metaphorically (through fright), **petroglyph** rock-carving, **petrology** the science of rocks, **petroleum** rock oil – because it is found in rocks (and **petrol** is refined petroleum)

PHAG(O) Gk *phagein* to eat; or related Greek words. Eg **anthropophagous** human-eating, **dysphagia** (state of) eating badly – ie difficulty in swallowing, **entomophagous**

146

insect-eating, **monophagous** eating a single (food) – ie eating only one kind of food, **phagocyte** eating cell – ie a blood cell that 'eats up' bacteria, **polyphagous** eating many (things) – ie having a varied diet, **sarcophagus** flesh-eating (stone) – the original Greek word was applied to a type of limestone thought to consume flesh and for this reason used by the Greeks to make coffins; hence a 'sarcophagus' is a stone coffin

PHAN(T) Eg **diaphanous, phantasm, phantasy** – see FAN(T)

PHARMAC(O) Gk *pharmakon* drug, medicine. Eg **pharmaceutical** relating to drug (administration), **pharmacist** druggist, **pharmacology** the science of drugs, **pharmacopoeia** (text on) drug making – ie a catalogue of drugs with instructions for preparing them; or a stock of drugs

PHAS(IA) Gk *phanai* to speak. Eg **aphasia** speechlessness – ie loss of the ability to express oneself in words, or of the ability to understand words

PHEN Eg **phenomenon** – see FAN(T)

PHER Eg **periphery** – see PHOR

PHIL(O) Gk *phileein* to love; or related Greek word elements. Eg **anemophilous** wind-beloved, wind-loving – ie wind-pollinated, **anglophile** lover of England (and things English), **bibliophile** book-lover, **entomophilous** insect-beloved, insect-loving – ie pollinated by insects, **francophile** lover of France (and things French), **haemophiliac** (US **hemophiliac**) blood-loving – ie bleeding-loving, having a tendency to excessive bleeding, **hydrophilic** water-beloved, water-loving – ie attracting water, **ornithophilous** bird-beloved, bird-loving – ie bird-pollinated, **paedophile** (or **pedophile**) child-lover – ie person who desires children sexually, **Philadelphia** (land of) brotherly (and sisterly) love, **philanderer** (should mean:) man-lover, (in fact taken to mean:) loving man – ie flirtacious man, man given to casual love-affairs, **philanthropist** human-lover – ie lover of humankind, person who does good works, **philatelist** lover of exempt-from-charge (literally 'no charge') (stamps) – ie lover of postage stamps, stamp-collector (the original postage 'stamps' were receipts impressed on to letters indicating that the postage charge had been paid and that the letter was therefore now exempt from charge), **philharmonic** harmony-loving – ie music-loving, **philology** love of words – ie the science of language, **philoprogenitive** progeny-loving – ie loving one's children, or inclined to produce children, **philosophy** love of wisdom, **philtre** (US **philter**) love-potion

PHILIPPIC Gk *Philippikos* Philippic (discourse), from *Philippos* – Philip II, king of Macedonia (to the north of Greece) in the fourth century BC. (He was the father of Alexander the Great.) The Philippics were a series of speeches made by the Athenian orator Demosthenes attacking Philip and warning of the threat posed to Greece by his ambition to dominate it. Thus a **philippic** is an attacking speech

PHOB Gk *-phobos* -fearing, -dreading; *-phobia* -fear, -dread. (In derivative English words, the 'phob' element often implies aversion or hatred rather than fear.) Eg **agoraphobia** fear of assemblies (ie public places), **claustrophobia** fear of enclosures (ie confined places), **homophobia** hatred of homo(sexuals), **hydrophobia** fear or hatred of water – or (because an aversion to water is a symptom of rabies in humans) rabies, **hydrophobic** water-hating – ie repelling water, **phobia** fear (or aversion or hatred) (of one particular thing), **photophobic** light-hating – ie shrinking from the light, **xenophobe** (person who) fears or hates foreigners

PHON(O) Gk *phone* voice, sound. Eg **cacophony** bad (ie ugly) sound, **euphonious** well-sounding – ie making a pleasing sound, **francophone** French-voiced – ie French-speaking, **megaphone** (instrument for making a) big sound – ie instrument for amplifying sound, **microphone** small-sound (instrument) – ie instrument for amplifying small sounds, **phon** sound – name of a unit of loudness level, **phonetic** relating to the sounds (of language), **phonolite** sound-stone – ie clinkstone (which rings when struck), **quadraphonic** four-voiced – ie (of a stereophonic system) issuing sound through four speakers fed by different sound channels, **stereophonic** (producing) solid sound – ie using two or more different sound

148

channels to give an effect of 'all-round' sound, **symphony** a sounding together – ie (loosely) a large musical work for a full orchestra, **telephone** far-voice (instrument) – ie instrument for transmitting sound over a long distance, **xylophone** wooden voice – name of a musical instrument consisting of a series of wooden bars

PHOR, PHER Gk *-phoros* -bearing, -bearer; *pherein* to bear. Eg **electrophoresis** a bearing electrically – ie the migration of suspended particles under the influence of an electric field, **metaphor** a bearing across (from one place to another) – ie the use of a word (or phrase) to describe or refer to something to which it does not literally apply, **periphery** a bearing around – ie a boundary line round, boundary, **phosphorus** light-bearing (substance) – because it shines in the dark, **semaphore** signal-bearing (apparatus) – ie apparatus for sending signals

PHOT(O), PHOS Gk *phos, phot-* light. Eg **phosphorus** light-bearing (substance) – because it shines in the dark, **photograph** light writing – ie production of an image by the action of light on a special surface, **photophilic** light-loving – ie turning towards the light, **photophobic** light-hating – ie shrinking from the light, **photosensitivity** sensitivity to light, **photosynthesis** light synthesis – ie process by which plants build up complex compounds using the energy provided by light

PHRAS Gk *phrasis* a speaking, speech; *phrazein* to indicate, tell. Eg **paraphrase** a speaking beside – ie saying the same thing in different words, **periphrasis** a speaking around – ie a roundabout way of expressing oneself, **phrase** a speaking

PHREN(O), FREN, FRANTIC Gk *phren* heart, mind; *phrenesis* or *phrenitis* disorder of the mind, derangement. Eg **frantic** deranged, **frenetic** (or **phrenetic**) deranged, **frenzy** derangement, **phrenology** science of the mind – ie supposed science according to which mental characteristics can be deduced by feeling the bumps on the outside of the head, **schizophrenia** (disease seen as involving a) split mind

PHYLACT, PHYLAX Gk *phylakter* or *phylax* guard; *phylassein* to keep guard; *phylakterion* garrison post, safeguard, amulet. Eg **phylactery** safeguard – ie a small box containing pieces of scripture worn by Jews, **prophylactic** keeping guard before – ie guarding over, guarding against (disease); or (as a noun), a guarding against conception – ie a condom

PHYLL(O) Gk *phyllon* leaf. Eg **chlorophyll** green (colouring matter of) leaves, **erythrophyll** red (colouring matter of) leaves, **phylloid** leaf-shaped – ie leaf-like, **phyllotaxis** leaf arrangement – ie the arrangement of leaves on the stem

PHYSI(O) Gk *physis* nature. Eg **physical** relating to nature – ie to matter (eg the human body), **physics** natural (science) – originally; later came to be applied only to a specific part of natural science, **physiognomy** interpreting from nature (ie from bodily characteristics) – ie the art of judging people's characters from their physical characteristics (especially those of the face); or the face itself, **physiolatry** nature-worship, **physiology** the science of nature – ie of living things, **physiotherapy** nature treatment – ie treatment using methods such as exercise, massage and heat rather than drugs

PHYT(O) Gk *phyton* plant. Eg **hydrophyte** water plant – ie plant growing in water (or in very damp conditions), **neophyte** newly planted (person) – ie new convert, novice, **phytogenesis** plant birth – ie the evolution of plants, **phytotoxin** plant toxin – ie toxin produced by a plant

PI Gk *pi* – sixteenth letter of the Greek alphabet (equivalent to the English 'p'), written π and adopted as a symbol for the ratio of a circle's circumference to its diameter (3.14159)

PIEZO Gk *piezein* to press. (In English, the prefix 'piezo' is used to mean 'pressure'.) Eg **piezochemistry** pressure chemistry – ie the chemistry of substances under high pressure, **piezo-meter** pressure meter – ie instrument for measuring pressure

PIL(I) Lat *pilus* a hair; *pilare* to deprive of hair. Eg **depilatory** (thoroughly) depriving of hair – ie hair-removing, **pile** hair (of a carpet etc), **piliform** hair-shaped – ie hair-like, **pilosity** hairiness

PIN(N) Eg **pinnacle, pinnate** – see PEN(N)

PISC(I) Lat *piscis* fish. Eg **piscator** a fisher – ie an angler, **Pisces** the Fishes – sign of the zodiac, **pisciculture** fish-farming, **piscina** fish(pond) – ie (in churches) a basin at the side of the altar, formerly used for pouring away water in which vessels had been washed, **piscine** relating to fish, fishy, **piscivorous** fish-eating

PLAC Lat *placere* to please; *placare, placat-* to appease, calm; *placidus* pleasing, peaceable, calm. Eg **complacent** (thoroughly) pleasing – came to mean thoroughly 'pleased' (with oneself), self-satisfied, **implacable** unappeasable, **placate** to appease, calm, **placebo** 'I shall please' – ie a medicine given to please the patient rather than because of any direct physical good it will do him/her, or a neutral substance given (eg in research experiments) so that the recipient thinks he/she has, or may have, been given a drug (etc)

PLAGIAR Lat *plagiarius* abductor, kidnapper. Eg **plagiarist** kidnapper (of someone else's work) – ie person who steals from somebody else's writings (etc), passing off the other's work as his/her own

PLASM, PLAST Gk *plassein* to mould, form, shape; *plastikos* relating to moulding, forming or shaping; *plasma* thing moulded, formed, shaped. Eg **plasma** moulded thing – ie the coagulable liquid part of blood etc, **plaster** (substance) moulded on – ie daubed on, **plastic** relating to moulding or shaping (eg the 'plastic' arts are sculpture, modelling etc, and 'plastic' surgery involves remodelling parts of the body) – or mouldable ('plastics' are 'mouldable' substances), **plasticity** (quality of) moulding – ie mouldability, or a 'three-dimensional' quality in a picture, **protoplasm** first moulded-thing – ie basic moulded-thing, the semifluid substance constituting the basis of life in animals and plants

PLATONIC Gk *Platon* Plato – name of an Athenian philosopher (c429-c347BC) (see also ACADEM). Plato's *Dialogues* are our main source of information on the thought and philosophical method of Socrates (469-399BC), who left no written works himself. The term **platonic** love (for a union of spirits, with no sexual element) arose as an alternative way of describing 'Socratic love' (*amor socraticus*) – the type of love Socrates was supposed to have felt for the young men who joined him in discussion

PLATY Gk *platys* flat, broad. Eg **platypus** flat-footed (creature), **platyrrhine** broad-nosed (eg of a division of monkeys)

PLAUD, PLAUS, PLOD, PLOS Lat *plaudere* (or *plodere*), *plaus-* (or *plos-*) to clap the hands. Eg **applaud** clap to (something) – ie express approval for something, **explode** clap out – ie drive out by clapping, hiss off the stage, drive out (air etc) forcefully, burst into pieces, burst out, **implosion** a clapping in – ie a bursting inwards, **plaudit** – shortening of *plaudite!* (clap your hands!) which was used as an appeal for applause at the end of a performance; thus a 'plaudit' is an expression of approval, **plausible** clappable – ie worthy of approval, acceptable, fairly convincing

PLEB(I) Lat *plebs*, *pleb-* the plebs or common people (see PATRICIAN, also TRIB(UN)). Eg **plebeian** relating to the common people – ie lower-class, **plebiscite** decree of the common people – ie (in ancient Rome) a law enacted by the vote of the *plebs* as a distinct political entity, (now) a referendum

PLECT, PLEG, PLEXY Gk *-plegia* a -striking, a blow; *plessein* to strike. Eg **apoplexy** a (thorough) striking – ie sudden loss of the powers of sensation and motion, **hemiplegia** a half-striking – ie paralysis of one side of the body only, **monoplegia** a single striking – ie paralysis of one part only, **paraplegia** a striking beside – ie a striking on one side, partial paralysis, paralysis of the lower half of the body, **plectrum** (implement for) striking (ie plucking) – originally for plucking the strings of a lyre, now usually for the strings of a guitar, **quadriplegia** (or **tetraplegia**) a four(fold) striking – ie paralysis of all four limbs

PLEIO Eg **pleiomerous** – see PLEO

PLEISTO Gk *pleistos* most. Eg **Pleistocene** – see CENE

152

PLEN(I), PLET Lat *plenus* full; *-plere, -plet-* to fill. Eg **completed** (thoroughly) filled – ie filled-up, finished, **depleted** de-filled – ie emptied, (of a stock of something) run-down, **expletive** (word or phrase) (thoroughly) filling (speech) – ie word or phrase filling up speech, filling it out, serving only to fill it out: an oath or swear-word, **plenary** full, **plenilunar** relating to the full moon, **plenipotentiary** fully powerful – ie (of, eg, an ambassador) vested with full powers, **plenitude** fullness, **replenish** fill again – ie restock, **replete** filled again – ie filled-up, full

PLEO, PLEIO, PLIO Gk *pleion* or *pleon* more. Eg **pleiomerous** (having) more parts – ie having more than the usual number of parts, **pleonasm** a more-ness (of words) – ie a superfluity of words, a using of more words than are necessary to express something, **Pliocene** (or **Pleiocene**) – see CENE

PLET Eg **expletive, replete** – see PLEN(I)

PLEX, PLIC Lat *plectere, plex-* to interweave, plait; *-plex, -plicis* -fold; both related to *plicare* – see PLI(C). Eg **duplex** twofold – ie (of an apartment) on two floors, (of a house) divided into two (for two households), **duplicity** twofoldedness – ie double-dealing, deceitfulness, **multiplicity** a manyfoldedness – ie a numerousness, a great number, **perplexed** (thoroughly) interwoven – ie intricate, made confused, **triplicate** threefold, **plexus** an interweaving – ie a network

PLEXY Eg **apoplexy** – see PLECT

PLI(C) Lat *plicare, plicat-* to fold (see also PLEX). Eg **application** a folding to – ie the placing of something on to something else (eg the 'application' of ointment to a wound, or the giving of one's attention to something (one can work with 'application'), or the making of an address to someone (as in a job 'application'), **complicated** folded together – ie twisted together, entangled, intricate, **explicable** fold-out-able – ie unfoldable, explainable, **explicit** folded out – ie unfolded, clearly stated, **implicate** to fold in – ie intertwine, involve (in guilt etc), **implicit** folded in – ie intertwined, present as an inference but not actually stated, **replica** a folding again – ie a

153

repetition, a reproduction, **pliable** foldable – ie bendable, flexible

PLIO Eg **Pliocene** – see PLEO

PLOD, PLOS Eg **explode, implosion** – see PLAUD

PLUMB(I) Lat *plumbum* lead. Eg **plumber** lead(-worker) – ie person who attends to water-pipes etc, **plumbiferous** lead-bearing, **plumbism** lead (poisoning), **plumb-line** lead-line – ie line to which lead weight (or similar) is attached

PLUM(I), PLUMUL Lat *pluma* feather (the small soft type); *plumula* little feather, down-feather. Eg **plume** feather – or a bunch of feathers, **plumiped** (having) feathered feet, **plumose** feathered, feathery, **plumule** little feather, down-feather – or the rudimentary shoot in a seed

PLUR(I), PLU(S) Lat *plus, plur-* more. Eg **nonplussed** (in a state in which) no more (can be said or done) – ie brought to a standstill, thoroughly confused, **pluperfect** more (than) perfect – ie (in grammar) going back further than the perfect tense, **plural** more (than one), **pluriserial** (in) more (than one) series or row – ie in several series or rows, **plus** more – ie with the addition of, **surplus** over-more – ie more in addition, more than is required

PLUTO Lat *Pluto*, Gk *Plouton* Pluto – name of the god of the underworld. The planet **Pluto** was named after him, and the element **plutonium** was named after the planet. This classical god, with his hellish realm, is also responsible for the geological term **plutonic** (relating to, formed by, etc, underground heat)

PLUTO Gk *ploutos* wealth. Eg **plutocracy** rule by the wealthy, **plutolatry** worship of wealth

PLUVI(O) Lat *pluvia* rain. Eg **pluviometer** rain-measure – ie rain-gauge, **pluviose** rainy

PNEUM(O), PNEUMAT(O), PNEUMON(O) Gk *pneumon* lung; *pneuma, pneumat-* wind, air, breath, spirit. Eg **pneumatic** relating to (or driven by, containing, etc) air or wind (or gas), **pneumatometer** breath-measure – ie instrument for measuring breathing, **pneumoconiosis** dust-(in-the-)lung disease – ie disease amongst miners etc caused by inhaling dust, **pneumonia** (inflammation of the) lung(s)

POD(O), PUS Gk *pous, pod-* foot. Eg **antipodean** (having) feet opposite – ie (of a person) living on the other side of the globe, **chiropodist** (one who treats) the hands and feet – now just the feet, **octopus** eight-footed (creature) – ie creature with eight tentacles, **platypus** flat-footed (creature), **podophthalmous** foot(stalk)-eyed – ie (of crabs etc) having eyes on footstalks (stalks which fit into a 'foot' or base), **tetrapod** four-footed (creature), **tripod** three-footed (ie three-legged) (structure)

POE(IA), PO(I)ESIS Gk *poieein* to make. Eg **erythropoiesis** red (blood-cell) making – ie the formation of red blood-cells, **galactopoietic** milk-making – ie milk-producing, **onomatopoeia** name-making – ie word-making, the formation of words from the sounds made by the things meant, **pharmacopoeia** (text on) drug-making – ie a catalogue of drugs with instructions for preparing them; or a stock of drugs, **poet** maker (of verses), **prosopopoeia** a face-making – ie a person-making, personification

POENO Eg **poenology** – see PEN(O)

POL Gk *poleein* to sell. Eg **monopoly** selling alone – ie a situation in which there is only one seller of a particular product, so that this seller has all the market, **oligopoly** (situation of) few selling – ie situation in which there are only a few traders selling a particular product

POLEM(IC) Gk *polemos* war. Eg **polemical** relating to war, or war(-like) – ie controversial, disputatious

POLIC, POLIS, POLIT Gk *polis* city; *polites* citizen. Eg **acropolis** highest city – ie upper city, citadel, **cosmopolitan** citizen of the world, **metropolis** mother-city – ie (in ancient Greece)

155

the parent city or state from which colonies were sent out; (now also) capital city, chief cathedral city, **Neapolitan** relating to (ie belonging to etc) New City – ie to Naples, **necropolis** city of the dead – ie cemetery, **police** (force for maintaining) citizenship – ie force for maintaining the civil structure, force for maintaining public order, **policy** (proposal etc relating to) citizenship – ie relating to government (etc), **politics** (business) relating to citizens – ie the business of government

POLY Gk *poly-* much, many (see also HOI POLLOI). Eg **polyanthus** many-flowered (plant), **polygamy** many-marriage – ie marriage with more than one person at once, **polyglot** many-tongued (person) – ie one who speaks many languages, **polygon** many-angled (figure), **polymath** (person) having learnt much – ie person versed in several fields of learning, **polymer** (compound consisting of) many parts – ie compound of which the molecules are in effect a molecule of a simpler substance many times over, **polymorph** (substance that can take) many forms; or one of the forms themselves, **Polynesia** Many Islands, **polysyllabic** (having) many syllables, **polytechnic** (in the UK) (college of further education in) many skills – ie many subjects, **polytheism** (belief in) many gods

POM(I) Lat *pomum* fruit (later came to be applied particularly to the apple). Eg **pomade** apple (ointment) – ie hair ointment, apparently formerly made with apple, **pomegranate** seeded apple – ie apple-like fruit with many seeds, **pomiculture** fruit-growing, **pomiferous** apple-bearing, fruit-bearing, **pommel** little apple – ie knob (on a saddle etc)

PON Eg **exponent, postpone** – see POS

PONDER Lat *pondus, ponder-* weight. Eg **imponderable** (something) unweighable – ie something the weight (or importance etc) of which cannot be gauged, **ponder** to weigh (in the mind), **ponderous** weighty – or heavy, cumbersome, **preponderate** weigh in front – ie outweigh, outnumber

POR(C) Lat *porcus* pig. Eg **porcine** relating to pigs (or pig-like), **porcupine** spiny pig, **pork** pig (meat), **porpoise** pig fish

PORNO Gk *porne* prostitute. Eg **pornocracy** rule by prostitutes – ie a situation in which courtesans have an important influence on government (especially applied to the papal court in the first half of the tenth century), **pornography** writing relating to prostitutes – ie obscene writing (or pictures etc)

PORT Lat *portare, portat-* to carry. Eg **deport** carry away, **export** carry out (of a country), **import** carry in(to a country), **important** carrying (significance) (with)in – ie significant, **portable** carry-able, **porter** carrier (note that this 'porter' is etymologically distinct from the 'porter' listed in the next entry), **portly** (of impressive) carriage – ie of stout build (carried with dignity), **report** carry (news etc) back, **support** carry (from) under – ie bear (a load), hold up, endure, **transport** carry across – ie carry from one place to another

PORT Lat *porta* gate. Eg **portal** gate(way), **portcullis** sliding gate, **porter** gate(-keeper) (note that this 'porter' is etymologically distinct from the 'porter' listed in the preceding entry), **porthole** gate(way) hole – ie an opening in the side of a ship (note that the 'port' in 'porthole' does not derive from the word 'port' meaning harbour)

PORT Lat *portus* harbour (related to *porta* gate – see preceding entry). Eg **importunate** (originally, of a wind) not (blowing towards) harbour – ie not favourable (when one wants to go into harbour), untimely, inconvenient, inconveniently pressing, **opportune** (originally, of a wind) (blowing) towards harbour – ie favourable (when one wants to go into harbour), timely, convenient, **port** harbour

POS, PON Lat *ponere, posit-* to place, put. Eg **composite** placed together – ie amalgamated, joint, **deposit** place down – ie put down, put away, **exponent** (person) placing forth – ie person who sets something out, explains it, **imposition** a placing on (someone) (of a burden etc), **juxtaposition** a placing close (together), **opponent** (person) placing against – ie someone who fights against something, **opposition** a placing against – ie a fighting against, **posit** to place – ie lay down as an assumption, **position** a placing, placement, **postpone** place after – ie put off till later, **posture** a placing (of parts of the

157

body etc), **preposition** a placing before – ie a word placed before a noun, pronoun etc to indicate its relation to another word in the sentence, **proposition** a putting forward – ie a suggestion, contention etc put forward

POSS, POTEN Lat *posse* to be able; *potens, potent-* being able – ie having the power (to do something), powerful. Eg **impotent** powerless, **omnipotent** all-powerful, **plenipotentiary** fully powerful – ie (of, eg, an ambassador) vested with full powers, **posse** (short for *posse comitatus* power of the county) – ie a body of men called to arms by a sheriff (etc), **possible** able to be, **potent** powerful, **potentate** powerful (person) – ie ruler, **potential** able to be – ie not existing yet but having the capacity to exist

POST, POSTER Lat *post* after; *posterus* coming after, following; *posterior* coming 'more after' – ie coming still after, following after; *postumus* coming 'most after' – ie last, last-born. Eg **a posteriori** 'from (that which) comes after' – ie (of reasoning) from effect to cause, **postdate** date after – ie give a date that is after the actual date, **posterior** (part of the body) following after – ie hinder part, buttocks, **posterity** (those who) come after – ie later generations, **posthumus** – see second HUM, **pm** (abbreviation of **post meridiem**) after midday, **postmortem** (examination of a body) 'after death', **postnatal** after birth, **postpone** place after – ie put off till later, **post-prandial** after-dinner, **postscript** (thing) written after – ie added to the main text after it has been finished, **post-war** after the war, **preposterous** before-behind – ie back to front, absurd

POTAM(O) Gk *potamos* river. Eg **hippopotamus** river-horse, **Mesopotamia** (land) in the middle of the rivers – name of the region between the rivers Tigris and Euphrates, **potamology** the study of rivers

POTEN Eg **potent, potential** – see POSS

PRANDIAL Lat *prandium* morning or midday meal (used to mean dinner in the English derivatives). Eg **ante-prandial** before-dinner, **post-prandial** after-dinner, **pre-prandial** before-dinner

PRE Lat *prae* before, in front. Eg **precede** go before, **preclude** close (a door etc) in front (of something) – ie debar, block, rule out, **precursor** forerunner, **predict** say before – ie foretell, **predilection** a choosing apart before – ie a choosing out in preference to others, a preference, **pre-eminent** eminent before (all others) – ie eminent beyond others, **prehistoric** before history – ie going back further than historical record, **prelude** a playing before – ie an introductory performance or piece, **premonition** a forewarning, **preponderate** weigh in front – ie outweigh, outnumber, **preposterous** before-behind – ie back to front, absurd, **prescience** foreknowledge, **pre-war** before the war

PREC Lat *precari* to beg, pray, entreat; *precarius* begged for, obtained by entreaty. Eg **deprecate** pray away – ie pray against something, try to ward it off by entreaty, protest against it, **imprecation** a praying onto (someone) – ie a calling down by prayer of something upon someone (especially a calling down of something evil), **precarious** obtained by entreaty – ie dependent on the good will of another, uncertain, risky, **precatory** entreating

PRECI Lat *pretium* price. Eg **appreciate** (give) a price to – ie give a value to, be aware of the value of, or to go up in value, **depreciate** down-price – ie belittle the value of, or to go down in value, **precious** (of great) price – ie of great worth, very valuable

PRESBY(TER) Gk *presbys* old, old man; *presbyteros* older, an elder. Eg **presbyopia** old-person eyes – ie the long-sightedness common in old age, **presbyterian** (of a church) (governed by) elders

PRESS, PRIM Lat *premere*, *press-* to press. Eg **compress** press together, **depressed** pressed down – ie lowered, dispirited, **express** press out – or give voice to, **impress** press in, press on – ie stamp, imprint a mark on, make a mark on (eg when something 'impresses' one), **imprimatur** 'let it be pressed in' – ie 'let it be printed' (the formula used to license publication of a book); hence, a stamp of approval, **oppress** press down, **repress** press back – ie keep down, keep from coming out,

reprimand (a fault) to be pressed back – ie a fault to be checked, a checking of a fault, a rebuke, **suppress** press under – ie press down, keep from coming out

PRETER Lat *praeter* more than, beyond. Eg **preterhuman** more than human, **preternatural** beyond nature – ie not conforming to the laws of nature, abnormal

PRIAP Lat *Priapus*, Gk *Priapos* – name of the god of procreation, who was often treated as a comic figure and portrayed with a large detachable phallus. Thus **priapism** is a condition in which the penis is persistently erect, or licentiousness

PRIM Eg **imprimatur, reprimand** – see PRESS

PRIM(I), PRIM(O) Lat *primus* first. Eg **prim(a)eval** relating to (or belonging to etc) the first ages, **prima facie** 'at first face' – ie at first appearance, at first sight, **primate** (person etc of the) first (rank) – ie the chief bishop of a province, or a member of the highest order of mammals, **prime** first – ie first-rank, best-quality (and when one is in one's 'prime' one is in one's best period), **primigravida** (woman) first (time) heavy (with child) – ie a woman pregnant for the first time, **primipara** (woman) first (time) bringing forth – ie a woman giving birth for the first time, **primogeniture** (state of being) first-born (in a family) – or the practice of inheritance by the first-born child, **primordial** relating to (belonging to etc) the first beginning, **primula** – from *primula veris* little first (thing) of spring, apparently originally applied to the cowslip; 'Primula' was later used as the name of the whole genus

PRIOR Lat *prior* first (of two), former. Eg **a priori** 'from the former' – ie (of reasoning) from cause to effect, **prior** former – ie earlier, or ('prior to') before, **prior/prioress** (person who comes) first – ie the head (or second-in-command) of a religious house, **priority** (thing that comes) first – ie thing first in order of importance, something of top importance

PRO Gk *pro* before, in front, forward, forth, for, instead of. Eg **problem** (thing) thrown forward (to be dealt with) – ie a task, a difficulty, **procephalic** relating to the before-head – ie to the fore part of the head, **proembryo** a before-embryo – ie the group of cells from which the embryo develops, **prognosis** a knowing before – ie a forecast (of the course of a disease etc), **program(me)** a writing forth – ie a public notice, a schedule of events, a sequence of instructions for a computer, (etc), **prologue** before-speech – ie a speech made before a play, **proscenium** (space) before the *skene* (the background part of the stage) – ie (in the ancient theatre) the front part of the stage, on which the action took place; (in the modern theatre) the very front of the stage, between the curtain and the orchestra pit

PRO Lat *pro* before, in front, forward, forth, for, instead of, according to. Eg **procathedral** (church used) instead of a cathedral – ie church used temporarily as a cathedral, **proclamation** a calling forth – ie a calling out, an announcement, **produce** lead (ie bring) forth, **profession** a declaring forth – ie a public declaration (of faith etc), a calling, **pro forma** 'for form' – ie as a matter of form, **pro-French** 'for' the French – ie in favour of the French, **profusion** a pouring forth – ie an abundance, **progress** a stepping forward, **prohibit** hold in front – ie hold back, prevent, forbid, **pro rata** 'according to a rate' – ie proportional(ly), **pros and cons (contras)** (reasons) for and against, **proscribe** write forth – ie (in ancient Rome) write up publicly, publish the name of (someone who has been condemned or is to be outlawed); hence, to outlaw or denounce, **prospect** a looking forth, a looking forward – ie that which presents itself to the view, or what the future seems to hold, **pro tem** (short for **pro tempore**) 'for the time (being)', **provoke** call forth – ie cause to come forth, incite

PROB Lat *probare, probat-* to try, test. Eg **probable** testable – ie provable, believable, not impossible, likely, **probate** the testing (or 'proving') (of a will), **probation** a testing, **probe** to test – ie examine, investigate, **reprobate** tested back – ie tested and found wanting, disapproved of, given over to sin, unprincipled

PROLETARI, PROLI Lat *proles* offspring; *proletarius* person 'having offspring' – ie a citizen of the lowest class, equipped to serve the state only with offspring, rather than with property. Eg **proletarian** of the lowest (or poorest) class – or, more specifically, the wage-earning class, especially those without capital, **prolicide** the killing of offspring – or the destruction of the human race, **proliferate** bear (many) offspring – ie reproduce, multiply, **prolific** making (ie producing) many offspring – or having a large output

PROP(E)R Lat *proprius* one's own; *proprietas* that which is 'one's own' – ie something belonging to one, or peculiar to one. Eg **appropriate** belonging to, peculiar to – ie suitable (for), fit (for); or (as a verb) to make something one's own, take possession of something, or assign it to a particular purpose, **expropriate** (take) that which is owned away from (someone) – ie dispossess (someone), or take possession of (that which belongs to someone else), **proper** belonging – ie suitable, fit, genuine (or suitable, fit, respectable), **property** that which is one's own, **proprietor** owner, **propriety** that which belongs or is peculiar to (a situation etc) – ie that which is suitable for it, suitable behaviour, respectable behaviour

PROT(O) Gk *protos* first; *proteios* being the first, first-rank. Eg **protagonist** first (ie chief) actor – ie the chief person in a drama, conflict etc; or (loosely) a champion or advocate of a cause, **protein** first-rank (substance) – ie basic substance (in animals and plants), **protium** the first (hydrogen) – ie ordinary hydrogen, as distinguished from deuterium (see DEUT(ER)(O)) and tritium (see TRI), **protocol** first (leaf) glued – ie (originally) a leaf glued to the front of a manuscript listing the contents; hence, the original note of a transaction, or draft of a treaty, a diplomatic (or other) official formula, or a body of diplomatic (or other) etiquette, **proto-historic** relating to (belonging to etc) first history – ie the very beginning of history, after the 'prehistoric' period but before written records began, **protolanguage** first language – ie a hypo-thetical language deemed the ancestor of particular known languages, and whose existence and characteristics are inferred from these known languages, **proton** first (thing) – name of an elementary particle, **protoplasm** first moulded-thing – ie basic moulded-thing, the semifluid substance constituting the basis of life in animals and plants, **prototype** first type – ie the original model of something from which copies are made or other versions developed, **Protozoa** first animals – ie the most primitive animals (consisting of only one cell)

PROXIM Lat *proximus* nearest, very near. Eg **approximately** (coming) near to – ie about, 'roughly', **proximate** nearest – or next

PRURI Lat *prurire, prurit-* to itch. Eg **prurient** itching – ie dwelling on lewd thoughts, indulging in sexual curiosity, **prurigo** (skin disease causing) itching, **pruritus** an itching

PSALM Gk *psalmos* a plucking (of a musical instrument, with the fingers), from *psallein* to pluck, twang. Eg **psalm** a plucking – ie a song to be sung to the accompaniment of a stringed instrument (such as the harp)

PSEPH(O) Gk *psephos* pebble. Eg **psephite** pebble (rock) – ie a rock composed of pebbles, **psephology** the study of pebbles – ie the study of votes, the study of elections (from the fact that in one form of ballot used in ancient Greece a vote was cast by placing a pebble in an urn)

PSEUD(O) Gk *pseudes* false; *pseudos* falsehood. Eg **pseud** false (person) – ie pretentious person, **pseudaesthesia** false feeling – ie feeling something that is not there (eg when someone can 'feel' a leg that has in fact been amputated), **pseudo-Gothic** false Gothic – ie sham Gothic, **pseudology** the study of falsehood – ie the art of lying, **pseudonym** false name

PSYCH(O) Gk *psyche* spirit, soul, mind. Eg **metempsychosis** (putting of) soul in beyond – ie the passing of the soul (on death) into another body, **psyche** soul, spirit, mind, **psych-edelic** (making the) mind (see) clear – ie (of drugs etc) heightening perception and mental powers (or apparently doing so), **psychiatry** mind-healing – ie treatment of mental disease, **psychology** the science of the mind, **psychopath** mind-sufferer – ie (loosely) person ill in the mind, **psycho-somatic** mind-body – ie (of a disease) physical but with its origins in the mind

163

PTER(O) Gk *pteron* feather, wing. Eg **Coleoptera** sheath-winged (creatures) – name of the order of insects that have wings with sheaths (ie beetles), **helicopter** screw-winged (machine) – ie flying-machine with flying blades arranged in a screw shape, **Lepidoptera** scale-winged (creatures) – name of the order of insects with four scale-covered wings (ie butterflies and moths), **pterodactyl** wing-fingered (creature) – because of its 'winged' forelimbs, **pterygoid** wing-shaped – ie wing-like

PUD Lat *pudere* to be ashamed; *pudens, pudent-* ashamed, modest. Eg **impudent** immodest – ie brazen, 'cheeky', **pudenda** (things) to be ashamed of (or to be modest about) – ie the genitals

PUER Lat *puer* child, boy. Eg **puerile** relating to children, childish, **puerperal** relating to bringing forth a child – ie relating to childbirth, **puerperium** the bringing forth of a child – ie childbirth, labour

PUGN Lat *pugnare* to fight. Eg **impugn** fight against – ie attack (with words), call into question, **oppugn** fight against – ie attack (with words), call into question, **pugnacious** (given to) fighting, **repugnant** fighting back – ie contrary, incompatible, objectionable

PULMO Lat *pulmo, pulmon-* lung. Eg **pulmonary** relating to the lungs

PULS Eg **pulse**, repulsive – see PEL

PULVER Lat *pulvis, pulver-* dust. Eg **pulverise** (turn into) dust (or powder), **pulverous** dusty (or powdery)

PUN Eg **punitive, impunity** – see PEN(O)

PUNCT, PUNG Lat *punctum* point; *pungere, punct-* to prick, pierce. Eg **compunction** a (thorough) pricking (of the conscience) – ie remorse, **expunge** prick out – ie mark out for deletion using dots, delete, wipe out, **punctilious** (attentive to) little points – ie attentive to the fine points, precise, scrupulous, **punctual** relating to a point (or dot) – ie 'on the dot', on time, **punctuation** pointing – ie insertion of points (full-stops, commas etc), **puncture** a piercing, **pungent** pricking – ie sharp, stinging, tart

PUPA, PUPIL Lat *pupus* boy; *pupa* girl, doll; *pupillus* 'little boy' – ie orphan, ward; *pupilla* 'little girl' – ie orphan, ward. Eg **pupa** girl, doll – ie chrysalis, **pupil** (of the eye) 'little child' – apparently because of the tiny images of people (or things) that can be seen reflected there, **pupil** orphan, ward – ie a child in the care of a guardian, a child under instruction from a tutor or teacher, anyone who is being taught

PURG Lat *purgare* to cleanse. Eg **expurgate** cleanse out – ie remove the offending parts from (a book etc), **purgative** cleansing, **purgatory** (place or state in which one is) cleansed (of minor sins) (after death) – or (loosely) a period or state of suffering or discomfort, **purge** a cleansing, or (as a verb) to cleanse

PUS Eg **octopus, platypus** – see POD(O)

PUT Lat *putare, putat-* to reckon, think. Eg **compute** reckon together – ie calculate, **dispute** a reckoning apart – ie an assessing, a debate, an argument, **impute** reckon (someone) in – ie charge (someone) with (a wrongdoing etc), attribute (a wrongdoing etc) (to someone), **putative** (according to) thought – ie according to supposition, supposed, **reputation** a reckoning back – ie a thinking over, an opinion, the opinion generally held of someone or something

PUTR(E) Lat *puter, putr-* rotten. Eg **putrefacient** making rotten – ie causing rotting, **putrefaction** a making rotten – ie rotting, rottenness, **putrid** rotten

PYRET, PYREX, PYR(O) Gk *pyr* fire; *pyretos* burning heat, fever; *pyressein* to be feverish. Eg **pyre** fire (pile) – ie pile of material set alight to burn a corpse, **pyretic** relating to fever, **pyrexia** fever, **pyrolatry** fire-worship, **pyrolysis** loosening (by) fire – ie chemical decomposition brought about by heat, **pyromania** fire madness – ie an obsessive desire to set fire to

165

things, **pyrotechnics** fire artistry – ie the art of making fireworks, or the display of fireworks

PYTHON Gk *Python* – name, in Greek mythology, of the huge snake killed by the god Apollo near Delphi. Hence a **python** is a type of large snake

Q

QUA Lat *qua* in so far as, in as much as. The word **qua** is used in English to mean 'in the capacity of' (eg 'Qua teacher he had seen it one way; qua parent he soon saw it another')

QUADR(I), QUATERN Lat *quad-*, from *quat(t)uor* four; *quadrans*, *quadrant-* a fourth part, quarter; *quadraginta* forty; *quaterni* four together, four by four. Eg **quadragenarian** (person) of forty (years) – ie person in his or her forties, **quadrangle** four-cornered (figure, court etc), **quadrant** a fourth part (of the circumference of a circle) – or an angle-measuring instrument using this arc, **quadraphonic** four-voiced – ie (of a stereo system) issuing sound through four speakers fed by different sound channels, **quadrennial** (happening every) four years – or lasting four years, **quadriplegia** a four(fold) striking – ie paralysis of all four limbs, **quadruped** four-footed (creature), **quadruple** fourfold, **quaternary** four by four – or fourfold, or based on four, or of a fourth order

QUAL(I) Lat *qualis* of what kind. Eg **qualify** make a what-kind – ie specify what kind, specify more exactly; or to be of the right kind for something, fulfil the requirements of something, **qualitative** relating to what-kind – ie relating to the nature, character, degree of excellence (etc) of something

QUANT(I) Lat *quantus* how big, how much. Eg **quantify** make a how-muchness – ie assess as an amount, express as an amount, **quantitative** relating to how-much – ie relating to amount, **quantometer** how-much measure – ie instrument for measuring the relative amounts of the different constituent elements in a metallic sample, **quantum** a how-muchness – ie an amount (with a technical meaning in physics)

QUART Lat *quartus* fourth. Eg **quart** a fourth (part) (of a gallon), **quarter** a fourth (part), **quarto** (in) a fourth – ie printed on sheets each of which is then folded to make four leaves (eight pages); or a page size arrived at by folding a sheet into four, (etc)

QUAS(I) Lat *quasi* as if. Eg **quasar** (contraction of 'quasi stellar') – a quasar or 'quasi stellar object' is a heavenly body that is 'as though a star' (ie star-like) but not a star, **quasi** as if – ie as though, as it were, in appearance but not in fact

QUATERN Eg **quaternary** – see QUADR(I)

QUEST, QUIR, QUISIT Lat *quaerere, quaesit-* to seek. Eg **acquire** seek 'to' – ie seek additionally, add, gain, obtain, **acquisition** a seeking 'to' – ie a seeking additionally, an adding, gaining, obtaining (or the thing obtained), **enquire** (or **inquire**) seek into – ie ask, **exquisite** sought out – ie carefully sought, carefully done, delicately wrought, extremely fine, or (of a sensation) very keen, **inquest** a seeking into – ie an investigation (eg into cause of death), **inquisition** a seeking into – ie a (legal etc) examination, **perquisite** (thing) thoroughly sought – ie something sought for carefully, gratuities or some other benefit (apart from formal payment) that go with a job (and **perk** is short for 'perquisite'), **quest** a seeking, **question** a seeking – ie an asking, **request** a seeking back – ie a seeking hard, an asking (for something), **requisite** sought back – ie sought hard, necessary

QUID, QUO, QUOD Lat *quid* what, something; *quo* (by/in etc) which, (by/in etc) something; *quod* which. Eg **quiddity** the whatness (of something) – ie the essence of something, **quidnunc** a 'what-now'? – ie a newsmonger, gossip, **quid pro quo** 'something for something' – ie something given in return for something else, **quod vide** (abbreviated to qv) 'see which!' – a form of cross-reference in a text, **status quo** 'the standing in which (things are/were)' – ie things as they are/were. (Eng **quid**, slang for 'pound', may also come from Lat *quid*, perhaps via 'quid pro quo')

QUIEM, QUIES, QUIET Lat *quies, quiet-* rest; *requies, requiet-* rest;

167

quiescere, quiet- to rest; *requiescere, requiet-* to rest. Eg **acquiesce** to rest-to – ie to find rest in something, to be content to let something happen, to agree to it, **quiescent** at rest, **quiet** restful, **quietude** restfulness, **quietus** (from *quietus est*, he is at rest, ie he is free from obligations etc) – ie an acquittance (from financial obligation etc) or a discharge (eg from life), **requiem** – first word of the introit of the Mass for the Dead (*Requiem aeternam dona eis, Domine*, Rest eternal grant them, O Lord), **RIP** (abbreviation of *Requiescat in pace*) 'may he/she rest in peace'

QUINQU(E), QUIN(T) Lat *quinque* five; *quintus* fifth. Eg **quin-quennium** (period of) five years, **quintessence** fifth essence – ie (in ancient and medieval philosophy) a fifth basic substance, underlying the other four (the elements – earth, fire, air and water) and supposed to form the hidden essence of all things; thus the 'quintessence' of something is its very essence, the most perfect form of it, the embodiment of it, **quintuplet** (one of a) fivefold (set) – ie one of five children born together

QUIR Eg **acquire, enquire** – see QUEST

QUISIT Eg **acquisition, exquisite** – see QUEST

QUO Eg **status quo, quid pro quo** – see QUID

QUOD Eg **quod vide** – see QUID

QUONDAM Lat *quondam* formerly. In English **quondam** is used as an adjective to mean former, one-time (eg 'my quondam teacher')

QUORUM Lat *quorum* of whom. Eng **quorum** (the number of people who must be present at a meeting for it to be valid) arises from the form of words formerly used to commission (in Latin) a justice of the peace of special status whose presence was essential for a bench to be validly constituted: 'of whom we want you, X, to be one'

QUOT Lat *quot* how many; *quotiens* how many times. Eg **quota** a how-manieth (part) – ie a specified proportion, a specified

168

number or quantity, **quote** to how-many – ie to mark (a text) with numbers or references, to refer to a particular part of a text, to cite a text or repeat part of it, **quotient** a how-many-times – ie the number of times one number is contained in another (or a ratio – as in IQ, Intelligence Quotient)

R

RAD Eg **abrade** – see RAS

RADI(C)(I) Lat *radix, radic-* root. Eg **eradicate** root out, **radical** relating to the root – or fundamental, concerned with fundamental change, **radiciform** root-shaped – or root-like, **radish** root

RADI(O) Lat *radius* staff, rod, spoke, ray. Eg **irradiate** (send) rays onto – ie throw light on, light up; or expose to rays, **radial** relating to rays, or (having) spokes, or (arranged like) spokes – or (of a tyre) having layers of fabric wrapped round in the same direction as the radii (or 'spokes') of the wheel, **radiate** (send out) rays – or spread out from a centre like the spokes of a wheel, **radiation** (the sending out of) rays; or (energy transmitted in) rays (ie in electromagnetic waves, or by particles), **radio** (the transmission of signals etc by means of) rays (ie by means of electromagnetic waves), **radioactive** ray-active – ie sending out rays (of particles), **radiography** ray-writing – ie the picturing of the inside of the body etc by means of X-rays etc, **radiology** the science of rays – ie X-rays etc, and their use in medicine, **radius** spoke (of a circle) – ie line drawn from the circle's centre to its circumference

RAM(I) Lat *ramus* branch. Eg **ramification** a branch-making – ie a forming of branches or complexities, or a less obvious consequence, **ramose** branched

RAPID, RAP(T) Lat *rapere, rapt-* to snatch, take by force. Eg **rapacious** snatching – ie grasping, **rape** a taking by force – ie a forcing of sexual intercourse on a person (Note: the word 'rape' was formerly used in English without the sexual connotation; thus paintings of the 'Rape of the Sabine

Women' refer to the women's abduction by force, rather than rape in the modern, more restricted sense), **rapid** seizing, snatching – ie fast-moving, **rapt** seized – ie carried away, entranced, **rapture** a seizing – ie a state of entrancement, ecstasy

RAS, RAD, RAZ Lat *radere, ras-* to scrape, shave. Eg **abrade** scrape away – ie scrape off, rub off, wear down, **abrasive** scraping away – ie (of a substance) capable of scraping off, rubbing off, wearing down, scratching; (of a person) tending to 'rub' people up the wrong way, grating in manner, **erase** scrape out – ie rub out, **raze** scrape – ie (of a building, in the phrase 'raze to the ground') bring to the level of (the ground), demolish completely, **razor** shaving (instrument)

RATIO Lat *ratio, ration-* reckoning, account, judgement, reason; *reri, rat-* to reckon, think; *ratiocinari, ratiocinat-* to reckon, think out. Eg **rate** reckoned (part) – ie fixed part, fixed numerical relationship between one thing and another, **ratify** make (something) reckoned – ie make it fixed, validate it, **ratio** a reckoning – ie a fixed proportional relationship between two things, **ratiocination** a thinking out – ie the process of reasoning, **ration** a reckoning – ie an allowance (of food etc), **rational** relating to (according to etc) reason

RAZ Eg **raze, razor** – see RAS

RE Lat prefix *re-* back, again (or, occasionally, simply strengthens the word). Eg **recede** go back – ie draw back, fade away, **recline** lean back, **recurrent** running again – ie happening again (and again), **reduce** lead back – ie lessen, **regress** step back – ie go back (to an earlier stage), **reject** throw back – ie turn away, deem unacceptable, **rejuvenate** (make) young again, **remission** a sending back – ie forgiveness (of sins), a lessening (of a prison sentence etc), **remorse** a biting back – ie a biting afterwards, a troubling of the conscience, feelings of repentance, **remote** moved back – ie moved away, out-of-the-way, far away, **renascent** being born again – ie coming to life again, getting a new lease of life, **report** carry (news etc) back, **revert** turn back – ie go back (to a former state), **revive** to live again – ie come (or bring) back to life, **revoke** call back – ie annul, cancel

RE(AL) Lat *res* thing. Eg **re** (in) the thing (of) – ie in the matter of, concerning, **real** relating to things – ie being a thing, actually existing, genuine (or, as in 'real estate', constituting fixed property: land and buildings), **reify** make (into) a thing – ie think of as a thing, **republic** the thing of the people – ie the state, a state in which the people have supreme power

RECT, REG Lat *regere, rect-* to guide, straighten, rule (see also RECT(I)); *rex, reg-* ruler, king; *regina* queen; *regnum* reign; *regula* rule. Eg **correct** (thoroughly) straightened – ie in order, right, **direct** straightened apart – ie set straight, straightforward, **erect** to (set) straight forth – ie to set upright, build, **interregnum** (period) between reigns, **rector** ruler – ie principal (of a college, religious house etc), or the clergyman in a certain type of parish, **regal** kingly (or queenly), **regalia** kingly (or queenly) (insignia), **regent** ruling (person) – especially someone exercising royal authority in place of the monarch, **regicide** killing (or killer) of a king, **regime** rule – ie system of government, **regimen** rule – ie system of government, **regiment** rule – ie government, unit of government, unit of soldiers, **region** a ruling – ie a line, boundary, area, **regius professor** professor of the king/queen – ie the holder of a professorship founded by the Crown, **regular** (in accordance with a) rule, **regulation** a ruling

RECT(I) Lat *rectus* straight, right (related to *regere* – see RECT). Eg **rectangle** straight-angled (figure) – ie right-angled figure, **rectify** make right, **rectilineal** straight-lined, **rectitude** rightness – ie moral uprightness, **recto** right(hand) (page) – of a book, when the book is lying open, **rectum** straight (gut) – ie the straight part of the large intestine

REG Eg **interregnum, regal, regime** – see RECT

REN(I) Lat *renes* kidneys. Eg **adrenal** (gland) towards (ie near) the kidneys – and **adrenaline** is a hormone secreted by these glands, **renal** relating to the kidneys, **reniform** kidney-shaped

REPT(IL) Lat *repere, rept-* to creep. Eg **reptile** creeping (creature)

171

RET(I) Lat *rete* net; *reticulum* little net. Eg **reticulated** little-netted – ie in the form of a net, or marked with a network, **reticule** little net – ie small bag of a sort that was originally of net-work, **retiform** net-shaped. (The word **retina**, a part of the eye, may also derive from Lat *rete*)

RETRO Lat *retro* backwards, back, behind. Eg **retroactive** active backwards – ie (of a law etc) applying to the past, **retrograde** stepping backwards, **retrogress** step backwards, **retroject** throw backwards, **retrospective** looking backward, **retroversion** a turning back – or a falling back

RHEO Gk *rheos* stream, flow. (The element 'rheo' is often used in English words to denote an electric current.) Eg **rheometer** flow measure – ie instrument for measuring electric and other currents, **rheotome** flow-cutter – ie instrument for breaking an electric circuit

RHESUS Gk *Rhesos* – name of a mythical king of Thrace (a region now divided between Greece, Turkey and Bulgaria). His name was given, apparently for no particular reason, to an Indian monkey, and hence to a group of antigens (the presence of which is described as the **Rhesus factor**) first discovered in the blood of this **rhesus monkey**

RHIN(O) Gk *rhis, rhin-* nose; in plural, nostrils. Eg **antirrhinum** (plant) opposite (ie instead of, mimicking) a nose – because the flower resembles an animal's nose, **monorhine** (having a) single nostril, **rhinoceros** horned-nosed (creature) – ie animal with a horn on its nose, **rhinoplasty** plastic (surgery) of the nose

RHIZ(O) Gk *rhiza* root. Eg **rhizanthous** root-flowering – ie seeming to flower from the root, **rhizogenetic** root-producing, **rhizome** root(-like stem)

RHOD(O) Gk *rhodon* rose. Eg **rhodium** rose (element) – because it forms salts that produce rose-coloured solutions, **rhododendron** rose tree, **rhodolite** rose stone – because of its colour

RID, RIS Lat *ridere, ris-* to laugh. Eg **deride** (thoroughly) laugh (at) – ie mock, scoff at, **derision** a (thorough) laughing (at) – ie mockery, scoffing, **ridiculous** laughable – ie absurd, **risible** laughable – or inclined to laugh, **risus** a laugh – or grin (eg as brought about involuntarily by certain diseases)

RIG(ID) Lat *rigidus* stiff; *rigere* to be stiff. Eg **rigid** stiff – ie unbending, **rigor mortis** 'stiffness of death', **rigour** (US **rigor**) stiffness – ie hardness, severity

RIS Eg **derision, risible** – see RID

RIV Lat *rivus* stream; *rivalis* one who draws water from the same stream (as another). Eg **derive** to off-stream (water) – ie to divert water from a stream into a channel, to take from a source, or (of a word etc) to have its source, **rival** – thought to derive from *rivalis* (one who draws water from the same stream as another, hence one who is after the same thing as another, one who is in competition with another). Note that Eng 'river' derives not from Lat *rivus* but from Lat *ripa* (riverbank)

ROD, ROS Lat *rodere, ros-* to gnaw. Eg **corrode** (thoroughly) gnaw – ie gnaw away, eat away, wear away, **erosion** a gnawing away – ie an eating away, a wearing away, **rodent** gnawing (creature)

ROG Lat *rogare, rogat-* to ask, consult (eg the people, about a law), propose (a law). Eg **abrogate** propose (a law) away – ie repeal (a law), cancel, **arrogant** asking to (oneself) – ie claiming for oneself, claiming something to which one has no right, overbearing, presumptuous, **derogatory** asking away (from something) – ie taking away from, speaking ill of something or someone, **interrogate** ask (questions) between (someone) – ie ask questions of (someone), **prerogative** (right of being) asked before (others) – ie (in ancient Rome) the right to vote first, (hence) a privilege, right, **surrogate** asked (for) under (another) – ie asked for in place of another, taking the place of another

ROMANC, ROMANT Lat *Roma* Rome. The steps by which this place name gave rise to Eng **romance, romantic** etc can be

173

summarised as follows. From Lat *Romanus* (Roman), derives the Old French word *romanz*, applied to the language spoken in France that developed out of Latin. The word *romanz* was applied also to works written in this language, notably to the medieval tales of chivalry and adventure. Thus a 'romance' became a fictitious tale of wonderful or out-of-the-ordinary events; and hence more recently the word has come to mean more specifically a love affair or the genre of literature (etc) describing such.

The 'romance' languages are those that developed out of Latin – French, Spanish, Italian, Portuguese etc

ROS Eg **erosion** – see ROD

ROSTR Lat *rostrum* beak, snout. Eg **fissirostral** split-beaked – ie having a deeply cleft beak, **latirostral** broad-beaked, **rostrate** beaked, **rostrum** – from the *rostra* in Rome, the speaker's platform in the forum. (see FORUM), which was so called because it was decorated with the 'beaks' (prows, or iron projections used for ramming enemy vessels) of captured ships

ROTA, ROTUND Lat *rota* wheel; *rotundus* 'wheel-like' – ie round, circular. Eg **orotund** round-mouthed – ie round-voiced, full and rounded of speech, pompous-sounding, **rota** wheel – ie a circular taking of turns, list of people (etc) taking turns, **rotary** wheeling – ie turning like a wheel, operating in a circle, **rotate** to wheel – ie to turn in a circle, **rotund** round, **rotunda** round (building)

RRHAG(IA) Gk *-rr(h)agia* a bursting (forth). Eg **haemorrhage** (US **hemorrhage**) a bursting forth of blood – ie a discharge of blood from the blood-vessels, **menorrhagia** bursting of the monthly – ie excessive menstrual flow, **metrorrhagia** womb bursting – ie bleeding from the womb between monthly periods, **rhinorrhagia** nose bursting – ie excessive nose-bleeding

RRH(O)(EA) Gk *rhoia* a flow, flowing; *rheein* to flow; *-rhoos* flowing, streaming. Eg **amenorrhoea** (US **amenorrhea**) no monthly flow – ie non-occurrence of menstruation, **catarrh** a down-flow (from the nose etc), **diarrhoea** (US **diarrhea**) a through-flowing, **galactorrhoea** (US **galactorrhea**) (excessive) milk flow (in nursing mothers), **gonorrhoea** (US **gonorrhea**) seed flow – from the belief once held that the discharge characterising the disease was semen, **haemorrhoids** (US **hemorrhoids**) blood-flowing (veins) – ie a swelling of the veins of the anus (sometimes with bleeding), piles, **leucorrhoea** (US **leucorrhea**) white flow – ie an abnormal white discharge from the vagina, **logorrhoea** (US **logorrhea**) (excessive) flow of words

RUB Lat *ruber* red; *rubere* to be red; *rubellus* reddish; *rubrica* red earth, the title of a law (originally written in red ochre), hence a law. Eg **rubefacient** red-making – ie that reddens the skin, **rubella** (disease giving) reddish (skin) – ie German measles (which gives a pink rash), **rubescent** reddening, **rubicund** red(dish) – ie ruddy, **rubric** – an instruction as to action, gesture etc (traditionally written or printed in red) appearing in the text of a religious service, or a heading or title (originally one written in red), or a guiding rule, (etc)

RUD Lat *rudis* rough, raw, not worked on, unpolished; *rudimentum* a first 'go' at something, a beginning in something. Eg **erudite** (brought) out of the raw – ie worked on, educated, learned, **rude** rough, unpolished etc, **rudiments** beginnings

RUG Lat *ruga* wrinkle. Eg **corrugated** (thoroughly) wrinkled, **rugose** wrinkled

RUPT Lat *rumpere, rupt-* to break. Eg **abrupt** broken away – ie broken off, sharp, sudden, **corrupt** (thoroughly) broken – ie destroyed, ruined, tainted, dishonest, **disrupt** break apart – ie break up, **erupt** break out, **interrupt** break between – ie break in(to), **rupture** a breaking, break

RUR, RUS Lat *rus, rur-* the country. Eg **rural** and **rustic** relating to (in, belonging to, etc) the country

S

SAC(E)R, SECR Lat *sacer, sacr-* sacred; *sacerdos, sacerdot-* priest, priestess. Eg **consecrate** (thoroughly) (make) sacred – ie dedicate to a sacred purpose, **desecrate** de-sacred (something) – ie put something sacred to a non-holy use, violate, **execrate** (thoroughly) (make) sacred – ie make sacred right to the bitter end, sacredly vow (something or someone) to its/his/her end, curse, loathe, **sacerdotal** priestly, **sacrament** sacred (rite), **sacrifice** a sacred-doing – ie the killing of an animal as an offering to the gods, any offering made to a god, the giving up of something for the sake of something else, **sacrilege** a gathering (up) of sacred things – ie theft of sacred things, violation of something sacred, **sacrosanct** made holy by sacred (rite) – ie inviolable

SAGITT(I) Lat *sagitta* arrow. Eg **Sagittarius** the Archer – sign of the zodiac, **sagittiform** arrow-shaped – ie shaped like an arrow-head

SAL(T), SIL, SULT Lat *salire, salt-* to leap. Eg **desultory** relating to (ie like) a leaper-down – ie like a vaulter, jumping from one thing to another, disconnected, in fits and starts, **exult** leap forth – ie leap up, rejoice, triumph, **insult** a leaping on or against – ie an expression of scorn, an affront, **resilient** leaping back – ie returning to the original position, 'bouncing back', able to recover quickly from a 'knock', **result** a leaping back – ie a consequence, **salacious** leaping – ie (originally of male animals) lustful; hence also exciting lust, **salient** leaping – ie sticking out, prominent, striking (Note: the phrase 'salient point' was originally applied to the first visible form of the heart, appearing as a leaping speck, in an embryo; hence it came to mean a first beginning or first rudiment; the phrase is also used to mean the striking point or main point)

SAL(I) Lat *sal* salt. Eg **desalinate** de-salt – ie take the salt out of, **salad** salted (greenery etc), **salary** salt (money) – ie money paid to Roman soldiers to buy salt with; hence pay, **saliferous** salt-bearing, **saline** salty

SALU(T) Lat *salus, salut-* health; *salutare, salutat-* to wish someone health – ie to greet him/her. Eg **salubrious** healthful, **salutiferous** health-bearing – ie health-giving, **salutary** healthful – ie promoting health or safety, **salutation** a greeting, **salute** to greet

SALV Lat *salvus* safe. Eg **salvage** to save – ie to rescue (eg a ship's cargo) from loss, **salvation** a saving

SAN Lat *sanus* healthy. Eg **sanatorium** (place for making) healthy – ie place where the sick are treated, **sane** healthy (in mind), **sanitary** relating to (ie promoting etc) health, **sanitation** (measures promoting) health – especially those concerned with drainage and sewage disposal

SANCT(I) Lat *sanctus* holy; *sancire* make holy. Eg **sacrosanct** made holy by sacred (rite) – ie inviolable, **sanctify** make holy, **sanctimonious** (pretending) holiness, **sanction** a making holy – ie a making sacred or inviolable, a decreeing or forbidding under penalty, a giving of approval (to a course of action); or a penalty threatened in order to persuade another party to adopt a certain course of action, **sanctity** holiness, **sanctuary** holy (place) – or a sacred place such as a church in which, in medieval times, a fugitive from justice could not be touched by the law; hence a place of refuge or retreat, **sanctum** – short for *sanctum sanctorum* the 'Holy of Holies' of the Jewish temple, hence a private room

SANGUI(N) Lat *sanguis, sanguin*- blood. Eg **consanguinity** (a having of) blood together – ie a having of the same blood, a blood relationship, **sanguinary** bloody, **sanguine** bloody, blood(-red) – or in a state in which the blood is predominating over the other 'humours' (see CHOL(ER)), ie optimistic

SAPIEN Lat *sapiens, sapient*- wise, having judgement. Eg **Homo sapiens** human (species) having judgement – name of the currently existing human species (as distinct from its ancestors, such as *Homo erectus*), **sapience** wisdom

SAPPH Eg **sapphism** – see LESBIAN

SARC(O) Gk *sarx, sark*- flesh; *sarcazein* to tear off flesh (as dogs do). Eg **sarcasm** a tearing off of flesh – ie the use of cutting (usually ironic) remarks, **sarcoma** fleshy (growth)- ie a tumour derived from connective tissue, **sarcophagus** flesh-eating (stone) – the original Greek word was applied to a type of limestone thought to consume flesh and for this reason used

177

by the Greeks to make coffins; hence a 'sarcophagus' is a stone coffin

SARTOR Lat *sarcire, sart-* to mend, patch; *sartor* a 'patcher' – ie a tailor. Eg **sartorial** relating to tailors – or relating to clothes

SATELLIT Lat *satelles, satellit-* an attendant. Eg **satellite** an attendant – ie a follower or 'hanger on' of an important person; or a body revolving round a planet (eg round the earth); or ('satellite state') a state that is dependent on and accepts the dictates of a larger one

SATI(S) Lat *satis* enough. Eg **satiate** (fill etc) enough (or more than enough) – ie fulfil (a desire etc) even to the point of overfulness, **satisfy** do enough (for something or someone) – ie fulfil the wishes or requirements (of something or someone)

SATUR(N) Lat *Saturnus* – name of an old Italian god of agriculture, later identified by the Romans with the Greek Cronos, who was one of the Titans (see TITAN) and father of Zeus (see JOV). The planet **Saturn** was named after him, and the day **Saturday** was named after the planet. Those born under the planet are supposed to be the opposite of fun-loving in temperament; hence the word **saturnine**, meaning cold, gloomy. The Roman festival of Saturn, the Saturnalia, consisted of several days of riotous merrymaking (in which even slaves were involved, sometimes being waited on by their masters); hence the word **Saturnalia** is sometimes used in English to mean an orgy. The name Saturn was adopted by alchemists as the name for lead; hence (eg) **saturnism** is lead-poisoning

SATYR Gk *satyros* satyr. Companions of Bacchus (see BACCH), the satyrs were first pictured by the Greeks as having long pointed ears and a tail; later they acquired goat's legs, so that they were half man and half beast, and were identified by the Romans with the fauns (see FAUN(A)). They had great appetites – for wine and lechery. Hence **satyriasis** is uncontrollable sexual desire in a man

SAUR(O) Gk *sauros* lizard. Eg **brontosaurus** thunder lizard,

178

dinosaur terrifying lizard, **megalosaurus** great lizard, **saurognathous** lizard-jawed – ie having a lizard-like arrangement of the palate bones

SCAT(O) Gk *skor, skat-* dung. Eg **scatology** the study of dung – ie the study of faeces for the purpose of medical diagnosis or to assess diet; or obscene literature; or interest in the obscene; **scatophagous** dung-eating

SCEND, SCENS, SCENT Lat *scandere, scans-* to climb. Eg **ascend** climb to – ie climb up, **ascension** a climbing to – ie a climbing up, a rising, **condescend** (thoroughly) climb down – ie stoop, graciously waive one's superior status, **descent** a climbing down, **transcend** climb across – ie climb over, climb beyond, surpass

SCEPTIC (US SKEPTIC) Gk *skeptesthai* look about, examine, consider. The first 'sceptics' were the followers of the Greek philosopher Pyrrho of Elis, who lived in the fourth century BC. He doubted that certain knowledge was possible and taught that true wisdom and happiness would only be attained if judgement was suspended. So the Sceptics questioned ('examined') all generally accepted propositions, and a **sceptic** is now someone who tends to doubt what he/she is told

SCHIS, SCHIZ(O) Gk *schizein* to split, cleave; *schistos* split, cloven; *schisma* a split, rent, cleft. Eg **schism** a split (in a church), **schist** split (stone) – ie crystalline rock tending to split, **schizogenesis** (re)production by splitting (ie by dividing), **schizoid** schizo(phrenic)-shaped – ie schizophrenic-like, displaying schizophrenic-like behaviour (without positively suffering from the disorder), **schizophrenia** (disease seen as involving a) split mind

SCI Lat *scire* to know. Eg **conscience** knowledge with – ie a being privy to something (with another person), knowledge in oneself, awareness of right and wrong (or of the fact that one has done right or wrong), **conscious** knowing with – ie privy to something (with another person), knowing in oneself, aware, **nescient** not knowing – ie lacking knowledge,

179

omniscient all-knowing, **prescience** foreknowledge, **science** knowledge, **scientific** knowledge-making – ie producing knowledge, relating to the pursuit of knowledge

SCLER(O), SKELET Gk *skleros* dry, hard; *skellein* to dry up. Eg **sclerodermous** hard-skinned, **sclerosis** a hardening (eg of the arteries), **sclerotic** hard (coating of the eye-ball), **skeleton** dried-up (body)

SCOP Gk *skopeein* to look at, view; *skopos* object looked at or aimed at, a shooting mark. Eg **episcopal** relating to (or governed by etc) overviewers – ie overseers, bishops, **horo-scope** time-viewing – ie a charting of the heavens at a particular time, eg the time of a person's birth; hence a prediction from the stars of a person's future, **hygroscopic** (enabling) moisture-viewing – ie (of a substance) readily absorbing or reacting to moisture and therefore serving to indicate how much moisture is present, **kaleidoscope** beautiful-shape viewer, **microscope** small viewer – ie instrument for looking at small things, **periscope** around-viewer – ie instrument for looking around (eg above the surface of the water, when in a submarine), **scope** shooting mark – ie something aimed at, the aim of something, or its range, or the area it covers, **stethoscope** chest viewer – ie instrument for examining the chest, **telescope** far-viewer – ie instrument for looking at far-away things, **thermoscopic** (enabling) heat-viewing – ie (of a substance) sensitive to changes in temperature and therefore serving to indicate such changes

SCRIB, SCRIPT Lat *scribere, script-* to write. Eg **ascribe** write to (something) – ie add to a list of something, enrol as something, assign (eg something to someone), attribute (eg something to someone), **circumscribe** write (ie draw) (a line) round – ie define the limits of, limit, **conscript** (person) written together (with others) – ie person enrolled (in an army) (compulsorily), **describe** write from (something) – ie write down, represent in words, **inscription** (words) written on (something), **manuscript** (thing) written by hand, **post-script** (thing) written after – ie added to the main text after it has been finished, **prescribe** write before – ie set before (someone) in writing, lay down as a rule or recommendation,

proscribe write forth – ie (in ancient Rome) write up publicly, publish the name of (someone who has been condemned or is to be outlawed); hence, to outlaw or denounce, **scribe** writer, **script** (thing) written, writing, **scripture** writing, **subscription** a writing under – ie a signature at the end of a document, a giving of assent or support, a financial contribution, a membership fee, **transcribe** write across – ie write out in another place, make a copy of, write out (from shorthand etc), adapt (for a different medium)

SCRUP Lat *scrupulus* little sharp stone. Eg **scruple** little sharp stone – ie a niggling anxiety, a moral doubt making one hesitate before action

SCRUT Lat *scruta* rags, rubbish, trash; *scrutari* to search through (as a rag-picker searches through rubbish). Eg **inscrutable** un-search-through-able – ie impenetrable, revealing nothing, **scrutiny** a searching through – ie a detailed look

SE, SED Lat *se, sed* without, apart. Eg **secede** go apart – ie withdraw (formally – from an alliance etc), **secluded** shut apart – ie shut off, shut away, **secure** without care – ie safe, **sedition** a going apart – ie a quarrel, a rebellion, fermenting of rebellion, **seduce** lead apart – ie lead astray, **segregate** (move) apart (from) the flock – ie separate from the flock, set apart

SEC Eg **consecutive, second** – see SEQ

SECR Eg **consecrate, desecrate** – see SAC(E)R

SEC(T) Lat *secare, sect-* to cut. Eg **bisect** to cut into two, **dissect** to cut apart – ie cut up, **insect** cut-into (creature) – ie cut-up creature, segmented creature, **intersect** to cut between – ie cut across, (of two lines etc) cross each other, **secateurs** cutters, **section** a cutting – or a part cut off, a part, **trisect** to cut into three, **vivisection** an alive cutting – ie the cutting up of an animal while it is still alive

SED Eg **sedentary, sediment** – see SID

181

SED Eg **sedition** – see SE

SELEN(O) Gk *selene* the moon. Eg **selenium** moon (element) – so named because it shares many properties with tellurium, named after the earth (see TELLUR(O)), in reference to the fact that the moon has a similarly close relationship with the earth (in that the moon revolves around the earth), **selenography** moon writing – ie the mapping or description of the moon, **selenomorphology** study of moon shapes – ie the study of the surface of the moon

SEMEN – see SEMIN

SEMI Lat *semi-* half-. Eg **semicircle** half-circle, **semi-monthly** half-monthly, **semi-official** half-official – ie partly official, **semiquaver** half a quaver

SEMIN(I), SEMEN Lat *semen, semin-* seed. Eg **dissemination** a seeding apart – ie a scattering around, a spreading around, **inseminate** (put) seed in – ie plant seed (or semen) in, **semen** seed – ie fluid carrying sperm, **seminal** relating to seed (or semen) – or acting like seed (eg by giving rise to a new movement or a development in thought), **seminar** seed(-plot) – ie meeting for educational or training purposes, **seminary** seed(-plot) – ie place where priests (etc) are nurtured or trained, **seminiferous** seed-bearing

SEMPER, SEMPIT Lat *semper* always. Eg **sempiternal** (lasting) always – ie everlasting

SEN Lat *senex* old, old man; *senior* older; *senescere* to grow old; *senilis* relating to an old man. Eg **senate** (body of) old men – ie governing body of elders (or distinguished people), governing body, **senescent** growing old – or on the verge of old age, **senile** relating to an old man – ie relating to old age, or suffering from the mental decay characteristic of old age, **senior** older – or higher in rank

SENS, SENT Lat *sentire, sens-* to feel, think; or related Latin words. Eg **assent** think towards – ie give one's agreement (to), **consensus** a thinking together – ie a general agreement,

consent think together (with another) – ie agree, **dissent** think apart – ie think differently, disagree, **insensible** not feelable – ie imperceptible; or not feeling – ie unconscious, or unfeeling, **resent** feel back – ie feel in response, feel pain, feel offended by (eg by the action of another), **sensation** a (physical) feeling, **sense** feeling – ie faculty of feeling, faculty of perception; or a feeling, an impression; (etc), **sentence** a feeling, a thought – ie a grammatical structure suitable for expressing a thought; or (in the context of a court) a judgement, the punishment decided on, **sententious** (full of) thoughts – ie full of pithy sayings or fine-sounding generalisations, **sentient** feeling – or capable of feeling, conscious, aware, **sentiment** a feeling – or emotion

SEPSIS, SEPTIC Gk *sepein* to rot. Eg **antiseptic** anti-rotting (substance) – ie substance that fights bacteria, **aseptic** non-rotting – ie free from bacteria, **sepsis** a rotting – ie infection with bacteria, **septic** rotting – ie infected with bacteria, or involving the action of bacteria (as in 'septic tank'), **septicaemia** (US **septicemia**) rotten blood – ie infection of the blood with bacteria

SEPT(I) Lat *septem* seven; *septuaginta* seventy; *septuagenarius* containing seventy. Eg **September** seventh (month) – our ninth month was the seventh month of the Roman year, which began in March (see also OCTAV, NOV, DEC(I)), **septilateral** seven-sided, **septuagenarian** (person) containing seventy (years) – ie person in his/her seventies, **Septuaginta** (work of the) Seventy (translators) – ie the Greek Old Testament, traditionally held to have been translated into Greek by seventy (or, more precisely, seventy-two) translators

SEPTIC Eg **antiseptic, septicaemia** – see SEPSIS

SEQ, SEC Lat *sequi, secut-* to follow; *secundus* 'following' – ie next (after the first), second. Eg **consecutive** (thoroughly) following – ie following on closely, following on without a break, **consequence** (thing) (thoroughly) following (something else) – ie following on closely from it, resulting from it, **non-sequitur** an 'it-does-not-follow' – ie the drawing of a conclusion that does not follow logically from the premises, or such a conclusion, **persecute** follow through, (thoroughly) follow – ie follow constantly, hunt down, hound, **prosecute** follow (someone) forth – ie go with or follow after someone, chase him/her, undertake a legal action against him/her, **second** next (after the first), **sequel** (that which) follows – ie something that follows on from something else, **sequence** a following – ie a number of things following on from each other, or the order in which a number of things follow each other, **subsequent** following under – ie following after

SERP Lat *serpere* to creep. Eg **serpent** creeping (creature), **serpigo** creeping (skin disease)

SESS Eg **sessile, session** – see SID

SEX(I) Lat *sex* six; *sextus* sixth; *sexaginta* sixty; *sexagenarius* containing sixty. Eg **sexagenarian** (person) containing sixty (years) – ie person in his/her sixties, **sex(i)valent** of valency six, **sextant** a sixth (of the circumference of a circle) – or an angle-measuring instrument using this arc, **sextet** (group of) six, **sextuplet** (one of a) sixfold (set) – ie one of six children born together

SIC Lat *sic* so, thus. The word **sic** appears in brackets in text to confirm that something that is surprising or seems a mistake (eg a misspelling or grammatical error) has been done deliberately for some reason; usually the circumstances are that another text is being quoted, in which the mistake (or apparent mistake) is present and, as it is wished to reproduce the original text exactly, the 'mistake' is reproduced also

SICC Lat *siccus* dry. Eg **desiccated** (made) (thoroughly) dry, **siccative** drying – ie that dries up moisture

SID, SED, SESS Lat *sedere, sess-* to sit; *insidiae* a 'sitting in' or 'sitting on' – ie ambush. Eg **assiduous** sitting towards (something) – ie sitting by its side, attending to it, devoting oneself to it, consistently working hard at it, **dissident** (person) sitting apart – ie not agreeing, **insidious** ambushing – ie treacherous, creeping up unnoticed, **obsession** a sitting against – ie a besieging, an idea besieging a person, **preside** sit before – ie sit in front, be in charge, **resident** (person) sitting back – ie staying seated, staying, living (in a particular place), **residue** (that which) sits back – ie that which is left, **sedentary** sitting – ie involving a lot of sitting, not involving much moving about, **sediment** a sitting – ie a settling, matter settled at the bottom of a liquid, **sessile** sitting – ie (of a flower or leaf) stalkless (so that it 'sits on' the base), **session** a sitting, **supersede** sit above (something) – ie override it, take its place

SIDER(O) Lat *sidus, sider-* constellation, star. Eg **sidereal** relating to (or like) the stars, **siderostat** star make-stander – ie instrument used when observing a star to keep its image in the same position in the field of a telescope

SIDER(O) Gk *sideros* iron. Eg **siderite** iron (meteorite) – ie meteorite mainly of iron (also used to refer to ferrous carbonate, an iron ore), **siderolite** iron (and) stone (meteorite) – ie meteorite made of iron and stone, **siderosis** iron (disease) – ie lung disease caused by breathing in fragments of iron

SIL Eg **resilient** – see SAL(T)

SILV(I) Eg **silviculture** – see SYLV(I)

SIMIL, SIMUL Lat *similis* like; *simul* at the same time. Eg **assimilate** make like (the rest) – ie absorb, **facsimile** a 'make-the-like!' – ie an exact reproduction (eg of handwriting), **similar** like, alike, **simile** a likening (of one thing to another), **simulate** (make) like – ie pretend, imitate, **simultaneous** (happening) at the same time, **verisimilitude** likeness to the truth – ie appearance of truth, plausibility

SINE Lat *sine* without. Eg **sinecure** (clergyman's post) without care (of souls) – ie clergyman's post without pastoral duties, or some other appointment not involving any work, **sine qua non** a 'without-which-not' – ie an essential condition

SINISTER, SINISTR(O) Lat *sinister* left, on the left. Left-handedness was associated with awkwardness and something being

'wrong' (whereas right-handedness was associated with skill –
see DEXTR(O)); thus *sinister* also meant awkward, wrong,
unfavourable. Eg **sinister** on the left – ie unfavourable,
threatening evil, **sinisterity** left(-handedness), **sinistral** left –
ie (of a shell) spiralling to the left, (of flatfish) lying left side
up, (etc)

SIN(U) Lat *sinus* a bend, curve, fold of a toga. Eg **insinuate**
bend in – ie get in by twists and turns rather than directly, get
in stealthily, hint, **sinuous** bendy, curvy, **sinus** curve – ie
cavity (in a bone etc), especially those affecting the nose

SIREN Gk *Seirenes* the Sirens – in mythology, sea-nymphs who
lured sailors to their deaths with their sweet singing. Hence a
siren is an alluring but dangerous woman, or an instrument
that broadcasts a loud noise (eg to warn of air-raids)

SIST, STIC, STIT, STAT, STET Lat *stare, stat-* to stand; *sistere, stat-* to
make to stand, stop, stand (still); *statuere, statut-* to make to
stand, set, place; or related Latin words. Eg **armistice** a
standing (still) of arms – ie a stopping of fighting, a truce,
assist stand to – ie take up a position, stand by, help,
circumstance (fact) standing around – ie surrounding fact,
consistent (thoroughly) standing (still) – ie standing one's
ground, unvarying, free from self-contradiction, **constant**
(thoroughly) standing – ie standing firm, unwavering, continuous, **desist** stop from – ie leave off, **insist** stand on – ie
emphasise, be firm about something, refuse to give way,
institution (thing) set in – ie arranged, set up, established,
interstice a standing between – ie a (small) space between,
(small) gap, **prostitute** (person) set forth – ie laid out for sale,
offered for (sexual) sale, **resist** (make a) stand back (against
something or someone) – ie make a stand against, withstand,
fight against, **restitution** a making to stand again – ie a
setting-up again, or a giving back, **solstice** a standing (still) of
the sun – ie point at which the sun is at its greatest distance
from the equator and appears to be standing still, **station** a
standing (still) – ie a post, position, or a stopping-place (eg for
a train), **stationary** standing – ·ie not moving, **status** a
standing, **status quo** the 'standing in which (things are/were)'
– ie things as they are/were, **statute** (thing) made to stand – ie

a law, **stet** 'let (it) stand' – written beside a crossed-out word (etc) to indicate that it should have been left in

SIT(U) Lat *situs* place. Eg **in situ** 'in place', **site** place, **situate** to place

SKELET Eg **skeleton** – see SCLER(O)

SKEPTIC (US) – see SCEPTIC

SOCI(O) Lat *socius* sharing, allied, (as a noun) companion, ally. Eg **associated** (made) sharing, allied – ie linked, joined, **sociable** companionable, **society** companionship, or an alliance (of people with an interest in common) – or a body of people and the way it works as a body, **sociology** the study of companionships, alliances – ie of bodies of people and the way they work as bodies

SOL Lat *sol* the sun. Eg **solar** relating to the sun, **solarium** sun(dial) – or place for sunbathing, **solstice** a standing (still) of the sun – ie point at which the sun is at its greatest distance from the equator and appears to be standing still

SOLEC(ISM) Gk *soloikos* speaking incorrectly. According to ancient writers, the Greek word was a reference to the debased form of Attic Greek (see ATTIC) developed by the Athenian colonists at Soloi (now in Turkey). Thus a **solecism** is a grammatical or other mistake in the use of language, or some other breach of correct form, or a glaring mistake

SOL(I) Lat *solus* alone, only. Eg **desolate** (left) (thoroughly) alone – ie lonely, uninhabited, laid waste, (etc), **sole** only, **soliloquy** a lone-speaking – ie a talking to oneself, a speech made to oneself, **solipsism** oneself alone – ie the view that the only thing one can know is oneself, and even that the only certainty one can have is that one exists, **solitaire** (game to be played) alone, **solitary** only – or having aloneness as a characteristic, **solo** (performance etc done) alone

SOLU(T), SOLV Lat *solvere, solut-* to loosen. Eg **absolute** loosened away – ie freed, free from imperfections, perfect, unconditional, **absolve** loosen away – ie to set free (from sin, an obligation etc), **dissolute** loosened apart – ie loose or unrestrained (in morals), **dissolution** a loosening apart – ie a breaking up, or a moral looseness or lack of restraint, **dissolve** loosen apart – ie melt (especially, melt in a liquid), or break up, **resolve** loosen back – ie untie, unravel or dispose of (a dilemma etc), or make a decision (to do something), **soluble** loosenable – ie (of a substance) capable of being melted in a liquid, (of a problem) capable of being unravelled or disposed of, **solve** loosen – ie untie, unravel or dispose of (a problem etc), **solvent** loosening (agent) – ie substance that melts another substance, or the liquid in which a substance melts; or (as an adjective) loosening – ie paying off (debts), able to pay all debts

SOM(A)(TO) Gk *soma, somat-* body. Eg **chromosome** colour body – see CHROM(AT)(O), **microsome** little body (in a cell), **psychosomatic** mind-body – ie (of a disease) physical but with its origins in the mind, **somascope** body-viewer – ie instrument for producing television images of the inside of the body

SOMN(I) Lat *somnus* sleep. Eg **insomnia** sleeplessness, **somnambulism** sleep-walking, **somniferous** sleep-bearing – ie sleep-bringing, **somniloquy** sleep-talking, **somnolent** sleepy

SON Lat *sonus* sound; *sonor* sound. Eg **consonant** sounding together – ie in harmony; or (as a noun) a letter that is not a vowel and can only be used in speech when 'sounded together' with a vowel, **dissonant** sounding apart – ie out of harmony, **sonic** relating to sound – or to sound-waves, **sonorous** (full of) sound – ie sounding richly or powerfully, resounding, **supersonic** above sound – ie travelling faster than sound, **ultrasonic** beyond sound – ie relating to (or using etc) vibrations like sound-waves but of a frequency beyond the range of human hearing

SOPH Lat *sophos* wise, clever; *sophisma* clever or cunning device, trick. Eg **philsophy** love of wisdom, **sophism** cunning device (in argument) – ie a fine-sounding but false argument,

sophisticated (subjected to) clever devices – ie subjected to tampering, taken away from the pure or natural state, worldly-wise, complex, subtle, advanced, **sophistry** (use of) cunning devices (in argument) – ie reasoning that sounds plausible on first hearing but is of doubtful validity

SOPOR(I) Lat *sopor* deep sleep. Eg **soporific** deep-sleep making – ie sleep-bringing

SORB, SORPT Lat *sorbere, sorpt-* to suck in, swallow. Eg **absorb** swallow away – ie suck up, **adsorption** a swallowing to – ie a sucking to (itself) (by a solid), an attracting of vapour so that it forms a surface layer (rather than being sucked up)

SOROR(I) Lat *soror* sister. Eg **sororal** sisterly, **sororicide** killing (or killer) of (one's own) sister, **sorority** sisterhood

SORPT Eg **adsorption** – see SORB

SPARS Eg **sparse** – see SPERS

SPARTAN Gk *Sparte* (or *Sparta*) – name of the capital city of the Greek state of Laconia (see LACONIC). Apart from the 'laconic' characteristic of using few words, the Spartans had the reputation of being a hardy people, well adapted to military discipline and having a simple, rigorous lifestyle. Thus, today a **spartan** lifestyle (for example) is a disciplined one without luxuries

SPECT, SPECUL, SPIC Lat *specere, spect-* to look (at), see; *spectare, spectat-* look at (carefully), watch; *specula* lookout, watch-tower; *speculum* mirror. Eg **circumspect** looking around – ie wary, cautious, **conspicuous** (thoroughly for) looking at – ie thoroughly visible, readily noticed, notable, **despicable** able to be looked down (on) – ie worthy of scorn, vile, **inspect** look into – ie examine, **introspection** a looking within (oneself), **perspective** (the art of) thoroughly looking – ie seeing correctly, drawing things so that they look three-dimensional and the right size in relation to other things (etc), **perspicacious** (thoroughly) seeing – ie sharp-sighted, having insight, **prospect** a looking forth, a looking forward – ie that

189

which presents itself to the view, or what the future seems to hold, **prospectus** a looking forward – ie a description of a proposed venture etc (or of a school etc already existing), **respect** to look back at – ie think about, have regard for, think well of, **retrospective** looking backward, **spectacle** (thing) looked at, watched – ie sight, show, entertainment, **spectacles** (pair of lenses for) seeing (through), **spectator** (on)looker, **speculate** (watch, spy out, as from a) watch-tower – ie observe, consider, wonder about, guess, buy goods etc in the hope that the market price will rise and a gain will be made on selling, **speculum** mirror – or an instrument for viewing inside the body

SPERS, SPARS Lat *spargere, spars-* to scatter, sprinkle. Eg **aspersion** a sprinkling to – ie a sprinkling over, a besmirching (of someone else's reputation), **disperse** scatter apart, **intersperse** scatter among or between – or diversify, **sparse** (thinly) scattered – ie scanty

SPHINX Gk *Sphinx* – name of a monster in Greek mythology, with the head of a woman and the body of a lionness. The creature also exists (in a slightly different form) in Egyptian mythology, but the name 'sphinx' is Greek. The version that has come down to us of the story of the 'riddle of the sphinx' is also Greek, though the legend may have originated in Egypt. According to this story, the monster terrorised the Greek city of Thebes, killing all those who, presented with a riddle, failed to solve it. Hence to describe someone as a **sphinx** is to suggest that he or she is full of puzzles or mysteries

SPIC Eg **conspicuous, perspicacious** – see SPECT

SPIN(1) Lat *spina* thorn. Eg **spine** thorn; or thorn(-like bone) – ie backbone, **spiniferous** thorn-bearing, **spiniform** thorn-shaped – ie thorn-like

SPIR Lat *spirare, spirat-* to blow, breathe. Eg **aspire** breathe towards – ie breathe on, favour, hope to have, have ambitions towards, **conspire** breathe together – ie agree, join together, plot together, **expire** breathe out – ie breathe one's last, or (of a period of time etc) come to an end, **inspire** breathe into – ie uplift or excite the mind (of someone), move (someone) to action (etc), **perspiration** a breathing through – ie a sweating out, sweating, **respiration** a breathing back – ie a taking of breath, breathing, **spirit** breathing, breath – ie breath of life, soul, bodiless being, ghost, disposition, cast of mind, (etc), **transpire** breathe across – ie give off as a vapour, pass off through the skin, (of a fact) leak out, come to light, (of events) come to pass

SPLEND Lat *splendere* to shine, be bright. Eg **resplendent** shining back – ie shining out, glittering, magnificent, glorious, **splendid** shining, bright – ie magnificent, glorious, excellent

SPOND, SPONS Lat *spondere, spons-* to pledge oneself, promise. Eg **despondent** promising away – ie promising to give something, giving something up, giving up hope, losing heart, **respond** promise back – ie promise in return, answer, **responsible** able (to be called to) promise back (for something) – ie able to be called to answer for something, answerable for something, or trustworthy, **sponsor** (person who) pledges himself/herself (on behalf of another) – ie person who undertakes to answer for another, (etc)

SPOR Gk *speirein* to sow, scatter; *spora* a sowing, seed; *sporas, sporad-* scattered. Eg **Diaspora** a scattering apart – collective term for the Jews scattered amongst non-Jews (ie, now, the Jews outside Israel), **sporadic** scattered – ie occurring here and there (and not in a regular pattern), **spore** seed – ie (in plants) a tiny reproductive body

STADIUM Gk *stadion* – name of a unit of length of about 200yd (185m); hence a race-course of this length, or a race-course in general. Hence Eng **stadium**

STAMEN, STAMIN Lat *stamen, stamin-* warp (ie the threads stretched lengthwise in a loom, to be crossed by the weft; ancient looms stood upright, so the warp threads stood vertically), warp thread, thread, thread spun by the Fates (see FAT). Eg **stamen** warp thread – ie (in a flower) the pollen-producing organ (which includes a thread-like stalk), **stamina** warp threads, threads – ie basic elements, basic structure, inborn constitutional capacities affecting lifespan, constitutional strength, capacity for physical endurance. (Note: the development of the meaning of the English 'stamina' was affected both by the 'warp threads' sense of the Latin and by the association with the threads spun by the Fates)

STANC Eg **circumstance** – see SIST

STAPHYL(O) Gk *staphyle* bunch of grapes. Eg **staphyle** bunch of grapes – ie the uvula (fleshy appendage of the palate, hanging over the back of the tongue), **Staphylococcus** bunch-of-grapes berries – ie rounded bacteria clustered like bunches of grapes

STAS, STAT Gk *histanai* to make stand, set, place, place in the balance, weigh; *stasis* a standing, stoppage; *statikos* making to stand, relating to weighing; *statike* the science of bodies at rest, the science of weighing; or other related Greek words. Eg **apostasy** a standing away from – ie abandonment (of one's religion etc), **barostat** weight make-stander – ie device for regulating pressure, **ecstasy** a placing out (of the mind) – ie a putting out of place of the mind, a trance, frenzy, state of being 'beside oneself' (with joy etc), **hygrostat** wetness make-stander – ie device for regulating humidity, **stasis** a stoppage (eg of a body fluid), **static** (of bodies) at rest – or (of forces) in equilibrium, **thermostat** heat make-stander – ie device for regulating temperature

STAT Eg **station, stationary, status** – see SIST

STELL Lat *stella* star. Eg **constellation** stars together – ie group of stars, **interstellar** among the stars (ie beyond the solar system), between the stars, **quasar** – contraction of 'quasi stellar (object)': name given to a type of heavenly body that is 'as though a star' (ie star-like) but not a star, **stellar** relating to stars – or star-like, **stellate** star(-shaped)

STENTOR Gk *Stentor* – name of a member of the Greek army in the Trojan War (as described in Homer's Iliad) who was famous for his loud voice. Thus a **stentorian** voice is an extremely loud one

STER(E)(O) Gk *stereos* solid. Eg **cholesterol** bile solid – ie solid substance found in (amongst other places) bile-stones (gall-stones), **stereo** (abbreviation of **stereophonic**) (producing) solid sound – ie (in sound reproduction) using two or more different channels to give the effect of sounds coming from different directions, **stereochemistry** solid chemistry – ie the study of the way atoms are arranged in molecules, **stereotype** solid type – ie (in printing) solid metal printing plate (made from a mould taken from movable 'types' of the letters, assembled to make up the words required); hence, an image etc that is fixed or constantly recurring, a conventionalised image etc

STET – see SIST

STHEN, ASTHEN(O) Gk *sthenos* strength; *astheneia* 'not strength' – ie weakness. Eg **asthenosphere** weakness sphere – ie a less rigid sphere thought to exist between the crust and solid centre of the earth, **callisthenics** (exercises promoting) beauty and strength, **myasthenia** muscle weakness, **neurasthenia** nerve weakness

STIC Eg **armistice, solstice** – see SIST

STIC(H) Gk *stichos* row, line. Eg **acrostic** (poem or puzzle in which other words are formed by the) outermost (letters of the) lines – ie in which the first or last letters of each line spell other words, **distich** two lines (of verse) – ie a couplet, **distichous** (having, or in) two rows, **hemistich** half-line (of verse)

STIG Eg **instigate** – see STINCT

STIGMA(T) Gk *stigma, stigmat-* mark made with a pointed instrument, branding-mark, point, spot. Eg **astigmatism** no-point (condition of the eye) – ie eye defect in which rays of light reaching the eye fail to come together at one point on it (resulting in defective focusing), **stigma** branding-mark – ie mark of disgrace; or point, spot (in various technical senses), **stigmata** marks made with a pointed instrument (resembling the wounds of Christ), **stigmatise** to brand – ie to mark out as being bad

STIL(L) Lat *stillare, stillat-* to drip. Eg **distil** (make) drip down – or heat a liquid so that it becomes a vapour and then allow it to cool and become liquid ('drip down') again, **instil** drip in – ie put in gradually (eg ideas into the mind), **still** (apparatus for) dripping – ie for distilling spirits etc

STINCT, STING, STIG Lat *-stinguere, -stinct-* to prick, goad; *stigare, stigat-* to prick, goad; *stinguere, stinct-* to quench. Eg **distinct** pricked apart – ie marked out with pricks or dots, marked out, separate, clearly marked out, definite, **distinguish** to prick apart – ie to mark out with pricks or dots, mark out, separate, tell apart, **extinct** quenched out – ie died out, **extinguish** quench out – ie put out (light etc), wipe out, **instigate** goad on – ie spur on, set in motion, **instinct** a goading on – ie a spurring on, an impulse, an innate impulse

STIT Eg **institution, restitution** – see SIST

STOIC Gk *stoa* colonnade, porch. The Stoics were a school of philosophers founded by Zeno of Citium (c300 BC). The group acquired its name from the *Stoa Poikile*, the Painted Colonnade, where Zeno used to teach, in Athens. The Stoics held that happiness could only be achieved through virtue and freeing oneself from enslavement to the passions and appetites. Whether one experiences pleasure or pain is in itself irrelevant, and both should be accepted with indifference. Thus someone who endures hardship **stoically** endures it patiently

STOL Gk *stellein* to place. Eg **diastole** a placing apart – ie a drawing apart, a widening, the rhythmic expansion of the heart and arteries, **systole** a placing together – ie a drawing together, a narrowing (especially the rhythmic contraction of the heart and arteries)

STOM(ATO) Gk *stoma, stomat-* mouth. Eg **amphistomous** (having) a mouth on both sides – ie (of a worm etc) having a sucker at each end, **astomatous** mouthless, **colostomy** (the making of a) mouth(-like opening) (in the) colon, **stomato-plasty** plastic (surgery) of the mouth. (Eng **stomach** also derives from Gk *stoma*, via Gk *stomachos* which first meant

194

throat or gullet, then the 'neck' of an organ such as the stomach, then the stomach itself)

STRATAG, STRATEG, STRATO Gk *stratos* army; *strategos* an 'army-leader' – ie commander of an army, general. Eg **stratagem** (piece of) generalship – ie a plan for deceiving an enemy, or for gaining an advantage generally, **strategy** generalship – ie the art of conducting a military campaign, a plan of campaign, **stratocracy** rule by an army – ie military rule

STREPTO Gk *streptos* twisted, flexible. Eg **Streptococcus** twisted berries – ie rounded bacteria arranged in twisted chains

STRICT, STRING Lat *stringere, strict-* to draw together, draw tightly together, bind. Eg **astringent** drawing together to, binding to – ie drawing together closely, binding closely, causing contraction of organic tissues (and so stopping bleeding), (of manner, sensation etc) sharp, harsh, **constrict** bind together – ie to squeeze together, to cramp, to narrow, **restrict** bind back – ie limit, **strict** drawn tightly together – ie tightly delimited, precise, rigid, severe, **stringent** drawing tightly together, binding – ie (of rules etc) rigorous, tightly adhered to, (of reasoning) convincing

STRU(CT) Lat *struere, struct-* to build. Eg **construct** build together – ie heap up together, build up, put together, **construe** build together – ie heap up together, build up, analyse the way in which something is put together, explain, interpret, **destruction** a building down – ie an unbuilding, a reducing to nothing, a doing away with, **instruct** build in – ie set up, furnish, teach, tell (someone) what to do, **obstruct** build against – ie block, **structure** (thing) built, building – or the way in which something is put together

STYL Lat *stilus* the pointed metal or bone instrument used to write on wax tablets. (Note: the 'y' in the derivative English words arises through a confusion of the Lat *stilus* with the Gk *stylos*, see next entry; some of the meanings of derivative English words may also have been influenced by the confusion.) Eg **style** (work produced with a) writing instrument – ie piece of writing, mode of writing, fashion in which something is presented, (etc), **style** (part of a plant resembling a) pointed writing instrument, **stylus** (instrument resembling a) pointed writing instrument – used (eg) to cut gramophone records, or a gramophone needle

STYL Gk *stylos* pillar (see also previous entry). Eg **peristyle** pillars round – ie a colonnade round a building or courtyard etc

SUB (or SUC, SUF, SUG, SUM, SUP, SUR before 'c', 'f', 'g' etc) Lat *sub* under. Eg **subaqua** relating to underwater (sport), **subdivide** divide under – ie divide secondarily, divide further, **subhuman** under-human – ie less than human, **sub judice** 'under a judge' – ie currently being dealt with by a court, under consideration, **submarine** under-sea, or (as a noun) a vessel going under the sea, **subplot** under-plot – ie secondary plot (in a play etc), **subscript** (letter, number) written under – ie written below the main line of text, **subsoil** under-soil – ie layer of soil just below the surface soil, **subterranean** under the earth – ie underground, **subtitle** under-title – ie secondary title, **subtropical** under-tropical – ie nearly tropical, relating to the regions bordering on the tropics, **suburb** (settlement) under the city – ie settlement next after the city, the outlying part of a city, **subway** under-way – ie passage under a road etc, or underground railway, **successor** (person who) goes under – ie goes next, follows on, **suffix** (word element) fixed under – ie fixed on the end (of a word), **suggest** carry (from) under(neath) – ie bring forward, put forward (eg into the mind), **supplication** a folding under – ie a bending the knee, a humble begging, **suppress** press under – ie press down, keep from coming out, **suspend** hang under – ie hang (up), or bring to a temporary halt, put off until later, **surrogate** asked (for) under (another) – ie asked for in place of another, taking the place of another

SUBTER Lat *subter* beneath, below. Eg **subterfuge** flight below – ie secret flight, secret escape, device used to escape, **subternatural** below the natural – ie less than natural

SUD(ORI) Lat *sudor* sweat; *sudare* to sweat. Eg **exude** to sweat out – or ooze with, **sudorific** sweat-making – ie promoting sweating

SUI Lat *sui* of oneself, of itself. Eg **suicide** killing of oneself – or a person who kills him- or herself, **sui generis** 'of its (or his/her etc) own kind' – ie the only one of its (or his/her etc) kind

SULT Eg **insult, result** – see SAL(T)

SUM, SUMPT Lat *sumere, sumpt-* to take, buy, spend; *sumptus* cost, expense. Eg **assume** take to (oneself) – ie take on, claim, take for granted, take to be the case, **consume** take (thoroughly) – ie take completely, use up, devour, eat (or drink), **resumption** a taking back, a taking again – ie a taking up again, **presume** take before – ie anticipate, take for granted, take to be the case, or take it upon oneself (to do something that one has no right to do), **subsume** take under – ie bring (a concept etc) under (a more general concept), include in a larger category, **sumptuous** costly – or lavish, luxurious

SUM(M) Lat *summus* highest. Eg **consummation** (a bringing to the) (thoroughly) highest (point) – ie a bringing to the very highest point, a bringing to completion or perfection, **sum** highest (thing) – ie a total (of a number of things added together), an adding together (or some other arithmetical calculation), an amount (of money), **summarise** (state) the highest (things) – ie state the chief points (of a text etc), give a brief account of, **summit** highest (point), **summum bonum** 'the highest good'

SUMPT Eg **resumption, sumptuous** – see SUM

SUPER, SUPREM Lat *super* above; *superus* upper; *superior* 'more upper' – ie higher; *supremus* 'most upper' – ie highest. Eg **insuperable** not able to be (passed) above – ie that cannot be overcome, **superabundant** above-abundant – ie over-abundant, **superfluous** above-flowing – ie overflowing, present in greater quantity than is needed, **superimpose** impose (something) above (something else) – ie place something on top of something else, **superior** higher – or better, **supernatural** above the natural – ie beyond the

197

natural, **supernumerary** above the (normal or necessary) number, **supersonic** above sound – ie travelling faster than sound, **superstratum** above stratum – ie overlying stratum, **supreme** highest. Note: Eng **superb** also derives from Lat *super* – via Lat *superbus*, which meant proud (raising oneself 'above' others), distinguished, magnificent

SUPRA Lat *supra* above. Eg **supranational** above the national – ie going beyond purely national concerns, **suprarenal** above the kidneys

SUPREM Eg **supreme** – see SUPER

SURG, SURRECT Lat *surgere, surrect-* to rise. Eg **insurgent** (person) rising into – ie person who rises up, a rebel, **insurrection** a rising into – ie a rebellion, **resurgence** a rising again, **resurrection** a rising again, **surge** to rise (up)

SYBARIT Gk *Sybaris* – name of a town founded by the ancient Greeks in southern Italy and noted for the luxurious and pleasure-seeking lifestyle of the inhabitants. Thus a **sybarite** is a person who pursues pleasure and luxury

SYCA, SYCO Gk *sykon* fig. Eg **sycamore** (or **sycomore**) fig-mulberry (tree) – name of a species of fig-tree, but commonly applied in Britain to a different tree (and in the US to other trees again), **sycophant** (person who) shows figs – The Greek original of this word, *sycophantes*, was used to mean a common informer, but it is not clear why. It is possible that the original 'sycophants' were people who informed on those exporting figs while this was banned

SYLV(I), SILV(I) Lat *silva* (or *sylva*) wood. Eg **Pennsylvania** Penn's wooded (country) – name of the US state founded by William Penn, **silviculture** (or **sylviculture**) the farming of woods – ie forestry, **sylvan** (or **silvan**) relating to woods

SYN (or SYL, SYM, SYS, SY depending on the letter that follows) Gk *syn* with, together with. Eg **syllable** a taking together – ie a pronouncing together (of sounds), a word or part of a word uttered with a single effort of the voice, **symbiosis** life together – ie a situation in which one creature lives attached to another creature (in such a way that the attachment is to the advantage of both of them), **sympathy** a suffering or feeling together with (another) – ie fellow-feeling, **symphony** a sounding together – ie (loosely) a large musical work for a full orchestra, **symposium** a drinking together – ie a drinking-party, a meeting for discusssion, a collection of articles expressing different views on a subject, **symptom** a falling together – ie a falling upon, something that befalls one, a bodily change indicating disease, **synagogue** a leading together – ie a bringing together, a (Jewish) building for coming together (for worship), **synchronise** (bring to a state of) times together – ie (of clocks etc) bring to the same time, put at the same time, **syndrome** a running together – ie a set of symptoms occurring together, **synod** a way together – ie a coming together, an assembly (eg of bishops), **synonym** (word that is a) name together (with another one) – ie that is like another one (in that it has the same meaning), **synopsis** a seeing together – ie an overall view, a summary, **synthesis** a placing together – ie a bringing together of different parts into a whole, **system** a making to stand together – ie a placing together, a bringing together into an organised whole, an organised whole, a method of organisation, (etc)

T

TABERN, TAVERN Lat *taberna* hut; *tabernaculum* little hut, tent. Eg **tabernacle** tent – or canopied structure, temporary dwelling-place, place of worship, (etc), **tavern** hut (for refreshment)

TACHO, TACH(Y) Gk *tachys* quick; *tachos* quickness, speed. Eg **tachograph** speed-writer – ie instrument in a vehicle for recording its speed, distance travelled etc, **tachometer** speed measure – ie instrument for measuring speed, **tachycardia** (abnormally) quick heart(-beat)

TACIT, TIC Lat *tacere*, *tacit-* to be silent. Eg **reticent** (keeping) silent back – ie not saying much, not revealing much, **tacit** silent – ie unspoken, **taciturn** (tending to be) silent – ie not saying much

TACT, TAG, TANG, TIG Lat *tangere, tact-* to touch; or other, related Latin words. Eg **contact** a touching together with (something, someone), **contagion** a touching together – ie a touching of something infected, a disease caught by touching, **contiguous** touching together with (something) – ie adjoining, near, **contingent** touching together – ie befalling, happening, that may or may not happen, that is dependent on something else, **intact** untouched, **tact** (sense of) touch – ie the ability to handle people in such a way that upset is avoided, **tactile** relating to (perceived by etc) touch, **tangent** (line) touching (a curve), **tangible** touchable

TACTIC Eg **tactic** – see TAX(O)

TAG Eg **contagion** – see TACT

TANDEM Lat *tandem* at length, at last. The English noun **tandem** (first applied to a two-wheeled vehicle pulled by two horses harnessed so that one was in front of the other, and now used of a bicycle for two people seated one behind the other) is a pun on Lat *tandem*, which referred to length in time not to physical length

TANG Eg **tangent, tangible** – see TACT

TANTAL Lat *Tantalus*, Gk *Tantalos* – name of a mythical king, a son of Zeus (see JOV) by a nymph (see NYMPH(O)). He offended the gods in various ways, and was punished by having to stand in Tartarus (Hell) up to his neck in water that shrank away when he tried to drink it; while branches of fruit hung just out of his reach above his head. Thus to **tantalise** is to torment by exciting in the victim a desire for something that he/she cannot have. The metallic element **tantalum** was so named partly because it is non-absorbent (in reference to the fact that Tantalus was unable to take in water)

TAPH Gk *taphos* burial, tomb; *taphe* burial. Eg **cenotaph** empty tomb – ie tomb-like monument to someone buried elsewhere, **epitaph** (words) over a tomb – ie (in Greek) a funeral oration, (in English) words written on a tomb, **taphephobia** fear of burial (alive)

200

TARD(I) Lat *tardus* slow. Eg **retarded** slowed back – ie slowed down, held back, backward, **tardigrade** slow-stepping – ie walking slowly, slow-paced, **tardy** slow – ie slow to act (or to happen), or delayed, late

TAUTO Gk *tauto* the same. Eg **tautology** a saying the same (thing) (again) – ie using words that only say again what has already been said, **tautophony** a (making the) same sound (again) – ie repetition of a sound

TAVERN – see TABERN

TAX(O), TACTIC Gk *tassein* to arrange (especially a military formation); *taxis* an arranging, arrangement; *taktikos* fit for arranging, relating to arrangement. Eg **ataxia** no arrangement – ie disorder, lack of control over voluntary movements, **phyllotaxis** leaf arrangement – ie the arrangement of leaves on the stem, **syntax** the arranging together (of words – into grammatical structures), **tactic** (a piece of) arrangement (of forces for battle) – ie a manoeuvre in battle, a step taken in furtherance of a given policy, **taxidermy** the arrangement of skins – ie the stuffing and mounting of animal skins, **taxonomy** the regulation of arrangement – ie the principles of scientific classification, or such classification itself, **zootaxy** animal arranging – ie the classification of animals

TECHN(O) Gk *techne* art, skill. Eg **pantechnicon** – see second PAN, **polytechnic** (in the UK) (college of further education in) many skills – ie many subjects, **technical** relating to a skill, **technique** a skill – ie a procedure or method for doing something, **technology** the study of skills – ie the practical application of science, the skills and equipment needed to achieve a particular end

TECT, TEG Lat *tegere, tect-* to cover. Eg **detective** (person who) uncovers – ie makes discoveries, investigates crimes, **integument** a covering on – ie a covering over, a covering or skin, rind, (etc), **protect** to cover in front – ie to shield from harm

TECT(ON) Gk *tekton* carpenter, builder. Eg **architect** chief builder – ie master-builder, designer of buildings, **geo-**

tectonic relating to the building of the earth – ie to the structure of rock masses, **tectonic** relating to building – ie structural

TEG Eg **integument** – see TECT

TEL(E) Gk *tele* far, far off. Eg **telegram** a far-writing – ie a message sent over a long distance, **telepathy** far-feeling – ie far-perception, communication not through the medium of the senses but directly mind to mind (and therefore supposedly possible over a long distance), **telephone** far-voice (instrument) – ie instrument for transmitting sound over a long distance, **telescope** far-viewer – ie instrument for looking at far-away things, **television** (instrument for) far-seeing – ie for transmitting images over long distances

TEL(EO) Gk *telos* end, purpose; *teleos* (or *teleios*) finished, complete, perfect. Eg **teleology** the study of ends – ie the doctrine of final causes (which sees in nature evidence that things develop in accordance with the purpose they will fulfil), **teleostean** complete-boned – ie (of types of fish) having fully developed bones

TELLUR(O) Lat *tellus, tellur-* the earth. Eg **tellurium** earth (element) – so named by Klaproth as a counterpart to uranium (see URAN(O), and also SELEN(O)), **tellurometer** earth measure – ie instrument for measuring survey lines

TEMP(OR) Lat *tempus, tempor-* time. Eg **contemporary** (belonging to a) time together – ie belonging to the same time, **extempore** 'out of time' – ie not involving a period of time, immediately, on the spur of the moment, without advance thought, **temporal** relating to time – or relating to the time spent in this world (as opposed to the 'hereafter'), relating to this life, worldly, **temporary** (only for a) time

TEN Eg **tenable, tenet** – see TEN(T)

TEND, TENS, TENT Lat *tendere, tens-* (or *tent-*) to stretch. Eg **attention** a stretching towards – ie a turning of the mind towards, a heeding, **contention** a (thorough) stretching – ie a

202

stretching hard, a striving, the putting forward of an argument, an argument put forward, **distend** stretch apart – or swell out, **extend** stretch out, **extensive** stretching out – ie far-reaching, large, **intend** stretch into – ie stretch towards, aim (at), have a purpose in mind (for something), **intense** stretched into – ie stretched out, stretched tight, concentrated, or extreme in degree, **pretend** stretch before – ie stretch forward, hold out, claim, claim to be something that one is not, **subtend** stretch under – ie (of a line, in geometry) be opposite to (an angle etc), **tendency** a stretching (towards something) – ie a disposition towards something, an inclination, **tense** stretched – ie stretched tight, strained, feeling strained, **tent** (skin) stretched (out) – or similar shelter

TEN(T), TIN Lat *tenere, tent-* to hold. Eg **abstinence** a holding away from – ie a holding back, a refraining (from, eg, food, sex), **contents** (that which is) held together (in something) – ie that which is held inside something, **continence** a holding together – ie a holding in, self-restraint; or the ability to control one's bowel and bladder, **continuous** held together – ie unbroken, without a break, **detention** a holding away – ie a holding back, or a keeping in custody, **impertinent** not holding through (to something) – ie not reaching it, not relating to it, irrelevant; or inappropriate, insolent, **pertinent** holding through (to something) – ie reaching something, relating to it, relevant, **retention** a holding back – ie a keeping hold of, **sustenance** (that which) holds under(neath) – ie that which holds up, supports, nourishes, **tenable** holdable – ie capable of being held or defended, **tenacious** holding (fast) – ie holding on tightly, or persistent, **tenant** (person) holding (land) – ie person who rents property from someone else, **tenet** 'he/she holds' – ie a belief, principle etc held by a person or group

TENU Lat *tenuis* thin. Eg **attenuate** make thin – or weaken, **extenuate** make thin – ie lessen the importance of, partially excuse (a crime etc), **tenuous** thin – or slender, meagre

TER, TERN, TERTI Lat *ter* three times, thrice; *terni* three together, three by three; *tertius* third. Eg **tercentenary** relating to three hundred (years etc) – or (as a noun) three-hundredth aniversary, **ternary** three by three – or threefold, or based on three, or of a third order, **tertiary** third(-level), third(-degree) etc

TERA(TO) Gk *teras*, *terat-* marvel, prodigy, monster. (Note: in names of units 'tera' is used in English to mean a million million – see MEGA(LO).) Eg **teratogenic** monster-producing – ie causing malformations in the foetus, **terawatt** a monster watt – ie a million million watts

TERM(IN) Lat *terminus* boundary, limit. Eg **coterminous** (or **conterminous**) (having a) boundary together – ie having a boundary in common, meeting end to end, or having the same range, **determine** (thoroughly) bound, limit – ie fix the limits of, bring to a decision, make a decision, **exterminate** (drive) out of boundary – ie drive beyond the boundaries, banish, destroy, **interminable** boundless – ie endless, **term** boundary – ie time-limit, fixed period of time (eg a 'term' of office); or (in the plural) the limits of something, the conditions embodied in an agreement (etc), **terminate** to bound, limit – ie to bring to an end, **terminus** boundary – ie end-point (of, eg, a railway line)

TERN Eg **ternary** – see TER

TERPSICHOR Eg **terpsichorean** – see CHOR(EO)

TER(R)(ESTR) Lat *terra* the earth, earth. Eg **extraterrestrial** outside (or from outside) the earth, **inter** (put) in the earth – ie bury, **subterranean** under the earth – ie underground, **terracotta** cooked earth – ie baked earth (name of a type of pottery), **terra firma** 'firm earth' – ie solid land: formerly meant 'the mainland'; now used to mean 'dry land', **terrestrial** relating to (eg living on) the earth, earthly, **territory** earth – ie land

TERTI Eg **tertiary** – see TER

TESSARA (or TESSERA) Eg **tessaraglot** – see TETR(A)

TEST(I) Lat *testis* witness; *testari* to bear witness, call to witness,

204

make a will. Eg **attest** bear witness to (something), **contest** a (thorough) calling to witness – ie the bringing of a law suit, a dispute, a struggle for victory, **detest** call to witness away – ie call down the curse of a god (on something or someone), loathe, **intestate** unwilled – ie not having made a will, **protest** to bear witness forth – ie to declare publicly (eg to 'protest one's innocence'), or to declare oneself to be against something, **testicle** little witness – apparently because this semen-secreting gland is a 'witness' to virility, **testify** to witness-make – ie to bear witness, **testimony** witness borne – ie evidence

TETR(A), TESSARA (or TESSERA) Gk *tetra-* four; *tessares* (or *tesseres*) four. Eg **tessaraglot** (or **tesseraglot**) (in) four tongues – ie in four languages, **tetrachloride** four-chlorine (compound) – ie a compound with four chlorine atoms in every molecule, **tetrahedron** four-seated (figure) – ie solid figure with four faces, **tetralogy** (series of) four discourses – ie series of four plays, novels etc, **tetraplegia** a four(fold) striking – ie paralysis of all four limbs, **tetrarch** (one of) four rulers – ie the ruler of one of four divisions, a subsidiary ruler

TEXT Lat *texere, text-* to weave. Eg **context** a weaving together – ie the putting together or structuring of a piece of writing, the passages 'woven together' with (ie immediately before and after) a particular passage, the setting of anything, **pretext** a weaving in front – ie the weaving of a border, adornment, outward appearance, apparent reason, or excuse, **text** a weaving – ie a way of putting words together, the actual words of a book etc, a piece of writing, **textile** woven (fabric)

THANA(TO) Gk *thanatos* death. Eg **euthanasia** a well-dying – ie a peaceful and painless death, the deliberate bringing about of death (in˙a painless way) in cases of incurable suffering, **thanatophobia** fear of death

THE(O), THUS Gk *theos* god. Eg **apotheosis** a god(-making) – ie a deification, a glorification, **atheist** no-god (believer) – ie person who believes that there is no god, **enthusiasm** (state of having) god in(side) (one) – a state of being possessed by a god, state of feeling inspired by something, great eagerness,

monotheist one-god (believer) – ie person who believes that there is only one god, **pantheist** all-god (believer) – ie person who believes that everything is God, that God and the universe are the same thing, **pantheon** all the gods – ie the complete set of gods (of, eg, a particular religion); or a temple to all the gods (and now also applied to various buildings resembling the Pantheon in Rome), **polytheist** many-gods (believer) – ie person who belives that there are many gods, **theism** (belief in) (one) god, **theocracy** rule by God (or a god) – ie system of government in which God is deemed the direct ruler and the laws of religion form the laws of the state (adminstered by the priesthood), **theology** the study of God (or gods) – ie the study of religion(s)

THERAP Gk *theraps* attendant, servant; *therapuein* to wait on, attend, treat medically; *therapeutikos* curative, healing. Eg **hydrotherapy** water treatment – ie treatment using water externally, **physiotherapy** nature treatment – ie treatment using methods such as exercise, massage and heat rather than drugs, **therapeutic** curative, healing, **therapy** medical treatment

THERM(O) Gk *therme* heat; *thermos* hot. Eg **hypothermia** under-heat – ie low body temperature, **thermal** relating to heat – or warm, or designed to conserve heat, **thermometer** heat measure – ie instrument for measuring temperature, **thermo-nuclear** heat-nuclear – ie relating to nuclear reactions that take place only at very high temperatures, **thermoscopic** (enabling) heat viewing – ie (of a substance) sensitive to changes in temperature and therefore serving to indicate such changes, **thermostat** heat make-stander – ie device for regulating temperature

THES(IS), THET Gk *thesis* a placing, setting; *tithenai* to place, set. Eg **antithesis** a placing against – ie a placing of ideas in opposition to each other, an opposite idea, the opposite of something, **epithet** (word) placed on (a noun) – ie a word added to a noun (to denote some quality that the thing has), a descriptive term, **hypothesis** a placing under – ie a foundation, basic assumption, assumption for the purposes of discussion, or a theory put forward to explain something,

parenthesis a placing in beside – ie a comment or explanation inserted in a passage, or (usually in the plural: 'parentheses') the brackets used to mark off such a comment or explanation, **synthesis** a placing together – ie a building up, a bringing together of different parts into a whole, **synthetic** (made by) placing together – ie built up (rather than naturally occurring), artificial, **thesis** a placing (of an idea) – ie a proposition (put forward for discussion), or an academic work written in support of a proposition

TIC Eg **reticent** – see TACIT

TIG Eg **contiguous** – see TACT

TIM(ID) Lat *timere* to fear. Eg **intimidate** (put) into fear – ie frighten, **timid** (tending to) fear – ie easily frightened, **timorous** fearful

TIN Eg **continence, pertinent** – see TEN(T)

TITAN Gk *Titan* Titan. The Titans and Titanesses were a group of gods (see ATLANT and SATUR(N)), the children of Ge or Gaia (Earth) and Uranus (the Sky, or Heaven) (see URAN(O)). They were giants; hence **titanic** is used to mean huge in stature – physical or otherwise (eg intellectual stature). The metallic element **titanium** was named after the Titans by Klaproth, who had previously named uranium after the planet bearing their father's name (see URAN(O))

TOG Eng **togs** (slang for 'clothes') is thought to derive ultimately from Lat *toga* – the outer robe worn by Roman citizens

TOM Gk *-tomia* a cutting; *ektome* a cutting out (*ek* out – see EC); *temnein* to cut; or other related Greek words. Eg **anatomy** a cutting up (of the body) – ie the science of the structure of the body, or a dissection, analysis, **atom** (particle) not (able to be) cut – ie particle so small that it cannot be divided and is thus the ultimate particle of matter (or so it used to be thought), **appendectomy** a cutting out of the appendix, **dichotomy** a cutting into two, **entomology** (etc) – see ENTOM(O), **epitome** a cutting upon – ie a cutting into, a cutting short, an abridgement, a summary, **hysterectomy** a cutting out of the womb, **lobotomy** a cutting of a lobe (of the brain), **tome** (piece) cut – ie slice, volume of a work of more than one volume, book (especially a large or heavy one), **tonsillectomy** a cutting out of the tonsils

TOP(o) Gk *topos* place; *topion* small place; *topikos* relating to place or to commonplaces; *Ta topika* (the title of a work by Aristotle) matters relating to commonplaces, general ideas for use in argument. Eg **dystopia** bad place – ie place where the social and political system is the worst imaginable (the opposite of utopia – see below), **ectopic** out of place – ie (of a pregnancy) in which the foetus develops outside the womb, **isotope** (one of two or more forms of an element occupying the) same place (in the periodic table) – ie with the same atomic number; but differing in atomic weight, **topiary** small-place (works) – ie ornamental gardening, the clipping of trees into ornamental shapes, **topic** commonplace or general idea for use in argument – ie subject for discussion, subject, **topical** relating to commonplaces – ie relating to general ideas or subjects for discussion, relating to current affairs, **topography** place writing – ie the description of a place, the features of a place, **toponymy** (the study of) place-names, **utopia** no-place (Gk *ou* not) – name of an imaginary ideal republic described by Thomas More; hence any place with a perfect social and political system

TORP Lat *torpere* to be stiff, numb, sluggish; *torpedo* state of numbness, sluggishness. Eg **torpedo** (fish causing a) state of numbness – name of a type of fish that gives electric shocks; hence a type of underwater missile, **torpid** benumbed, sluggish

TORS, TORT Lat *torquere, tort-* to twist. Eg **contortion** a (thorough) twisting, **distort** twist apart – ie twist out of shape, (of facts etc) misrepresent, **extort** twist (something) out of (someone) – ie obtain it by force or threats, **retort** twist back – ie bend back, turn (an attack etc) back on (the attacker), answer sharply, **torsion** twisting – or the strain or force produced by twisting, **tortuous** twisty – ie full of twists and turns, not straightforward, **torture** a twisting – ie a writhing, great pain, the infliction of great pain (especially, by another, deliberately)

TOT Lat *totus* whole, all. Eg **factotum** a 'do-all!' – ie person taken on to do all sorts of tasks, **in toto** 'in the whole' – ie entirely, **total** whole – or complete, or (as a noun) the whole, the sum of a number of items

TOX(IC)(O) Gk *toxon* bow; *toxikos* relating to the bow, for the bow; *toxikon* (drug) for the bow – ie poison (which was smeared on arrows). Eg **intoxicate** (put) poison in – ie to poison, to drug (with alcohol etc), or to make as though drugged (with joy or excitement), **toxaemia** blood-poisoning, **toxic** poisonous – or caused by poison, **toxicology** the science of poisons, **toxophily** love of the bow – ie love of archery

TRA Eg **trajectory** – see TRA(NS)

TRACT Lat *trahere, tract-* to draw, drag; *tractare, tractat-* draw along, drag along, handle, treat. Eg **abstract** drawn away – ie removed (from the concrete), existing only as a mental concept, (etc), **attract** draw to (oneself/itself), **contract** a drawing together – ie an agreement, **detractor** drawer away – ie person who takes away from (the reputation of) somebody or something, criticises, **distract** draw apart – ie draw (someone's attention) in a different direction, **extract** draw out – or take out, or (as a noun) a passage taken out of a longer text, or a substance 'drawn out' of another substance (eg by distillation), **intractable** not draw-along-able – ie not easily handled, unmanageable, **protracted** drawn forth – ie drawn out, long-drawn-out, **retract** draw back – ie withdraw (eg something one has said), **subtract** draw (from) under – ie take from underneath, take away, **traction** a drawing – ie the medical procedure of pulling on a muscle etc to correct an abnormal condition; or the drawing of loads (as in 'traction engine'), or the driving forward of vehicles (as in 'steam traction'), **tractor** drawer – ie vehicle for drawing loads

TRAD Lat *tradere, tradit-* to give up, hand over. Eg **extradition** a handing over out – ie a handing over to another country (of someone accused of a crime), **tradition** a handing over – ie a handing down (of customs etc, from one generation to the next), the customs etc handed down

TRA(NS) Lat *trans* across. Eg **trajectory** (path of a body) thrown across – ie path of a body sent through the air, **transact** drive across – ie drive through, carry out (eg a piece of business), **transatlantic** across the Atlantic (Ocean) – ie the other side of the Atlantic, or crossing the Atlantic, **transcend** climb across – ie climb over, climb beyond, surpass, **transcribe** write across – ie write out in another place, make a copy of, write out (from shorthand etc), adapt (for a different medium), **transgress** step across – ie go beyond (the bounds), commit a fault, **transhume** (move) across ground – ie move livestock from summer to winter pastures or vice versa, **transient** going across – ie passing over, short-lived, **transit** a going across (from one place to another), **transmigration** a migration across – ie a removal from one country (etc) to another, or the passage of a soul from one body into another, **transparent** appearing across – ie appearing through, showing through, that can be seen through, **transport** carry across – ie carry from one place to another, **transvestite** (person who) clothes across – ie who dresses in the clothes of the opposite sex

TRI, TRIT Lat and Gk *tri-* three; Gk *tritos* third; or related words. Eg **triad** (set of) three, **triangle** three-angled (figure), **tricolour** (or **tricolor**) three-coloured (flag) – especially that of France, **tricycle** three-wheeled (vehicle), **trident** three-toothed (ie three-pronged) (spear), **trilogy** (series of) three discourses – ie series of three plays, novels etc, **trimester** three-monthly (period) – ie period of three months, or an academic term, **trinity** a threefoldness – ie the 'three persons in one God' of Christians, or a set of three, **tripod** three-footed (ie three-legged) (structure), **trisect** to cut into three, **tritium** the third (hydrogen) – ie hydrogen with three times the mass of ordinary hydrogen (see PROT(O) and DEUT(ER)(O))

TRIB(O) Gk *tribein* to rub. Eg **diatribe** a rubbing through – ie a rubbing away, a wearing away, a spending of time, study, discussion, an attacking harangue, **tribo-electricity** (the generation of) electricity by rubbing (ie by friction)

TRIB(UN) Lat *tribus* tribe (see also next entry); *tribunus* tribune – title of various officers of the Roman state, including the Tribunes of the People, who were elected by the plebeians (see PLEB(I)) to defend their rights. The forerunners of these tribunes were the representatives of the three old Roman tribes – hence the derivation of the Lat *tribunus* (tribune) from Lat *tribus* (tribe). Eng **tribunal** (a court, or some other body sitting in judgement) derives from Lat *tribunal* – a raised platform on which officials such as the tribunes sat to administer justice or carry out other formal duties

TRIBUT Lat *tribuere*, *tribut-* to allot, bestow, give (originally, to divide amongst the tribes, from *tribus* – see previous entry). Eg **attribute** (quality, characteristic etc) allotted to (someone or something), **contribute** bestow together with (others) – ie make a payment or offering to a joint fund or effort, **distribute** allot apart – ie share out, deal out, **retribution** a giving back – ie a 'paying back' (for wrongdoing), **tribute** (tax) bestowed – ie tax paid (in Roman times, a payment made by one state etc to another, in acknowledgement of the former's dependence on or submission to the latter); hence an offering due (to someone), an offering of words of praise; and a **tributary** is a stream or river that 'pays tribute' to (makes an offering to, flows into) a larger one

TRICH(O) *thrix*, *trich-* hair. Eg **trichologist** (person who) studies the hair – or a hairdresser

TRIT Eg **tritium** – see TRI

TRIT Lat *terere*, *trit-* to rub. Eg **attrition** a rubbing against – ie a rubbing away, a wearing down (of, eg, an enemy), **contrite** (thoroughly) rubbed – ie worn away, crushed, penitent, **detritus** (that which is produced by) rubbing away – ie matter worn away (from, eg, rock), **trite** rubbed – ie well-worn, overused, hackneyed

TRIUMPH Lat *triumphus* a triumph – ie the processional entry into Rome awarded to a commander and his army after an important victory. The procession included prisoners and booty, and the commander, drawn in a carriage, wore a crown

211

of laurel leaves. Lat *triumphus* (which probably derives from Gk *thriambos* a hymn to Bacchus – see BACCH) came to be applied more generally to a victory or glorious achievement, as is the derivative Eng **triumph**

TROP Gk *-tropos* turning; *trepein* to turn. Eg **heliotropy** sun-turning – ie (in plants) property of turning under the influence of light (either towards it or away from it), **hydrotropic** water-turning – ie (of plants etc) that turn under the influence of moisture (either towards it or away from it), **tropic** (circle) relating to the turning (of the sun) – ie one of the two parallels of latitude corresponding to the two circles on the celestial sphere touching the path of the sun where it reaches its furthest point north or south and 'turns'

TROPH(O) Gk *trophe* nourishment; *trephein* to nourish. Eg **atrophy** no nourishment – ie a wasting away, **dystrophy** ill-nourishment – or a wasting away (of the muscles), **troph-ology** the study of nutrition

TRUD, TRUS Lat *trudere, trus-* to thrust. Eg **abstruse** thrust away – ie hidden, difficult to penetrate, hard to understand, **extrude** thrust out, **intrude** thrust (onself/itself) in – ie enter uninvited or unwelcome, **obtrude** thrust (oneself/itself) in the way of (someone/something else) – ie thrust oneself/itself on someone/something, thrust forward, **protrusion** a thrusting forward – or a sticking out, or that which thrusts forward or sticks out

TSAR (or TZAR) Eg **tsar** – see CAESAR

TUBER Lat *tuber* a swelling; *tuberculum* little swelling. Eg **protuberance** a swelling forward – ie a swelling out, a bulge or lump, **tuber** a swelling – ie thick, round plant root or underground stem, **tuberculosis** (disease characterised by) little swellings (eg in the lungs)

TUM(UL) Lat *tumere* to swell; *tumulus* 'little swelling' – ie mound; *tumultus* a 'swelling' – ie an upheaval, uproar, commotion. Eg **tumescent** (in the process of) swelling, **tumour** (US **tumor**) a swelling (in the body) – or an abnormal growth of cells,

tumult upheaval, uproar, commotion, **tumulus** (burial) mound

TURB Lat *turba* uproar, disorder, commotion, crowd; *turbare, turbat-* to throw into disorder. Eg **disturb** throw apart into disorder – ie to disquiet (someone), or to break up, interrupt (something), **perturb** thoroughly throw into disorder – ie to disquiet, **turbulent** disorderly, in uproar

U

UBI(QUIT) Lat *ubi* where; *ubique* everywhere. Eg **ubiquitous** (found) everywhere

ULTERIOR, ULTIM Lat *ulterior* further away, further; *ultimus* furthest away, furthest, last. Eg **penultimate** almost last – ie last but one, **ulterior** further – ie beyond, beyond what 'meets the eye', **ultimate** furthest – ie last, or that goes as far as it is possible to go

ULTRA Lat *ultra* beyond. Eg **ultramarine** (colour from) beyond the sea – name of a colour the pigment of which was originally obtained from lapis-lazuli brought from abroad ('beyond the sea'), **ultramicroscope** a beyond-micro-scope – ie a microscope with which things can be seen that are too small to be seen with an ordinary microscope, **ultra-modern** beyond modern – ie beyond the ordinary in modernity, extremely modern, **ultramundane** beyond the world – or beyond the solar system, **ultrasonic** beyond sound – ie relating to (or using etc) vibrations like sound-waves but of a frequency beyond the range of human hearing, **ultraviolet** beyond violet – ie beyond the violet end of the visible spectrum, relating to (or using) radiations of lesser wave-length than those of visible light, **ultra vires** 'beyond (one's) power' – ie beyond that which one has the authority or legal power to do

UMBEL(LI), UMBR(A) Lat *umbra* shade, shadow; *umbella* 'little shade' – ie sunshade. Eg **adumbrate** (make) shadow – ie shade in, sketch (or foreshadow, or overshadow), **penumbra** almost shadow – ie partial shadow, **umbelliferous** sunshade-bearing – ie member of a family of plants having groups of flowers arranged like sunshades, **umbrage** shade, shadow – ie a feeling of having been slighted, **umbrella** sunshade(-like device) – used to protect from the rain rather than the sun

UND Lat *unda* wave (of the sea); *undare* to flow. Eg **abundant** flowing away – ie overflowing, plentiful, **inundate** to flow into – ie to flood, **redundant** flowing back – ie surging up, streaming over, present in excess, not needed, **undulate** (move in, or look like) little waves

UN(I) Lat *unus* one; *unicus* one and only. Eg **unanimous** of one mind, **unicorn** one-horned (creature), **uniform** of one shape – ie the same, unvarying, **unify** make (into) one, **unilateral** one-sided – ie affecting one side (or party) only, **unique** one and only, **unit** a one – ie a single thing, a distinct thing, (etc), **unity** a oneness, **universe** (that which has been) turned (into) one – ie everything taken together, the whole, the whole world, the whole of creation

URAN(O) Gk *ouranos* sky, heaven(s); *Ouranos* Uranus – name of a very ancient Greek god personifying the Sky. Eg **uranium** metallic element named after the planet **Uranus**, itself named after the god Uranus (see also TELLUR(O) and TITAN), **uranometry** measurement of the heavens – ie astronomical measurement

URB Lat *urbs* city. Eg **conurbation** a citying together – ie a large built-up area formed from a city and surrounding settlements, **suburb** (settlement) under the city – ie settlement next after the city, the outlying part of a city, **urban** relating to (ie belonging to etc) a city or cities, **urbane** city (-mannered) – ie polished, courteous, smooth in manner

URG(Y) Eg **metallurgy** – see ERG(O)

UR(O) Gk *ouron* urine. Eg **diuretic** (promoting) urine through – ie promoting urination, **haematuria** (US **hematuria**) blood (in the) urine, **uric** relating to (or got from, or found in) urine, **urolith** urine stone – ie 'stone' (calculus) in the urine or urinary tract uv(ul) Lat *uva* grape; *uvula* little grape. Eg **uvula** little grape – ie fleshy appendage of the palate hanging over the back of the tongue

V

vaccin Lat *vacca* cow. Eg **vaccine** cow(pox) (virus) – applied to any substance used to introduce a mild form of a disease into the body in order to provide immunity to the disease: so called because the first such inoculations used the cowpox virus (to provide immunity to smallpox)

vac(u) Lat *vacuus* empty (of), free from. Eg **evacuate** to empty out – or withdraw from (somewhere), **vacant** empty, **vacate** to empty – or withdraw from (somewhere), **vacation** a being empty of or free from (one's usual occupation) – ie a holiday, **vacuum** empty (space)

vad, vas Lat *vadere, vas-* to go, rush. Eg **evade** go out of – ie get out of, escape, avoid, **evasion** a going out of – ie a getting out of, an escape, an avoiding, **invade** go into (as an enemy), or rush into, **pervasive** going through – ie spreading through-out, **vade-mecum** a 'go-with-me!' – ie a 'companion' (book), handbook

vag Lat *vagus* wandering. Eg **extravagant** wandering outside (the bounds) – ie going beyond reasonable bounds, **vagabond** (person) wandering (about), **vagrant** wandering (person), **vague** wandering – ie ill-defined, unclear

val Lat *valere* to be strong, to have the power to do something, to be well, to be worth; *vale!* 'be well!' – ie farewell!, goodbye!; *valescere* to grow strong. Eg **ambivalent** strong on both sides, (seeing) worth on both sides – ie both attracted and repelled by something, having 'mixed feelings' about something, **convalescent** growing (thoroughly) strong (after an illness), **equivalent** (having) equal power, equal worth – ie corre-sponding, the same, **invalid** (person who is) not strong, (who is) unwell, **prevalent** being strong in front – ie very strong, stronger (than others), more influential or widespread (than

215

other things), widespread, **valediction** a saying farewell, **valency** power (to combine) – ie the relative capacity of an atom to combine with other atoms, **valiant** strong – ie brave, **valid** strong, having the power to do something – ie well-founded, having force, **valour** strength – ie courage, **value** the worth (of something)

vas Eg **evasion, pervasive** – see vad

vascul, vas(o) Lat *vas* vessel; *vasculum* little vessel. Eg **vascular** relating to (or having) little vessels – ie tubes carrying, eg, blood (the blood-vessels) or (in a plant) sap, **vas deferens** 'vessel carrying away' (sperm) – ie tube carrying sperm, **vase** vessel (for cut flowers etc), **vasectomy** a cutting out of a (piece of each) vas (deferens), **vasoconstriction** constriction (ie narrowing) of a (blood-)vessel, **vasodilatation** dilatation (ie widening) of a (blood-)vessel

vect, veh Lat *vehere, vect-* to carry. Eg **convection** a carrying together – ie a carrying into one place, a carrying of heat or electricity in currents through (eg) air or water, **invective** (words that) carry into (someone or something) – ie a 'laying into' someone or something, an attack with words, **vector** carrier – ie (in mathematics) a quantity having direction as well as size (which quantity can be shown as a straight line positioned in space), **vehicle** (means of) carrying

velo(ci) Lat *velox, veloc-* swift. Eg **velocipede** swift foot-(machine) – name given to various early forms of bicycle, **velocity** swiftness, **velodrome** swift (race-)course – ie cycle-racing stadium

ven(e), ven(i) Lat *vena* vein. Eg **intravenous** within a vein (or veins), **venepuncture** (or **venipuncture**) the puncturing of a vein (especially with a hypodermic needle), **venesection** the cutting of a vein (to let blood out)

ven(er) Lat *Venus, Vener-* Venus – name of the Roman goddess of love (especially sexual love), identified with the Greek Aphrodite (see aphrod). Eg **mons veneris** 'mountain (ie mound) of Venus' – ie the mound of flesh over a woman's

216

pubis, **venereal** relating to sexual love – ie (of disease) passed on by sexual intercourse, **Venus** – planet named after the goddess

VEN(I) Eg **venipuncture** – see VEN(E)

VEN(T) Lat *venire, vent-* to come. Eg **advent** a coming to – ie an arrival, **circumvent** come around – ie surround (eg in order to capture someone, or stop him/her doing something), assail, undermine, outwit, **contravene** come against – ie go against, **convene** come together – ie call together, **convenient** coming together – ie in harmony, fitting, suiting one's purposes, saving trouble, **convent** a coming together (of nuns) – ie a community of nuns, **convention** a coming together – ie an assembly; or an agreement; or something that has been agreed on, something that is generally accepted, established usage, **event** a coming out – ie an outcome, a happening, **intervene** come between – or act to alter the course of events, **invent** come upon – ie find, devise, **inventory** (list of things) come upon – ie list of things found (eg in someone's possession on his/her death, or in a property to be rented out), **prevent** come before – ie get a head start on, forestall, stop something from happening (or someone from doing something), **revenue** (that which) comes back – ie a return or yield (eg from property owned or investments), income, **supervene** come above – ie come on top of, happen in addition, follow on closely, **venue** (place for) coming – ie place where a meeting, concert etc is held

VENT(I) Lat *ventus* wind; *ventilare, ventilat-* toss to and fro in the air, fan, winnow. Eg **vent** to wind (forth) – ie to air, to let out, express, **ventiduct** a leading of wind – ie a passage to allow air in, **ventilate** toss to and fro in the air – ie air (a subject, in discussion), or fan, let air into

VENT(RI), VENTRIC Lat *venter, ventr-* belly; *ventriculus* 'little belly', stomach. Eg **ventricle** little belly – ie a small bodily cavity, **ventriloquism** a belly-speaking – ie a speaking from the belly (as it were) rather than through the mouth (as it were) so that the sound appears to be coming from some source other than the speaker

217

VERB Lat *verbum* word. Eg **proverb** word(s) (put) forth – ie familiar saying embodying a supposed general truth, **verb** word – the term for a particular part of speech, **verbal** relating to (or expressed in, etc) words – or to the spoken word (as opposed to the written word), **verbalise** (put into) words, **verbatim** 'word-ly' – ie word for word, **verbiage** (excessive) wordage, **verbose** wordy

VER(I) Lat *verus* true; *verax, verac-* truthful. Eg **veracity** truthfulness, **verdict** a true saying – ie a finding, judgement, **veridical** saying the truth, **verify** make true – ie provide confirmation of the truth of, check the truth of, **verisimilitude** likeness to the truth – ie appearance of truth, plausibility, **veritable** true

VERM(I) Lat *vermis* worm. Eg **vermicelli** (pasta, or chocolate, in the form of) little worms, **vermicide** worm-killer, **vermiform** worm-shaped, **vermin** worms (and other troublesome creatures), **vermivorous** worm-eating

VERN Lat *ver* spring. Eg **pre-vernal** (flowering, or coming into leaf) before the spring – or early, **vernal** relating to (or appearing in etc) spring

VERNACULAR Lat *verna* slave born in the house; *vernaculus* relating to a slave born in the house, (hence) home-born, native. Eg **vernacular** home-born, native – ie (of a language) naturally spoken by the people of an area, (of, eg, architecture) characteristic of an area, local

VERS, VERT Lat *vertere, vers-* to turn; *versare, versat-* to turn-and-turn-about, turn round; *versus* towards, in the direction of. Eg **adverse** turned towards or against – ie hostile, unfavourable, **advertise** turn (people's attention) towards, **anniversary** yearly (re)turn (of a date), **averse** turned away – ie disinclined, **avert** turn away – or ward off (a disaster etc), **controversy** a turning against – ie a dispute, **convert** (thoroughly) turn – ie change into something else, or change to acceptance of a belief or religion, **diversify** make turned-apart – ie make different, make varied, add variety, **diversion** a turning apart – ie a turning aside, a going a different way; or

218

a turning aside of the mind, something that captures one's attention, entertainment, **extrovert** (person) turned outside (ie outwards), **introvert** (person) turned inwards, **invert** turn in – ie turn over, turn inside out or upside down, turn the opposite way round, **pervert** to turn thoroughly – ie to overthrow, bring to ruin, turn from the right course, corrupt, **reversal** a turning back – ie a turning in the opposite direction, a turning the opposite way round; or a going backwards, **revert** turn back – ie go back (to a former state), **subversive** (tending to) turn (from) under(neath) – ie tending to overturn, overthrow, **universe** (that which has been) turned (into) one – ie everything taken together, the whole, the whole world, the whole of creation, **versatile** (tending to) turn-and-turn-about – ie changeable, adaptable, **version** a turning – ie a translation, or a particular form of something, **versus** towards – ie turned towards, against

VEST Lat *vestis* garment, clothing. Eg **divest** unclothe – or strip (of something), **invest** (put) clothing on (someone) – ie clothe with the insignia of office; or give to money some other 'clothing', put it into another form, turn it into (eg) stocks and shares, **transvestite** (person who) clothes across – ie who dresses in the clothes of the opposite sex, **travesty** a clothing across – ie a change in dress, a disguise or dressing-up, a grotesque imitation, **vest** garment – now applied only to a particular type of garment, **vestment** garment, **vestry** clothing(-room) (in a church)

VETER Lat *vetus, veter-* old. Eg **inveterate** made old – ie grown old, long-standing, **veteran** old (soldier) – ie experienced soldier (etc)

VETO Lat *veto* 'I forbid'. Hence in English a **veto** is the power to forbid something

VI(A) Lat *via* way, road. Eg **deviant** (turning) off the way – ie leaving the straight track, differing from the norm, **devious** off the way – ie removed from the straight track, following a winding course, underhand, **impervious** not (allowing a) way through – ie impenetrable, or unaffected (by something), **obviate** (get) in the way of (someone's, or something's) way –

ie block the path of, get rid of, **obvious** (lying) in the way of (one's) way – ie lying across one's path, clearly to be seen, self-evident, **previous** (taking the) way before – ie going before, former, **trivial** relating to (places where) three ways (meet) – ie such as may be found on every street-corner, commonplace, unimportant, **via** 'by way of', **viaduct** a leading of a way – a carrying of a way, a structure to carry a road or railway across (eg) a valley

VICT, VINC Lat *vincere, vict-* to conquer. Eg **convict** (thoroughly) conquer – ie prove guilty, pronounce guilty, **convince** (thoroughly) conquer – ie prove (a point), win over (to a point of view), **evict** (thoroughly) conquer – ie drive away, drive out (a tenant etc), **invincible** unconquerable, **victor** conqueror

VID, VIS Lat *videre, vis-* to see. Eg **evident** making (itself) seen – ie obvious, clear, **provide** see before – ie foresee, make preparation for, attend to, supply, **quod vide** (abbreviated to qv) 'see which!' – a form of cross-reference in a text, **supervise** above-see – ie oversee, **television** (instrument for) far-seeing – ie for transmitting images over long distances, **video** 'I see' – used in various terms connected with the electrical transmission of images, **visa** '(things) seen' – a word put on a document to indicate that it has been checked and found valid; hence a passport endorsement needed in order to enter a particular country, **visible** seeable, **vision** a seeing – ie the faculty of sight, or something that is seen, **visual** relating to seeing

VINC Eg **convince, invincible** – see VICT

VIN(I) Lat *vinum* wine; *vinea* vine, vineyard. Eg **vinegar** sour wine, **viniculture** the farming of vines – or the making of wine, **vinous** relating to (or like) wine

VIR, VIRTU Lat *vir* man, male person; hence, *virtus* manly excellence, courage, moral goodness, excellence. Eg **triumvirate** (group of) three men (sharing power) – or any group of three people, **virile** manly, **virtue** moral goodness, **virtuosity** excellence (in a particular art). (Note: Eng **virago**, used of a fierce or strident woman, reproduces Lat *virago*, which appears to derive from *vir* man. Lat *virago* meant a man-like woman, a female warrior, a heroine)

VIS Eg **supervise, vision** – see VID

VIT(AL) Lat *vita* life. Eg **curriculum vitae** (summary of the) 'course of (one's) life', **vital** relating to life – or essential to life, essential, **vitality** life (force) – or hold on life, energy, liveliness, **vitamin** life amine – so named in the mistaken belief that vitamins (which are essential for health – hence the 'vit') were an amino-acid

VITR(I), VITR(O) Lat *vitrum* glass. Eg **vitreous** glassy, **vitrify** make (or turn) (into) glass (or into a glass-like substance), **vitriol** glass(-like) (substance) – so named from the glass-like appearance of the salts referred to by this term

VIV(I) Lat *vivere* to live; *vivus* alive, living. Eg **modus vivendi** 'way of living' – ie a compromise arrangement enabling parties in dispute to get along for a time, **revive** live again – ie come (or bring) back to life, **survive** live above – ie live beyond (someone else, or some event etc), stay alive, **vivacity** liveliness, **vivarium** (enclosure for) living (animals) – eg for fish, **vivid** (full of) life, **viviparous** bringing forth living (young) – rather than eggs, **vivisection** an alive cutting – ie the cutting up of an animal while it is still alive

VOC, VOK, VOX Lat *vocare, vocat-* to call; *vox, voc-* voice. Eg **advocate** call to – ie call in, summon (in a court case) as a witness or to speak on behalf of someone, hence to speak in favour of, recommend, **convocation** a calling together – ie an assembly, **equivocal** calling equally – ie having the same name (but being in fact different), capable of more than one meaning, of doubtful meaning, questionable, **equivocate** call equally – ie have the same name (sound) as, use words capable of more than one meaning (in order to mislead), **evoke** call forth – ie summon up, **invoke** call in – ie call upon (in prayer, or to support one's case), **provoke** call forth – ie cause to come forth, incite, **revoke** call back – ie annul, cancel, **vocabulary** (list or set of) callings – ie of words, **vocal**

221

(having a) voice – or relating to or uttered with the voice, **vocation** a calling, **vociferous** voice-carrying – ie uttering (or uttered) in a loud voice, noisy, **vox pop** (abbreviation of **vox populi**) 'the voice of the people' – ie public opinion

VOL Lat *velle* (present participle *volens, volent-*) to will, wish. Eg **benevolent** well-wishing – ie good-willed towards others, **malevolent** ill-wishing – ie ill-willed towards others, **volition** (act or faculty of) willing, **voluntary** (depending on) will – ie on free choice

VOLCAN, VULCAN Lat *Vulcanus* (or *Volcanus*) – name of the Roman god of fire. He was also smith to the gods, forging their weapons. His name gives us both the word **volcano** and the name for a particular chemical process involving great heat, **vulcanisation**

VOLUT, VOLV Lat *volvere, volut-* to roll. Eg **convoluted** rolled together – ie rolled up, coiled, twisted, **devolution** a rolling down – ie a handing down or passing on (eg of power, from central government to regional governments), **evolution** a rolling out – ie the unrolling of a scroll, gradual development, **involve** roll in – ie roll up, wrap up, wrap (something/ someone) up (in something), entangle (something/someone) (in something), **revolution** a rolling back – ie a rolling round, or a complete change, the overthrow of a government, **revolve** roll back – ie roll round, turn round and round

VOR Lat *vorare* to eat (greedily). Eg **carnivorous** flesh-eating, **herbivore** eater of grass (etc), **insectivorous** insect-eating, **omnivorous** all-eating – ie eating all kinds of food, **voracious** eating greedily – or greedy

VOX Eg **vox pop** – see VOC

VULCAN Eg **vulanisation** – see VOLCAN

VULG Lat *vulgus* the masses, the common people; *vulgare* to make common to all, make generally known. Eg **divulge** make generally known apart – ie spread around, let it be known, reveal, **vulgar** relating to the common people – ie common, lacking refinement, in bad taste (and a 'vulgar' fraction is one written in the common or ordinary way – ie as two numbers one above the other with a line between them). Also, the word **vulgate** is applied to a version of the Bible, or some other text, in common use; notably to St Jerome's Latin version of the Bible, which was once the version in common use

X

XANTH(O) Gk *xanthos* yellow. Eg **xanthoma** yellow (tumour), **xanthophyll** yellow (pigment in) leaves

XEN(O) Gk *xenos* guest, host, stranger (entitled to hospitality), foreigner. Eg **pyroxene** stranger (to) fire – a type of mineral, so named because it was thought that, although commonly found in igneous (see IGN) rocks, it was alien to these, having been caught up in the lava only by chance, **xenogamy** foreign marriage, marriage with a stranger – ie cross-fertilisation, **xenophobia** fear or hatred of foreigners

XER(O) Gk *xeros* dry. Eg **xerography** dry writing – name of a photographic process not involving liquid developing agents (and **Xerox** is a trademark of a manufacturer of machines using this process), **xerophilous** dry-loving – ie (of a plant) able to exist in dry conditions, **xerosis** (abnormal) dryness (of the skin, mouth, etc)

XYL(O) Gk *xylon* wood. Eg **xylometer** wood measure – ie instrument for measuring the specific gravity of wood, **xylophone** wooden voice – name of a musical instrument consisting of a series of wooden bars

Y

YL, HYL(O) Gk *hyle* wood, matter. (In English, the element -yl is often used to indicate a chemical radical.) Eg **carbonyl** carbon matter – ie carbon radical (carbon monoxide), **ethyl** ether matter – ie the radical forming the base of ether,

hylophyte wood(land) plant, **hylozoism** (theory that) (all) matter (has) life

Z

zo(o) Gk *zoe* life; *zoion* living thing, animal; *zoidion* 'little living thing', 'little animal' – ie carved or painted figure. Eg **azoic** no-life – ie (of rocks) belonging to a period so early that there was no animal life on earth, **Palaeozoic** (or **Paleozoic**) ancient-life – name of the first great geological period (bearing the first evidence of animal life), **Mesozoic** middle-life – name of the second great geological period (the age of reptiles), **Cainozoic** new-life – name of the third great geological period (animal life as we know it develops), **Protozoa** (singular: protozoon) first animals – ie the most primitive animals (consisting of only one cell), **spermatozoa** (singular: spermatozoon) living things (contained in) sperm (ie in semen) – ie male germ-cells, **zodiac** (circle of the) carved figures – ie circle of the signs, **zoochemistry** the chemistry of animals, **zoology** the science of animals – and **zoo** was originally an abbreviation for 'zoological gardens'